HISTORY WARS

THE *ENOLA GAY* AND OTHER BATTLES FOR THE AMERICAN PAST

EDITED BY

EDWARD T. LINENTHAL

AND

TOM ENGELHARDT

An Owl Book

Henry Holt and Company | New York

Henry Holt and Company, LLC
Publishers since 1866
115 West 18th Street
New York, New York 10011

Henry Holt® is a registered trademark of
Henry Holt and Company, LLC.

An earlier version of "History at Risk" appeared in *The Journal of
American History* 82 (1995) as "History of the Culture Wars: The
Case of the Smithsonian Institution's *Enola Gay* Exhibition,"
© *The Journal of American History.*
An earlier version of Michael S. Sherry's "Patriotic Orthodoxy and
American Decline" appeared in *The Bulletin of Concerned Asian
Scholars* 27 (1995) as "Patriotic Orthodoxy and U.S. Decline,"
© *The Bulletin of Concerned Asian Scholars.*
"Culture War, History Front" is an abridged version of "The Battle
of the Enola Gay," the full text of which is available in Mike Wallace,
Mickey Mouse History and Other Essays on American Memory
(Philadelphia: Temple University Press, 1996).

Library of Congress Cataloging-in-Publication Data
History wars: the Enola Gay and other battles for the American past/
edited by Edward T. Linenthal and Tom Engelhardt.—1st ed.
1. United States—History, Military—20th century—Historiography.
2. Hiroshima-shi (Japan)—History—Bombardment, 1945—
Historiography.   3. Nagasaki-shi (Japan)—History—Bombardment,
1945—Historiography.   4. Vietnamese Conflict, 1961–1975—
Historiography.   I. Linenthal, Edward Tabor.   II. Engelhardt, Tom.
E840.4.H57   1996   96-886
940.54′25—dc20   CIP

ISBN 0-8050-4386-1
ISBN 0-8050-4387-X (pbk.)

Henry Holt books are available for special promotions
and premiums. For details contact: Director, Special Markets.

First Edition 1996

Designed by Victoria Hartman

Printed in the United States of America

10 9 8 7 6 5 4 3 2 1
10 9 8 7 6   (pbk.)

CONTENTS

HISTORY
WARS

INTRODUCTION: HISTORY UNDER SIEGE

TOM ENGELHARDT AND
EDWARD T. LINENTHAL

On November 23, 1994, National Public Radio's *Morning Edition* informed its listeners that one of the iconic artifacts of World War II had arrived at the Smithsonian Institution's National Air and Space Museum on the Mall in Washington, D.C. "At about a quarter to one, under a cloud-covered moon," the reporter began, "four police cars cruised down Independence Avenue, escorting what looked almost like a float in the Macy's Thanksgiving Day Parade. A flatbed truck carried a huge tube more than fifty feet long, wrapped in what seemed to be white plastic. The tube was the front half of the plane that carried the bomb that killed thousands of Japanese on August 6, 1945."

Here, under wraps, was the imposing fuselage of the *Enola Gay*, the famed B-29 Superfortress that dropped the first atomic bomb on Hiroshima. The aircraft, credited by many with ending a war of unparalleled ferocity, saving countless American lives, and bringing peace to a war-weary world, was now to rest temporarily in the museum that displayed the Wright brothers' first plane, Charles Lindbergh's ocean-spanning *Spirit of St. Louis*, and the Apollo spacecraft that brought humans to the moon.

Even though it entered the museum in the dead of night, the *Enola Gay* was shadowed by another story of war's end. For National Public Radio's reporter pointed out that the aircraft's route to the museum was not deserted. One protester sang a song of the *hibakusha,* those who had survived the atomic bomb the *Enola Gay* dropped on Hiroshima (a "national peace song in Japan," the reporter noted). Elsewhere en route, demonstrators from the pacifist Catholic Worker movement unfurled a banner that read "Disarm."

For fifty years, these two stories—of a weapon that brought peace and victory, and of a weapon that brought destruction and fear to the world—rested uneasily in American consciousness. Now, the aircraft's fuselage was headed toward an exhibit that promised to bring those two narratives together in a single museum space. With the plane as its central icon, that show was to explore the end of a hot war and the beginning of a cold one. As conceived by the Smithsonian's curators and advisers, the exhibit was to examine the bomb's creation, the decision to use it against Japanese cities, the *Enola Gay's* mission, the ground-level effects of atomic weaponry, the bomb's role in ending the war, and the new era it inaugurated—as well as the ways in which decades of historical research and debate on these topics had altered and deepened our understanding of them.

Such an exhibition, however, was not to be. For months, after a draft script of the proposed show was released to the media by the Air Force Association, a military lobbying group, the Smithsonian's managers and curators as well as the historians on whom they relied were subjected to increasingly angry charges: they had "hijacked history"; they were "anti-American"; they were practicing "politically correct" curating; they were projecting the "countercultural values" of the Vietnam era onto America's last good war. The fierceness of this response eventually doomed the National Air and Space Museum's planned show amid a remarkable controversy that pitted museum curators and historians against military officials and veterans' lobbying groups, as well as much of the media and Congress.

The exhibit was abandoned by a humiliated museum administration in January 1995 (to be replaced by a blandly upbeat display of the *Enola Gay* itself). Meanwhile, there were surprisingly few other memorial festivities celebrating the fiftieth anniversary of

World War II's end—the greatest military victory in U.S. history—even if the final moments of that war were anything but dead in public memory. In fact, it soon became apparent that they still held a rawness startling for events so long past. A once-familiar triumphant tale of a victory over Germany and Japan that was to lead to an American Century now seemed to end in disarray on August 6, 1945, in the rubble of Hiroshima. As August 6, 1995, approached, Peter Jennings anchored an ABC television documentary questioning the decision to drop the bomb, while Ted Koppel defended that decision on the same network's *Nightline*. Countless talk-radio programs, magazine and news articles, editorials, books, and book reviews argued over the minutiae of policymaking in 1945 with a passion and vitriol more often associated with fast-breaking news; and increasingly upset World War II veterans struggled to reassert to an oddly resistant nation the victory story they believed was their due.

Even with August 1995 past, anger about the *Enola Gay* exhibit did not die. On September 25, for instance, Robert Dole, Senate Majority Leader, Republican presidential hopeful and World War II veteran, made a pilgrimage to Indianapolis to address the national convention of the American Legion. His right arm and shoulder shattered by an explosive shell in Italy half a century earlier, the seventy-one-year-old Dole stood before the Legionnaires—many of them also aging survivors of his war—on what he was calling his final "mission."

As undoubtedly the last member of that wartime generation to seek the presidency, he had the war on his mind—and not just because he had been reminding the media of his old injury (partly as a rebuke to a young Democratic president long accused of being a "draft dodger"). Facing an audience of sympathetic veterans fifty years after the Japanese signed the instruments of surrender, Senator Dole did not linger on positive memories of a war that had once unified America in righteous victory. Instead, after the briefest of surveys of "dark forces . . . multiplying in almost every corner of the world" from North Korea to Iraq, he launched a frontal attack on America's true enemies in a post–Evil Empire world: "the arbitrators of political correctness," "government and intellectual elites who seem embarrassed by America," and "educators and professors" engaged in "a shocking campaign . . . to disparage America" and destroy the "keys" to American unity, its "language, history, and values."

He proceeded to attack diversity, multilingualism, affirmative action, and the newly proposed national history standards (whose purpose, he said, was "to denigrate America's story while sanitizing and glorifying other cultures"). Then, perhaps in search of a little red meat to add to his stump speech diet, he decried the fact that "liberal academic elites control more than our schools," and began to gnaw on the proposed *Enola Gay* exhibit, now nine months dead, that had already nourished Pat Buchanan, Newt Gingrich, Rush Limbaugh, and so many other conservative and right-wing politicians and media commentators.

"The Smithsonian created a display to commemorate the anniversary of Hiroshima, the day we effectively won a global war against the forces of evil," he said indignantly. "The message was that the dropping of the bomb was an act of American violence against Japanese culture. Somehow the Japanese were painted not as the aggressors but as the victims of World War II. Veterans' groups like the American Legion that complained were dismissed as special interests who couldn't be objective. That's right," he added after a pregnant pause, "if you love this country so much you're willing to die for it, maybe you do belong to a 'special interest,' but that special interest used to be called the people of the United States of America."

The fiftieth anniversary of any major event that put large numbers of people in peril naturally tends to establish a protective membrane around the commemorative moment. This accounts, in part, for the outrage that Senator Dole and other veterans expressed over the possibility that America's preeminent national museum might display historical material complicating or questioning more glorious tales of World War II's end. At the same time, however, Senator Dole's comments also reflected familiar themes in recent Republican party politics. After all, appeals to "traditional values" and attacks on the "elitist, liberal" media, the politically correct, and the racially other for supposedly undermining those values (as well as desecrating once-popular American conceptions of the past) have done much to keep the various factions of the party together.

The opening of a history front in the decade-old culture wars, even if only a new twist on an old act for Republicans and right-wingers, has been a genuinely shocking experience for historians committed to examining cherished national narratives. Indeed, the uproar over the *Enola Gay* show joins a number of other controversies of the 1990s in which historians became unexpected players on a public stage. They found their work debated or attacked, misused and abused, and themselves accused of aiding and abetting the post–Vietnam War fragmentation of an American consensus.

The act of challenging sacred historical narratives is a thankless task at any time, but especially so in periods of great uncertainty. Unquestionably, some of the most incisive scholarship of recent decades has taken on just that task, focusing on groups and experiences previously ignored in American history. But even as historians have seen their influence reach beyond the academy into various forms of public space—from museums to theme parks, CD-ROM "textbooks" to battlefield memorials—their work has often become contested (and detested) terrain, material for editorialists to condemn, politicians to denounce, and citizens to complain about or protest.

As political players, historians are relatively powerless and unorganized. Facing attacks that may grossly simplify and misrepresent their ideas and intentions, as in the *Enola Gay* controversy, they have few immediate ways to defend themselves. Whether they fight back or cave in to pressure (as the Smithsonian administration finally did in canceling the original *Enola Gay* show), they may find themselves in the uncomfortable position of being blamed for creating the very problems whose complexities they set out to explore. As stand-ins for more profound, elusive threats, they present remarkably easy targets and so are likely to take it on the chin—not just from right-wingers and various cultural warriors but from the media in general.

Now that they have been added to the conservatives' list of domestic enemies, one thing historians can do in their own defense is what they do best anyway. They can consider the various controversies that are troubling us, including those in which they are actors and targets, in light of our past. They can begin to make some sense of the ways in which the past lives with and within us, the ways remembering—and forgetting—work on us, the ways cultural productions (museum exhibits, living history performances, textbooks) can bring to the surface conflicting readings of our national stories. They can examine what Americans can and cannot bear to look at or consider at any moment, and why. This is the simple goal of our book: to let a group of historians take up, explore, and begin to make sense of one highly publicized controversy in America's ongoing history wars, one which, in its not-so-brief life, continues to generate far more heat than light.

The contributors to this book take as their starting point a draft script for a modest four-room exhibition at the National Air and Space Museum. But they do so in order to see what the ensuing *Enola Gay* controversy tells us about the state of our nation. The surge of anger over the Smithsonian show would have been inconceivable had America's global role not been in question, its enemies less and less clearly defined, and its past seemingly disintegrating before our eyes while many historical mini-tales—each attractive to some but disturbing or repugnant to others—compete for attention. In such a situation, reconsideration of the past cannot remain a sheltered or marginalized undertaking.

The anger also reminds us of the ways in which the cultural fallout from the bomb that destroyed Hiroshima still reaches into our own time, of how we continue to underestimate the destabilizing force of that blast. For the *Enola Gay* controversy exposed the centrality of the "Good War" to a sacred narrative of American history that has become increasingly distant and imperiled. After all, the history wars in America burst into full force only when it appeared that World War II might be deconstructed and reassembled in possibly irreverent ways at the National Air and Space Museum—and that the bombings of Hiroshima and Nagasaki might be used to pry open the "Good War"; indeed to further destabilize a larger sacred myth of the country's origins and development.

The United States is not the first country to experience history wars—or to discover the potentially explosive nature of public memory about World War II. Until recently, however, conflict over how that global conflagration should be remembered was a feature most conspicuous on the landscapes of the defeated nations, not that of the victors. In Japan, a public struggle over how the war should be portrayed has been in progress for decades, only intensifying in recent years as growing numbers of citizens, historians, and even politicians challenged the official government version of that war. Similarly, though from a different direction, in Germany in the early 1980s, conservative historians attempting to reframe the accepted version of the war (and of German responsibility for it) became the focal point of an emotional national debate. However, only as the fiftieth anniversary of the war's end approached did the victors join the vanquished in anguished and angry public controversy.

Americans like to think that they are capable of looking at their own history soberly, that they have avoided the snares of trivializing, sanitizing, and sanctifying the past into which other nations have fallen. Our own recent history wars, however, reveal otherwise. Here, then, is an anatomy of a thoroughly American controversy, and of an uncertain and unsettled nation at the edge of the millennium.

1

ANATOMY OF A CONTROVERSY

• EDWARD T. LINENTHAL •

When, in the fall of 1993, Martin Harwit, director of the National Air and Space Museum (NASM), asked me to serve on an advisory committee for that museum's upcoming *Enola Gay* exhibit, I was excited. After all, for many years I had studied battles over battlefield memorialization, clashes over "sacred ground." In the late 1980s, I had spent much time with National Park Service personnel as they struggled to transform the Little Bighorn battlefield from a shrine to George A. Custer and the Seventh Cavalry into a historic site where different—often clashing—stories could be told. There, I had first heard curatorial decisions attacked and derided as "politically correct history," and as a craven caving in to "special interests"; but there, too, I had watched as a complex interpretation of a mythic American event had successfully supplanted an enduring "first take."

In the early 1990s, I studied the National Park Service's preparations for the fiftieth anniversary of the beginning of World War II at the USS *Arizona* Memorial in Pearl Harbor. Watching members of the Park Service—and Pearl Harbor survivors—grapple with such a seemingly simple matter as whether a Japanese airman's uniform should be displayed (in an attempt to give a "human dimension" to the former enemy), I came to a fuller appreciation of the inevitable tension between a commemorative voice—"I was there, I know because I saw and felt what happened"—and a historical one that speaks of complicated motives and of actions and consequences often hardly considered at the moment of the event itself.

By the time Martin Harwit called me, I had published a book on the problems of memorializing American battlefields, from Lexington and Concord to Pearl Harbor, and had for more than a year been observing from within the volatile creation of the United States Holocaust Memorial Museum. In addition, as a historian I was aware of how uneasily the atomic bombing of Hiroshima rested in the American consciousness. Nonetheless, nothing in my experience with memorial exhibits prepared me for what happened when the National Air and Space Museum tried to mount its *Enola Gay* exhibit to mark the fiftieth anniversary of the end of World War II.

I certainly imagined that such a show would raise difficulties for the museum—problems between the commemorative and historical voices, between a reverently held story and its later reappraisal. But I expected, as had happened elsewhere, that the museum would overcome them and that a historically significant *Enola Gay* exhibit would open in 1995. In fact, I felt remarkably sanguine about the problems or issues that might arise, and the record of the advice my colleagues on the committee and I offered the museum during its early script preparations indicates how little any of us foresaw what lay in the museum's path. So the following reconstruction of the ugly controversy that doomed the exhibition is meant not just as a record of the failures and errors of others, but also of what I proved incapable of imagining as events began to unfold.

There is probably no better place to start that reconstruction than with a simple fact that was largely ignored while the controversy was under way. Although uneasiness about the *Enola Gay* and its mission would often be called a product of a disaffected Vietnam generation, left-wing historians, or the politically correct, its roots are half a century old. In the spring and summer of 1945, for example, the American press engaged in lively debate over alternatives to unconditional Japanese surrender. There was vigorous disagreement among Manhattan Project scientists who made the atomic bomb about the wisdom of the decision to use it, and after the war's end, there was strong criticism of its use from many prominent Protestant and Catholic spokespeople.

Influential conservative voices also criticized the decision. In 1948, Henry Luce, the founder of *Time*, wrote, "If instead of our doctrine of 'unconditional surrender,' we had all along made our conditions clear, I have little doubt that the war with Japan would have ended no later than it did—without the bomb explosion that so jarred the Christian conscience." Similar criticism was voiced by Hanson Baldwin, military affairs correspondent for the *New York Times*, David Lawrence, editor of *United States News*, and various conservative journals. For example, writing in William F. Buckley's *National Review* in May 1958, Harry Elmer Barnes argued that "the tens of thousands of Japanese who were roasted at Hiroshima and Nagasaki were sacrificed not to end the war or save American and Japanese lives but to strengthen American diplomacy vis-a-vis Russia." Within a few years, note media critics Uday Mohan and Sanho Tree, "this iconoclastic position taken in the conservative *National Review* would be labeled as 'left-wing revisionism' and would remain thus to this day."[1]

Artifact: The Uncomfortable Presence of the Enola Gay

Enduring uneasiness with the use of atomic weapons was also expressed in an enduring lack of enthusiasm for displaying the *Enola Gay*. After its mission, the plane returned to Tinian. On November 6, 1945, it was flown to Roswell Air Force Base, New Mexico. "After some modifications," a National Air and Space Museum report notes, it was flown back to the Pacific for Operation Crossroads, a test in the Marshall Islands "to determine the effects of atomic weapons on naval ships." However, the *Enola Gay* did not take part, because of engine problems. On July 2, 1946, it was stored at Davis Monthan Army Air Force Base, Arizona.[2]

Several months earlier, on March 5, 1946, New Mexico senator

Carl Hatch had drafted a bill to house the *Enola Gay* in an "Atomic Bomb National Monument" at Alamogordo, New Mexico, under the stewardship of the National Park Service. The site, Secretary of the Interior Harold Ickes wrote Robert Patterson, secretary of war, was appropriate for the *Enola Gay* because of its "links with Hiroshima" and because it "vividly demonstrates the ease with which atomic power could again be devoted to the destructiveness of war." Hillary A. Tolson, the acting director of the National Park Service, sought to assuage critics by stating that the use of atomic weapons would be "interpreted impartially without praise or blame. . . . Doubtless," he added, "the airplane would be a grim reminder of the destructive potentialities of this new power, but we hope to emphasize in contrast to it the medical and other constructive gains which atomic energy makes possible." The hope, said Tolson—clearly interested in portraying the "sunny side" of atomic energy—was that atomic power would in the future be used only for "peaceful ends." While the War Department soon agreed to transfer the *Enola Gay* to the National Park Service's care, Hatch's plan was never carried out, partly because the Atomic Energy Commission objected to it.[3]

On July 3, 1949, Colonel Paul W. Tibbets, Jr., the pilot for the Hiroshima mission, flew the *Enola Gay* to Park Ridge, Illinois—a facility that would eventually become O'Hare International Airport—where it was put under the jurisdiction of the Smithsonian's National Air Museum (the word *Space* would be added to its name in 1966). At the acceptance ceremony, a Smithsonian representative, delivering a speech written by head curator Paul Garber, called attention to the plane's "majesty." When the aircraft had "laid its egg, the Atomic Age was born." It would now rest in the nation's "Valhalla of the Air."[4]

On December 2, 1953, the plane moved to Andrews Air Force Base in Maryland, where it sat outside for seven years. In 1956, a journalist lamented that vandals had damaged the aircraft, and that "today, the once bright aluminum exterior is dull. The propellers are rusting, windows have been broken out, instruments smashed and the control surface fabric torn." Between August 10,

1960, and July 21, 1961, the *Enola Gay* was disassembled and its components moved to the Paul E. Garber Preservation, Restoration and Storage Facility for the Smithsonian's National Air Museum in Suitland, Maryland.

The *Enola Gay* was not entirely forgotten, however. Beginning in 1961, visitors could make appointments to see the plane's components, and in 1971, these became part of the Garber facility's daily tours. Still, a *Washington Post* reporter noted in 1979 that compared with the proud display of so many aircraft at the National Air and Space Museum on the Washington Mall, the *Enola Gay* sat "disassembled and virtually forgotten . . . in a suburban Maryland warehouse," for all practical purposes, hidden from sight. "Out of sight, out of mind" suited some members of the museum's staff, who in 1960 thought the plane would be "out of place alongside objects intended to engender pride." The matter seemed moot when budgetary concerns forced the Smithsonian to drastically scale back the size of the museum's new building—which would finally open on July 1, 1976—a decision that "effectively excluded the 'Enola Gay.'"[5]

Uneasiness with any future relocation of the *Enola Gay* was evident in congressional hearings on the Smithsonian in 1970. Senator Barry Goldwater of Arizona, an air force enthusiast who had been an Army Air Forces pilot during World War II, stated that "what we are interested in here [for the museum] is the truly historic aircraft. I wouldn't consider the one that dropped the bomb on Japan as belonging to that category." Congressman Frank Thompson agreed: "I don't think we should be proud of [the use of atomic weapons] as a nation. At least it would offend me to see it exhibited in the museum." The museum's acting director, Frank Taylor, defended the possible display of the *Enola Gay* only by claiming it would be of interest to "students in the future."[6]

During the early 1980s, a few B-29 veterans urged the museum to restore and display the *Enola Gay*. Others believed that the only solution was to move the aircraft to a different museum. In 1981, Ohio state auditor Thomas A. Ferguson led a move to bring the *Enola Gay* to the Air Force Museum in Dayton, Ohio. The Smithsonian, he thought, had buried an essential American artifact. "To me, storing the *Enola Gay* for thirty-four years is akin to mothballing the Statue of Liberty or the first space capsule that landed on the moon."[7]

Sensitive to such criticism, the Smithsonian finally did begin restoration work on the *Enola Gay* on December 5, 1984. "Components were returned to their original colors and appearance, decals were replaced and the instrument panels and throttle area were restored. . . . Plans are to retain only those markings that were on the airplane in August 1945." Although restoration only exacerbated the museum's ambivalence about the plane's eventual display, there would be a new drive to exhibit it in some fashion when Martin Harwit, a distinguished Cornell astrophysicist, became the museum's new director in 1987. His predecessor, Walter Boyne, a retired career air force officer, had opposed plans to display the *Enola Gay* because, he felt, the public did not have an "adequate understanding with which to view it." Even before accepting the job, however, Harwit had indicated to Smithsonian secretary Robert McCormick Adams that he was in favor of displaying the plane.[8]

Born in Czechoslovakia, Harwit brought with him vivid personal memories of the horrors of World War II. "There is just no question that this had a very big impact on the family. My father was counting up recently how many people had died in concentration camps. I think on his side of the family alone there were twelve." His father—dismissed from the German university in Prague in 1938—took the family to Istanbul, where he was a professor on the medical faculty at the University of Istanbul. Harwit remembered vividly the bombing of Hiroshima and Nagasaki. "I think everybody was glad the war was over within a few days. . . . I don't think at the time there was really much of a feeling of outrage. Don't forget that people had been worried about their kids getting killed off in the war. Lots of them had boys over there, and everybody was relieved that was over with."[9]

Harwit—who became an American citizen in 1953—was

drafted into the army and eventually went to the Pacific atolls of Eniwetok and Bikini to monitor nuclear tests. "The most impressive time I remember was when there was a hydrogen bomb blast very close to where we had put out the neutron monitors on a little island in the atoll chain. There was lush vegetation, a Japanese Betty plane was there, left over from World War II. . . . We went back afterwards by helicopter. There was a huge hole in the bottom of the atoll. Part of the island was missing, about half of it, no vegetation, just rubble, no Betty, no neutron counters."[10]

Under his leadership, he hoped that the museum could take up questions "that are under public debate." He wondered, for example, whether the museum could explore the controversy over Ronald Reagan's proposed Strategic Defense Initiative by considering "what we can expect technically from it. . . . What the investment in terms of dollars would be, and how long it would take to do, and whether the cost of constructing a [space] shield [against ballistic missiles] could be undermined by an adversary trying to circumvent it." He also believed that the public needed to be reminded of the dangers of warfare in the nuclear age. NASM could become a kind of public conscience. "I think we just can't afford to make war a heroic event where people could prove their manliness and then come home to woo the fair damsel."[11]

During Harwit's first year as director, veterans, who had formed the Committee for the Restoration and Proud Display of the *Enola Gay* to help raise funds for the restoration, accused the museum of delaying exhibition plans for fear of offending the Japanese. Responding in part to such accusations, museum staff members began to consider displaying the restored fuselage at the Garber facility, along with a film about the aircraft, its role in the bombing, its postwar history, and the process of its restoration. In July 1988, Secretary Adams envisioned an exhibit that contained "some account of what happened at Hiroshima—then and afterward. Probably the somewhat doubtful overall effectiveness of earlier and subsequent non-nuclear bombing—in Germany during World War II, and in Vietnam—also should be looked at, to provide a comparative perspective." Adams thought such a show would "cause us to reflect on how much of the extraordinary human achievement of ascending so far, and so abruptly, from the Earth has been funded and energized by the general scramble for superiority in ways of killing one another." The next month, writing in the museum's magazine *Air and Space*, Harwit remarked on the strong emotions engendered by the aircraft, adding that "the *Enola Gay* will be displayed in a setting that will recall the history of strategic bombing in World War II."[12]

Harwit had created the Research Advisory Committee, and the question of the *Enola Gay*'s display arose at one of its meetings in late October 1988. A majority of the committee members endorsed the museum's idea. While the act was "repugnant in retrospect," they declared, it was of "great importance." The sight of the aircraft would "emphasize the horrible devastation wrought by even so comparatively primitive a bombing capability." It would be displayed, they thought, at a proposed new NASM facility at Dulles Airport, for it must not have a "disproportionate presence on the Mall." The exhibit's message would be that "strategic bombing with nuclear weapons is too horrible an escalation of past warfare for any civilized society to contemplate."[13]

Admiral Noel Gayler, U.S. Navy (retired), who had been commander in chief of the Pacific Command, was, however, one committee member "staunch in his opposition" to the idea. There was nothing of unusual aeronautical interest about the *Enola Gay*, he thought, and the attack, "however much it may be justified in the aftermath as military necessity—incorrectly—was nonetheless genocide." He worried that no matter how sober the exhibit, "the impression cannot be avoided that we are celebrating the first and so far the only use of nuclear weapons against human beings." "Compared to the heroism of the bomber crews who went back again and again into flak," Gayler said, the Hiroshima and Nagasaki missions were "milk runs." Some committee members objected to Gayler's use of the term *genocide*; one offered a reminder that the goal of the attack was to bring the war to an end, and that "subsequent U.S. contributions to Japan's postwar recovery have led to a remarkable era of prosperity." The committee then decided to proceed with "great caution" and agreed that a symposium on strategic bombing would be a good way to begin exploring the history of strategic bombing.[14]

It was already clear, however, that the celebratory nature of the museum would be challenged by an exhibit on strategic bombing that, according to Steven Soter, special assistant to the director, was to "deal honestly and forthrightly with what might be called the dark side of aviation." With the fully restored *Enola Gay* as its centerpiece, the exhibit would call attention to the controversial nature of strategic bombing in World War II, when "the deliberate targeting of civilian populations became an acceptable practice, culminating in the atomic bombing of Japan, and opening the way to postwar strategic nuclear arsenals and deterrence by threat of mutual assured destruction." The *Enola Gay*, explained Soter, would not be displayed in the Mall museum, largely because the "appropriate mood to be evoked by the strategic bombing exhibit surrounding this airplane would clash with the predominantly soaring spirit of aviation which dominates the large open spaces of the main galleries." The main museum would only have some artifacts from the aircraft, including the bomb rack and casing.[15]

In 1990, as planning began in earnest, Tom Crouch, chairman of the museum's Aeronautics Department, reported to Martin Harwit that the planning group had discounted a special structure on the Mall—an option reportedly favored by Harwit—because of its cost (up to six million dollars) and potentially heavy security demands. The group preferred to display the *Enola Gay* at the Garber facility in the context of a special exhibit commemorating the end of World War II. Parts of this exhibit could then be incorporated into a traveling Smithsonian show that would "draw national and international attention to our museum and would avoid the impression that we are only 'celebrating' Hiroshima and Nagasaki—a very real possibility if the *Enola Gay* becomes the centerpiece of an exhibition on the Mall."[16]

The *Enola Gay* was to play an important part in the museum's ongoing investigation of what Secretary Adams called "the inter-

relationship between aerospace technology and modern warfare."
So, too, would a new exhibit the museum opened in November
1991, "Legend, Memory, and the Great War in the Air." According to Tom Crouch, its purpose was to contrast the "myths and
misconceptions that have grown up around [World War I] with
the reality of life and death in the air, 1914–1918." Soon after,
Martin Harwit informed Secretary Adams that historian Michael
Neufeld—a curator at the museum—would direct a follow-up exhibit on airpower in World War II, and that its "final installment"
would be the exhibition of the *Enola Gay*. Yet the plane's location
within early exhibit plans was still in question. Some of the museum's staff were fearful that too much visual emphasis on the
gleaming technological marvel that was the B-29 would, inevitably, lead to uncritical adulation and undermine the purpose of the
exhibit. Neufeld had already suggested to both Harwit and
Crouch that while the aircraft should be the "centerpiece" of the
exhibit, great pains should be taken to ensure that the exhibit not
be celebratory. "Through the use of proper lighting, sound insulation, black-and-white photographs, artifacts from the mission and
Hiroshima, and a restrained text, a quiet and contemplative mood
will be established in the exhibit. The morality of the bombing
will be addressed in particular in the section on the decision to
drop the bomb. The exhibit will not attempt to impose any particular point of view, but will give visitors enough information to
form their own views of a decision that to this day remains controversial." Only after moving through the exhibit would visitors
come to the aircraft, which would be surrounded by "giant black
and white photographs of Hiroshima after the attack."[17]

Throughout this period, Harwit was certainly aware of the exhibit's potential for controversy. It needed to be prepared, he
wrote, with the "greatest care and the forging of a strong consensus." He spoke encouragingly of support already received from
B-29 veterans for the restoration process, of the assistance of the
liberal John T. and Catherine MacArthur Foundation in funding
the strategic bombing symposium, and of positive discussions
held with museum officials in Hiroshima about the possible loan

of artifacts. He hoped as well that the Boeing Corporation, which had designed the B-29, would offer support. In a letter to former senator Mike Mansfield, special adviser to the Japan Foundation and former ambassador to Japan, Harwit expressed his hopes that the exhibit could offer a partial resolution of the "unarticulated issues" that had long haunted Japanese-American relations, and that it could make August 6—traditionally a day of "protest and recrimination"—into a day for reflection. "Without the most careful preparations," he said, "the display of the *Enola Gay* would arouse widespread anger among many groups." Harwit called attention to the potentially "serious problem" of seeming to stage a "U.S. celebration," and said that the museum had tried to "allay fears, by seeking to mount an exhibition sponsored both by the Japanese and the United States."[18]

At a December 1991 meeting of the Air and Space advisory board, members noted their uneasiness about the exhibit. They urged the museum to avoid discussion of the controversy about the decision to drop the bomb, and wondered whether an armed services museum might be a more appropriate place for the exhibit. They were, however, "unanimous in agreeing that the *Enola Gay* is an artifact of pivotal significance and that it should be exhibited."[19]

Over the next year, the show's focus shifted from strategic bombing to the use of atomic weapons and the opening of the nuclear age. By early 1993, a number of titles that reflected this change in emphasis were being considered: "Whirlwind: The Atomic Bomb and the End of World War II," "The Long Shadow," "Ground Zero," "Little Boy and Fat Man," among others. Eventually selected was "The Crossroads: The End of World War II, the Atomic Bomb, and the Origins of the Cold War."

Well before public controversy about the exhibit erupted, some B-29 veterans were privately expressing anger over the possibility that the *Enola Gay* would be part of an exhibit examining the controversy over the use of atomic weapons. In a letter to Supreme Court Chief Justice William Rehnquist, ex officio chairman of the Smithsonian Board of Regents, B-29 veteran W. Burr

Bennett, Jr., complained about the exhibit proposal, the museum's failure to care properly for the aircraft, and the strategic bombing symposium. He informed Rehnquist that he and four other veterans had collected eight thousand signatures calling for the "proper display of the *Enola Gay.*" It was "an insult to every soldier, sailor, marine and airman who fought in the war against Japan, or who were on their way to the invasion, to defame this famous plane by using it as the center piece of a negative exhibit on strategic bombing." Bennett made what would soon become a popular argument, stating that the museum was not living up to its mission, as set forth in Smithsonian legislation originally written for a proposed National Armed Forces Museum, but applying, in his view, to the National Air and Space Museum as well. According to this statute, "The valor and sacrificial service of the men and women of the Armed Forces shall be portrayed [by the museum] as an inspiration to the present and future generations of America."[20]

Even in 1993, it was evident that any exhibit that included the *Enola Gay* faced daunting interpretive issues unless it simply displayed the aircraft with minimal commentary. For several reasons, NASM did not choose to do that. Ironically, the motivation to display the *Enola Gay*—and to do so in an elaborate exhibit— came not from the Smithsonian's top managers or congressional leaders, those men of the World War II generation who might have seemed the most likely candidates to push for the display of the aircraft often credited with bringing the war to an end. As a group, they continued to show no great desire to display the aircraft. Rather, the impetus came from Martin Harwit and a new group of museum curators—mainly members of the postwar generation—who understood the power of the plane and the diverse stories connected with it. Sensitive to criticism that for too long their museum had merely been a showcase for aircraft, they now wanted to place their artifacts in historical context.

Artifacts like the *Enola Gay*, however, tend to establish a "commemorative membrane" around exhibit space within which the language of commemorative respect is often expected to dominate. For many NASM visitors, the *Enola Gay* could not help but transform exhibit space into commemorative space, where unambiguous narratives recalling the sacrifices of Americans at war could be expected to prevail, especially on the fiftieth anniversary of the war's end. Consequently, when it was decided that the proposed exhibit would focus on the difficult story of the bomb as both savior and destroyer, some people saw this as an offense to the heroic memory of the war and reacted as follows: they insisted that any ambiguous feelings about the mission of the *Enola Gay* were rooted in the subversive cultural impulses of the post-Vietnam left—located mainly in academia and among museum curators; they wanted to remove the aircraft lest it be symbolically soiled; they wished to punish those responsible both for the exhibit and for altering the celebratory nature of the National Air and Space Museum; and they desired to expunge the exhibit script of anything that might faintly offend American commemorative sensibilities.[21]

NASM: *Temple, Forum, Tribunal*

On August 12, 1946, President Harry Truman signed Public Law 722, creating the National Air Museum, whose purpose was "to memorialize the national development of aviation; collect, preserve, and display aeronautical equipment of historical interest and significance; serve as repository for scientific equipment and data pertaining to the development of aviation; and provide educational material for the historical study of aviation." The museum was born out of the desire of both the commanding general of the U.S. Army Air Forces, Henry H. "Hap" Arnold, and Congressman Jennings Randolph to create one central air museum to display "pioneering aircraft." Its most important objects—the *Wright Flyer* and the *Spirit of St. Louis,* for example—were initially housed in the Smithsonian's Arts and Industries Building. Head curator Paul Garber and a small staff ran the new museum.

By 1962, over two million people a year were flocking to see its aircraft, especially its latest addition, the Mercury space capsule *Freedom 7*, in which American astronaut John Glenn orbited the earth. The next year Congress began deliberations on a new building to house the museum.[22]

Besides being an aeronautical showcase, the new museum became a showcase for the aerospace industry and the military. When the navy and NASA wanted to get their stories on the Mall—through exhibits on the Navy Vanguard and the NASA Scout, for example—"they would do the exhibits and we would be the passive receptacle for them," recalled one NASM curator. The story of flight told in the museum was one of progress, of human achievement, of awe in the face of the remarkable—and often beautiful—technology that had allowed humankind to reach into space. The museum was a place designed to fire the imagination of visitors, to instill pride in the unmistakable triumph of American technology. Stanford historian of technology Joseph J. Corn noted that its "Milestones of Flight" gallery suggested that the "history of flying machines is simply a path, always headed in the same direction, along which clear milestones of progress may be discerned." Without any context, the artifacts became, according to Corn, "veritable icons" that the museum unabashedly celebrated "without raising any historical questions about their significance, let alone about the many antecedent failures and successes that made them possible."[23]

By the time Martin Harwit became director, a number of museums at the Smithsonian Institution had become places that did more than simply showcase curiosities or display beautiful artifacts. Many of their curators had become convinced that museums could "play a role in reflecting and mediating the claims of various groups, and perhaps help construct a new idea of ourselves as a nation." They had also been inspired by a heightened commitment among history museums around the nation to offer alternative readings of American history and to give voice to groups that had been silenced, or forgotten by traditional museum exhibitions. As a result, some Smithsonian museums began to organize provocative and controversial exhibits: in the National Museum of American Art, "The West as America: Reinterpreting Images of the Frontier, 1820–1920" called into question the heroic myth of the American frontier and raised questions about the relationship between art and politics; in the National Museum of American History, "A More Perfect Union" dealt with the internment of Americans of Japanese ancestry during World War II; "From Field to Factory," with African-American migration to the North; and "Science in American Life," with the promise and perils of science.[24]

In this atmosphere, NASM curators became ever more acutely aware of the need to change their institution from a temple to a forum where new and timely exhibits would seek to engage visitors in serious matters—like strategic bombing—in order to enrich civic culture. Martin Harwit saw some of the museum's provocative new exhibits as "trial balloons" for such a shift, and their success convinced him that the public was, in fact, ready to engage an exhibit that dealt with the dropping of the bomb and the end of the war. He took heart from the lack of opposition to the new interpretive labels and photographs for "Hitler's weapon," the museum's V-2 rocket, three thousand of which were launched against Britain, Belgium, and France in 1944 and 1945. Curator and historian David DeVorkin had long planned to build a "V-2 science mini-exhibit" that would focus as well on the Viking and the WAC Corporal, "American substitutes for the V-2" in the postwar U.S. rocket program. In 1990, Harwit approved a smaller version of DeVorkin's project, focusing only on the V-2 itself.[25]

The old exhibit had been a "temple" exhibit, ignoring the deaths of concentration camp inmates forced by the Nazis to build the rockets and of Allied civilians killed in V-2 attacks. The new V-2 labels and photographs provided a strikingly different interpretive framework. They spoke of the thousands of deaths among forced laborers and informed viewers that the attacks had killed approximately seven thousand people "and terrorized millions." Such sobering numbers were accompanied by a photograph of a dead civilian in Antwerp, "the first body shown in the museum," noted Martin Harwit, and a discomfiting photograph of Wernher von Braun—the creator of the V-2 and subsequently an important figure in the U.S. space program—chatting with Wehrmacht officers. The new exhibit was widely praised. The *Washington Post* hailed it as a "rare breakthrough" in "truth in labeling."[26]

Another successful "trial balloon" was the 1991 "Legends, Memory, and the Great War in the Air" exhibit. This, too, was greeted with admiration in the *Washington Post*—"a dose of reality such as has never before been seen in the Smithsonian's gee-whiz high-tech museum." The old World War I gallery, as Tom Crouch put it, had expressed the "spirit of romance that surrounds our memories of World War I aviation . . . one that reinforced the fantasy vision that many visitors brought with them of World War I in the air as a series of single combats fought mano-a-mano, high above the squalor of the trenches." Visitors to that show had seen a re-creation of part of an American airfield in France, with "sandbags, duckboards, and simulated mud providing a sense of time and place." Parked nearby was a German Fokker D.VII, and "visitors could overhear the conversation inside as U.S. intelligence officers interrogated the defecting German pilot." Hung overhead were several aircraft, including a SPAD XIII. Visitors then viewed exhibit cases "containing the uniforms and memorabilia of the great aces, whose names and faces were continually flashed on a screen at the exit." The old exhibit was, Crouch said, "a visual triumph . . . a jewel box, a stage setting in which the principal artifacts—the airplanes—could be displayed to best advantage."[27]

The new exhibit was designed to speak to visitors on a number of other levels as well. Crouch noted that although a "well-designed jewel box may help visitors appreciate the beauty of the Hope Diamond, it is not a very satisfactory way to communicate the meaning and importance of a complex social and technological artifact like a World War I airplane." In the new exhibit, airplane aficionados could find more aircraft than in the old one, an introduction to the wartime evolution of flight technology, and an examination of how the romantic mythology of air war could "cloud the reality of the historical experience in a remarkably short time."[28]

Harwit considered the fifteen-month-long strategic bombing symposium a success as well and was impressed with the fact that there was no public controversy over a four-minute video program set up at the entrance to the museum's permanent World War II exhibit that talked about the *Enola Gay* restoration program and included vivid evidence of the destructive power of the Hiroshima attack.

But there were undercurrents of discomfort with the National Air and Space Museum as forum, and some negative reactions to the World War I exhibit. When the *Enola Gay* controversy finally burst into the public arena, these feelings rose to the surface as well. For instance, John T. Correll, editor of *Air Force Magazine*, then described the exhibit as a "strident attack on airpower in World War I," with military aircraft characterized as an "instrument of death." In a letter to Tom Crouch on April 15, 1994, he argued that "in deploring the 'long shadow' that you say airpower has cast on the world for 75 years, you overlook the many contributions of military aviation to the defense of the nation and its interests. Your concept has little room for airpower's role in the deterrence of war and aggression." The editors of the *Wall Street Journal* characterized the exhibit as a "sneering look at aerial combat in World War I" and claimed that a weak Smithsonian administration allowed "revisionist social scientists," who had "overrun many university humanities programs," to work as Smithsonian curators.[29]

Long before any such criticism became public, before a draft script for an *Enola Gay* show even existed, some of the future critics of the National Air and Space Museum were already beginning to dream of a time when the museum would return to a style of exhibition making in which "facts" would be promoted instead of "interpretation." In the past, exhibits had supposedly allowed artifacts to "speak for themselves," and museum labels, wrote the

Smithsonian's director of American studies, Wilcomb E. Washburn, "identified particular objects and their use, without engaging in extensive interpretation or speculation about their larger meaning."[30]

The notion that once upon a time there were "neutral" museum exhibits or artifacts that "spoke for themselves" is, of course, illusory. "Agendas" and "points of view" have always been embedded in exhibits, even those that appeared authoritatively neutral and "objective." As museum critic Barbara Kirshenblatt-Gimblett has argued, every exhibit takes a position, has a "point of view," which becomes evident when one asks, "Why are some objects in museums of natural history and other objects in art museums and art galleries? . . . How are the exhibitions arranged? . . . The fact of the matter is those old style exhibitions were not random—they were not simply filled with lovely things to look at. . . . They were full of points of view, full of messages—full of interpretation."[31]

NASM's old V-2 exhibit was full of not just "facts"—information about rocket technology and its place in the evolution of rocketry—but choices, for it ignored information that would have given viewers a fuller but less upbeat "biography" of the rocket. The installation of new labels and photographs meant a change of interpretive perspective, not a change from a fact-filled exhibit to one with an agenda. The museum had simply decided that the human cost associated with building the V-2, its role as a weapon of terror, the thousands of deaths it caused, and the ease with which Nazi scientists later became American heroes were more important facts than those related to the rocket's technological development, although these by no means disappeared. What, after all, would a museum curator have said to a survivor of a camp that produced the V-2, or a descendant of someone who died in one of the camps, about the facts if the old labels had endured? Clearly, this artifact did not "speak for itself": there were many ways of telling the story of the V-2. NASM consciously jettisoned the technologically celebratory, believing that a more important story was being ignored.

The new World War I show also had a "point of view." It did indeed portray the evolution of war in the air from its genesis in World War I into the nuclear age as a shadow growing ever longer and darker. The exhibit catalog informed readers that "the atomic bombs dropped in Hiroshima and Nagasaki ended World War II, marked the dawning of the nuclear age, and represented the maturation of the strategic bomber as a weapon of total war." The exhibit certainly expressed a view of strategic bombing at odds with that of several important museum constituencies: the United States Air Force, the lobbying group the Air Force Association, and the aerospace industry. But what critics from these constituencies had refused to see, argued Richard H. Kohn, former chief of air force history and chair of the museum's advisory committee on research and collections management, was that the World War I exhibit was not hostile to airpower but presented the war "realistically" and explained "aviation's role in it." Airplanes, Kohn pointed out, had indeed been "instruments of death" in the war, and to ignore that fact was to "forfeit the opportunity to present balanced and realistic history." Kohn noted that by implication, critics advocated "a certain political use of the museum: to downplay war's reality and to glorify military aviation."[32]

Like "The Great War in the Air," "Crossroads" would soon be criticized as an exhibit that moved beyond the museum-as-forum to the museum-as-tribunal, where airpower, far from being celebrated, was "on trial" as a threat to human existence. "Crossroads" would question the decision to drop the bomb and call into question both the wisdom of and the necessity of its use, partially by focusing in graphic detail on Japanese victims of the bomb. The exhibit script would become a lightning rod in a bitter contest over the relationship between memory and history, as well as between celebratory and critical stances toward the American experience generally.

Script: Irreconcilable Narratives

"There are," University of Chicago historian Peter Novick informed a National Public Radio audience in January 1995, "all
sorts of different, alternative, and legitimate ways of framing the
story of Hiroshima. You can frame it as the veterans appear to
want, as the culmination of America's response to unprovoked
Japanese aggression. You can frame it as a chapter in the history of
white atrocities against nonwhites, as an episode in the escalating
barbarization of warfare in the twentieth century. You could talk
about it as the opening of the terrifying age of potential nuclear
devastation." There is, Novick argued, no one "truth" about Hiroshima. While truth may apply to straightforward matters of fact—
Paul Tibbets flew the *Enola Gay*, the city of Hiroshima was destroyed by an atomic bomb—historical accounts are always, in
Novick's words, "radically selective narrativizations of events."[33]

The curators who wrote the museum's first script chose to
emphasize the darker narrative of atomic destruction and fear.
This meant that atomic weapons had to be placed in the context
of the evolution of a war in which racial hatred on both sides had
reached a feverish pitch. In this narrative, the Pacific war was
largely a backdrop for the "freezing" of an epochal, horrific event,
which the museum considered worthy of intense examination
(much as the nearby United States Holocaust Memorial Museum
had "frozen" the Holocaust against the backdrop of war in Europe). In their proposed exhibit, the war was but prelude to the
use of the bomb, which drew back a curtain on a new age, revealing Japanese who were not so much the last civilian victims of
World War II as the first victims of the nuclear age. The commemorative message of this narrative was, in the words of a July
1993 exhibition planning document, embodied in "one common
wish: that nuclear weapons never be used in anger again."[34]

Organizing the script in this manner was anathema to those
who expected that the exhibition would linger on the barbarism of
Japan at war as well as on the bloody road to victory as an appro-

priate way to pay respects to America's war dead in the fiftieth anniversary year. For them, the exhibit's "emotional center" should have been the suffering of U.S. troops inexorably fighting their way across the Pacific until the atomic destruction of Hiroshima and Nagasaki brought the war that had begun at Pearl Harbor to a merciful end. The commemorative message of the narrative, then, should have been "remember what we did and the sacrifices that were made."

The museum's script, more than three hundred pages of text and illustrations divided into five sections, was completed on January 12, 1994. Its first section, "A Fight to the Finish," began with photos of cheering crowds in London, Paris, Moscow, and New York and of recently liberated prisoners from Dachau celebrating the end of the war in Europe, and of American soldiers shaking hands with their Russian allies at the Elbe River. The Allies had "won total victory in a just cause," the text read, "but the war was not over. In the Pacific, the battle with Japan was becoming increasingly bitter. Allied losses continued to mount. It seemed quite possible that the fighting could go on into 1946." Early on, the script also noted that "to this day, controversy has raged about whether dropping [the atomic bomb] on Japan was necessary to end the war quickly."

The opening text also informed readers that "Japanese expansionism was marked by naked aggression and extreme brutality. The slaughter of tens of thousands of Chinese in Nanking in 1937 shocked the world. Atrocities by Japanese troops included brutal mistreatment of civilians, forced laborers and prisoners of war, and biological experiments on human victims." Immediately following were words that would be used as weapons by exhibit critics long after they had been removed from subsequent drafts of the script: "For most Americans, this war was fundamentally different than the one waged against Germany and Italy—it was a war of vengeance. For most Japanese, it was a war to defend their unique culture against Western imperialism." What followed was a sober statement about the tenacity of Japanese resistance in the last bloody months of war; they kept fighting out of fear that "uncon-

ditional surrender would mean the annihilation of their culture."
For the Allies, the script noted, "the suicidal resistance of the
Japanese military justified the harshest possible measures. The
appalling casualties suffered by both sides seemed to foreshadow
what could be expected during an invasion of Japan. Allied victory
was assured, but its final cost in lives remained disturbingly uncertain."

The script's first section then set the context for the story of
the dropping of the bomb. It spoke of the horror of island fighting
on Iwo Jima and Okinawa, of kamikaze attacks—dramatized by
the display of a Japanese *Okha* piloted bomb—of the firebombing
of Japanese cities, and of the racial antipathy that had produced
"virulent hatred on both sides."

The second section of the script, "The Decision to Drop the
Bomb," detailed the history of the building of the bomb, including a display of Albert Einstein's famous letter to President Franklin D. Roosevelt. Dated August 2, 1939, the letter warned of the
potential for using "chain reactions for the construction of extremely powerful bombs" and urged that "some contact be established between the Administration and the group of physicists
who are working on the subject."

The text then turned to the factors involved in the decision to
use the weapon, declaring—all too definitively for some—that
"alternatives for ending the Pacific War other than an invasion or
atomic-bombing were available, but are more obvious in hindsight
than they were at the time." The script also raised a series of
questions, each of which encapsulated long-standing historical
controversy: "Would the bomb have been dropped on the Germans?" ("President Roosevelt would have used the bomb on Germany if such an attack would have been useful in the European
war.") Did the United States ignore Japanese peace initiatives?
("The United States should have paid closer attention to these
signals from Japan. . . . This matter will remain forever speculative and controversial.") Would the war have ended sooner "if the
United States had guaranteed the Emperor's position?" (In this
there might have been a "lost opportunity.") Significant space

was also devoted to a discussion of the "Soviet factor." Most scholars "believe that Truman and his advisers saw the bomb first and foremost as a way to shorten the war. . . . Still, virtually all now agree that the bomb's usefulness for 'atomic diplomacy' against the Soviets provided one more reason for Truman not to halt the dropping of the bomb."

Postwar objections to the use of the bomb by military figures like General Dwight D. Eisenhower and Admiral William D. Leahy were highlighted. The text asked whether a warning or demonstration of the bomb's power might have led to surrender and whether an invasion [of Japan] would have been "inevitable if the atomic bomb had not been dropped." The popularly held belief that an invasion would have resulted in half a million casualties or more was ruled improbable.

The script's third and largest section was entitled "Delivering the Bomb." Here, visitors were to encounter the *Enola Gay* itself, as well as a casing from a uranium atomic bomb, and learn about the creation of the B-29 "Superfortress," its role in the war, and the organizational genius of Colonel Paul Tibbets, the man put in charge of creating and commanding the almost two-thousand-man 509th Composite Group for the atomic missions. Tibbets offered "more than his stellar service record. . . . An innovator, he took on a project with an underdeveloped airplane and an undeveloped bomb and successfully executed it." Many individual and unit photographs of the men of the 509th were to be included, and their training from Wendover air base in Utah to Tinian Island carefully detailed. The postwar history of the *Enola Gay* and the Smithsonian's restoration process were noted, and a detailed examination of the bombing of Hiroshima and Nagasaki from the perspective of the pilots and crews of the 509th was offered. Tibbets was described as receiving a "Hero's Return" from his mission and shown being awarded a Distinguished Service Cross from General Carl Spaatz after he landed.

The fourth section, "Ground Zero," was meant to jar visitors out of the cockpits of American B-29s and into the horror of the bombing itself. The museum hoped to use numerous artifacts in this section to personalize and dramatize the story on the ground: the dial of a wristwatch retrieved from the Motoyasu River in Hiroshima marking the exact time of the explosion, a schoolchild's uniform, coins and bottles fused from the heat, a half-destroyed image of the Buddha, a fused rosary from Urakami Cathedral in Nagasaki, hairpins, infant garments, and the lunch box of a schoolgirl. There were horrific photographs of the dead, dying, wounded, and those still suffering from radiation sickness. The text allowed A-bomb survivors to offer their own graphic depictions of the horror and misery that engulfed them.

The final section, "The Legacy of Hiroshima and Nagasaki," used only twenty-four pages to deal with the role of the bombings in the eventual surrender of Japan, reminding readers that "even the news of the Nagasaki bombing did not change the situation" for hard-liners in the Japanese military ready to fight on. The script then touched on the beginning of the Cold War and the nuclear arms race, the failure to establish international atomic controls, the rise of an antinuclear movement, the creation of the doctrine of Mutual Assured Destruction (MAD), and the enduring dilemmas of nuclear waste, nuclear proliferation, and nuclear terrorism. It concluded: "A half century after the arrival of nuclear weapons in the world and their employment on Hiroshima and Nagasaki, the nuclear dilemma has not gone away. Some feel that the only solution is to ban all nuclear weapons. Others think that this idea is unrealistic and that nuclear deterrence—at a much lower level—is the only way that major war can be prevented. One thing is clear, the nuclear 'genie' is out of the bottle and, for the foreseeable future, the human race will not be able to eliminate the knowledge of how to build nuclear weapons. The dilemma is not about to disappear."

Controversy

As plans for the script first took shape in early 1993—a year before a first draft was completed—Martin Harwit believed the museum was adequately informing various constituencies about the exhibit's evolution. The planners felt they were taking "great pains" to acquaint various interested parties with the developing project: General Merrill A. McPeak, the air force chief of staff; Lieutenant General Claude M. Kicklighter (retired), the executive director of the Department of Defense's 50th Anniversary of World War II Commemoration Committee; members of several veterans' organizations; the crews of the *Enola Gay* and *Bock's Car* (the plane that dropped the second atomic bomb on Nagasaki); museum directors in Hiroshima and Nagasaki; and the Japanese ambassador to the United States. "With few exceptions," an early planning document stated, "we have been able to address and dispel concerns that the exhibition might present revisionist views on the history of World War II, or moralize on the bombings, or unfairly portray those who fought bravely and risked their lives to defend their country."

In April 1993, Martin Harwit and Tom Crouch spent ten days in Japan trying to obtain on loan a number of iconic artifacts from Japanese museums—"objects that tell touching human stories of death and suffering in the wake of the atomic bomb explosion." Harwit met with Takashi Hiraoka, the mayor of Hiroshima, who, according to Harwit, "voiced the strong sentiments of his city that all atomic weapons must be eliminated, and wanted to assure himself that our exhibition would not convey a message contrary to that spirit. I told the mayor that the museum was not in a position to make political statements, so that advocacy of the abolition of all nuclear weapons was not a message we would be presenting." Harwit was, however, willing to consider having the mayors of Hiroshima and Nagasaki contribute videotaped messages that might appear with others at the end of the exhibit. The mayor told him, Harwit recalled, that "he felt Japan owed the U.S.

an apology for Pearl Harbor, and that we owed one to Japan for the atomic bombings. Would our exhibit do that? I said that apologies were not as important as trying to learn lessons." Harwit informed the mayor that many of his family had been killed in the Holocaust, and said that "it made more sense to try to see how the holocaust had come about, rather than expecting an apology." Harwit agreed that the script would be sent to the mayor, who would then decide whether to loan the artifacts. Harwit and Crouch also met with Hitoshi Motoshima, mayor of Nagasaki, as well as with Japanese scholars and museum officials. Harwit hoped that since American veterans and the Japanese were reading the same script, the museum would soon reach a point where all constituencies "would be willing to trust us with their support."[35]

By the summer of 1993, when exhibit proposal drafts were first being written, the curators' greatest frustrations seemed to be coming not from their dealings with angry veterans but from the mixed messages they were receiving from Smithsonian secretary Adams and from Harwit. Adams wrote Harwit, for instance, "I cannot accept, that this will be 'an exhibit about the wartime development of the atomic bomb, the decision to use it against Japan and the aftermath of the bombings.'" It should instead commemorate the end of the war, calling attention to the crucial role of atomic weapons in the Pacific, and their decisive role in "decades of strategic and political thinking and action that followed." The introductory section, he argued, had to mention—in addition to the suffering of bomb victims—"prospective American losses if there were to be an invasion." He offered words of praise for the rest of the proposal, although he declared himself "uneasy" that later sections did not present in "adequate depth what were perceived as the horrors experienced by the Americans during all of the island invasions culminating with Okinawa."[36]

The curators, however, were not convinced that their show had serious problems of balance and context. Crouch complained to Harwit that Adams was "not consistent" in claiming that the planning document was both in "very good shape" and also a "risk to the Smithsonian." Crouch believed that Adams's unhappiness was simply due to the potentially volatile nature of the exhibit. "Any morally responsible exhibition on the atomic bombing of Japan has to include a treatment of the experience of the victims, [which would] certainly upset a lot of visitors." After arguing that various cosmetic changes sought by Adams would transform a "good, powerful, and honest exhibition into a mass of confused messages," Crouch wrote the following words, which would later be quoted repeatedly: "Do you want to do an exhibition intended to make veterans feel good, or do you want an exhibition that will lead our visitors to think about the consequences of the atomic bombing of Japan? Frankly, I don't think we can do both."[37]

The influential Air Force Association (AFA) first made known its displeasure with the planning document in 1993. A former AFA member, currently an NASM curator, described the group as an "effective lobbying organization representing the views of the Air Force to Congress, other members of the military coalition in the capital, and to the general public." The AFA would deftly organize and lead the battle against the exhibition, bringing the show's plans to its members in the pages of Air Force Magazine, edited by John T. Correll. Its executive director, Monroe W. Hatch, Jr. (U.S. Air Force, retired), wrote Harwit on September 12, 1993, that the planning document "treats Japan and the United States . . . as if their participation in the war were morally equivalent. If anything, incredibly, it gives the benefit of opinion to Japan, which was the aggressor. . . . Japanese aggression and atrocities seem to have no significant place in this account. Artifacts seem to have been selected for emotional value . . . in hammering home a rather hard-line point of view." That November, Hatch and Correll met with Harwit, Crouch, and Neufeld, but there was simply no way to reconcile the exhibit the museum was committed to and the one that the AFA thought appropriate. As Harwit and the curators saw the problem, the Air Force Association, representing an extreme position, sought to ignore the fifty-year history of controversy surrounding the decision to drop the bomb, to sanitize what had happened under the mushroom cloud, to defend strategic bombing against criticism, and, above all, to protect the heroic image of the air force. From the AFA's perspective, museum representatives seemed to be saying one thing—that they were open to criticism and suggestion, that the exhibit would honor American servicemen—while doing another—basically ignoring their criticisms.[38]

Certainly, Martin Harwit underestimated the formidable power and determination of the AFA. Two days before Christmas, still optimistic about achieving a rough consensus on the exhibit, he wrote Adams and Undersecretary Constance Newman that "veterans of the Enola Gay's crew . . . and Bocks Car's crew . . . have come forward with offers of memorabilia, and the two cities' [Hiroshima and Nagasaki] mayors have promised us the loans of artifacts from their respective museums." Furthermore, the air force chief of staff, General McPeak, "seems to be satisfied that we are going in the right direction." Several days later, however, McPeak wrote Harwit that he was concerned about lack of "balance" in the planned show. The script, he said, "should reflect the total context of the war and explain the potential American casualties Truman anticipated if an invasion were required. We're particularly concerned about portraying the American campaign as 'brutal' and highlighting only Japanese suffering."[39]

The nine-member exhibit advisory committee (of which I was a member), made up of academic and service historians and one combat veteran of the Pacific war, met on February 7, 1994, to discuss and critique the script. Historian Martin Sherwin, author of *A World Destroyed: The Atomic Bomb and the Grand Alliance*, raised fears that the exhibit might still prove too celebratory in nature. Ways to enliven the section on the decision to drop the bomb were also discussed, but no substantive objections to the structure or tone of the script were made. "The advisory committee did not serve us well," Harwit commented later. "It focused so much on the decision section that it did not help us identify other problem areas." The initial reaction of advisory committee member Edwin C. Bearss, former chief historian of the National Park Service, was typical of the moment. "As a World War II Pacific combat veteran," he wrote Tom Crouch, "I commend you and your colleagues who have dared to go that extra mile to address an emotionally charged and internationally significant event in an exhibit that, besides enlightening, will challenge its viewers. . . . The superior quality of the label texts and of the objects and illustrations identified by the exhibit designers and researchers set a pattern of excellence that all aspire to, but few achieve."[40]

Seemingly also comfortable with the script was Richard Hallion, chief of the air force historical program and a member of the advisory committee. Though he voiced no substantive objections during the daylong meeting, he and a colleague, Herman Wolk, submitted a three-page critique of the script to NASM. "Overall," they said, "this is a most impressive piece of work, comprehensive and dramatic, obviously based upon a great deal of sound research, primary and secondary." They were concerned, however, that "through sheer repetition, the script gives the impression that the Truman administration was more concerned with the atomic bomb as a diplomatic weapon against the Soviet Union than as a route to shorten the war and avoid heavy casualties." They also believed that the script did not clearly enough identify the Japanese as the aggressors in the Pacific, did not put sufficient emphasis on Truman's concerns with "potential American casualties," and did not do justice to "Japanese brutality to subject peoples." (Only "four or five sentences take us from 1931 to 1941.") At the bottom of the critique Hallion added a handwritten note to curator Michael Neufeld. "Again, an impressive job! A bit of 'tweaking' along the lines discussed here should do the job." In a personal note to Neufeld during the meeting, Hallion wrote, "Mike—chin up—you've got a great script, and nobody—except Marty [Sherwin]—is out to emasculate it."[41]

Harvard historian and advisory committee member Akira Iriye, who was unable to attend the meeting, wrote Neufeld that the script was "carefully written and reflects the authors' obvious intention to present as judicious interpretations of controversial events as possible." In late April, Iriye once again wrote Neufeld that as someone who was "fighting against political correctness in the academic disciplines . . . I do not see what is politically correct about the exhibit. My role as an advisor has been to assure the scholarly standards of the written material, and I believe the statements that go with the exhibit are accurate, well-balanced, and reflective of the most recent scholarship."[42]

A growing legion of military and veterans' group insiders felt differently. They believed that the proposed show did not appropriately attend to the commemorative voice, a failure that registered for them as an act dishonoring American veterans, even though the Air Force Association's John Correll admitted that the first script actually treated the men of the 509th Composite Group "extensively, and with respect."[43]

When Tom Crouch argued that the script could not both make veterans "feel good" and discuss the consequences of the use of atomic weapons, he pointed out the great gulf between the two narratives and worried that even though they were part of one story, no museum exhibit could bridge such a gulf. Harwit, on the other hand, continued to believe—through all the increasingly bitter public debates of 1994—that the exhibit could honor both narratives. In an August 7 editorial in the *Washington Post*, he wrote, "We want to honor the veterans who risked their lives and those who made the ultimate sacrifice. . . . But we also must address the broader questions that concern subsequent generations—not with a view to criticizing or apologizing or displaying undue compassion for those on the ground that day, as some may fear, but to deliver an accurate portrayal that conveys the reality of atomic war and its consequences." In the pages of the museum's *Air and Space* magazine, he commented that "the honor and bravery of our servicemen, their willingness to offer their lives in the fight against a ferocious aggressor, the heartbreak suffered by families who lost fathers, sons, and brothers, the strength of the nation's leadership in successfully fighting and concluding a war the United States had not sought, and the justice of the cause for which we were fighting—*all will be featured in our exhibition*." Harwit felt, in particular, that the films and videotapes in the show—especially the final moving video interviews with *Enola Gay* crew members—would honor commemorative expectations.[44]

In the increasingly angry atmosphere of the moment, many critics of the NASM exhibit questioned the motives or the sincerity of the museum's curators or of Martin Harwit himself. But in retrospect, it is easy enough to see how the very structure of the exhibition rather than any personal duplicity made the fulfillment of Harwit's double commitment an impossibility. After all, the plans called for the exhibit's "intellectual heart" to be the painstaking examination of the various controversies that now surround the decision to drop the bomb (a unit written by Michael Neufeld), and its "emotional heart" to be the horror of what the bomb did to the Japanese (written by Tom Crouch).[45]

In an internal review of the exhibit planning process, Preble Stolz, professor emeritus at the University of California School of Law at Berkeley, noted that while people at NASM knew how strongly veterans believed that the bomb had saved their lives, "no one thought about it or articulated very clearly the emotional significance of that set of ideas. . . . It is probably asking too much of people who have thought for fifty years that they owed their life to President Truman's decision to drop the bomb to reflect objectively about whether his decision was morally justified. At its core that asks people to consider the possibility that their life was not worth living." Similarly, Hubert R. Dagley II, internal affairs director of the American Legion, commented that it was easy for many veterans to believe the curators and historians were being condescending at best, contemptuous at worst, in dealing with the veterans' experiences. "As the press interpreted the script, vets felt that it said their lives had been purchased through racism and treachery, that their last fifty years were counterfeit, and they blamed the museum for this."[46]

In January 1994, draft copies of the script were sent to the Air Force Association. Martin Harwit expected that discussions on the script's further development would then continue in private. AFA representatives, however, had grown frustrated with what they believed was the museum's unwillingness to take their criticisms seriously, and decided to continue the argument very publicly in the pages of *Air Force Magazine*. John Correll's essay "War Stories at Air and Space," a slashing attack on every aspect of the proposed exhibit and its creators, appeared as the lead article in the April issue. Correll wrote that "US conduct of the war was depicted as brutal, vindictive, and racially motivated." He characterized the sentences about an American war of vengeance and a Japanese fight to preserve their way of life as a "curious call." Kamikaze pilots, he wrote, "are seen as valiant defenders of the homeland." Correll informed readers that Harwit had asked if "veterans really suspect that the National Air and Space Museum is an unpatriotic institution or would opt for an apologetic exhibition?" and responded, "the blunt answer is yes." The script's problems were due to "politically correct curating," which had "swept the Smithsonian complex" during the tenure of Secretary Adams, and "Crossroads" was an outgrowth of the same negative attitude toward airpower present in the World War I exhibit.[47]

Correll's essay was, in effect, a declaration of war, the first salvo in what would become a sustained campaign against the exhibition. For Martin Harwit, it seemed like nothing short of a surprise sneak attack, and he later said as much, if more politely. The Air Force Association, as he put it, had broken a trust with the museum by "going public." The AFA, on the other hand, maintained that going public was the only way to force a recalcitrant group of museum curators and managers to establish appropriate balance and context in the script. There was, Correll said, "a huge difference in impact between a few words in the script [about Japanese atrocities, for example] and an emotion-grabbing artifact like a little girl's burned lunch box. . . . We made an issue of the emotional impact of the school child's lunch box and pointed out that there was nothing on the other side for balance."[48]

There was also an enduring anger and sense of betrayal among many people at the museum over what appeared to be an almost immediate "about-face" by air force historian and advisory committee member Richard Hallion. Soon after the advisory committee meeting in February 1994, Hallion became a visible and influential critic of the script and characterized the use of the bomb as a "morally unambiguous act." Writing to Crouch in August in his own defense, he said that he and Wolk raised issues of "accuracy, context, fairness, and balance in our very first discussions. . . . Unfortunately, we believe that our comments—and those of our fellow military historians—have not been taken to heart." Their encouraging comments were meant as "polite . . . encouragement." Hallion was clearly uncomfortable with the widespread speculation that he had simply shifted his position given the intense opposition to the exhibit by veterans' groups and the military. He characterized as "downright insulting" the "implication" that he and Wolk had been "muscled by the Air Force leadership" into changing their position. "A friendly 'bridge-building' note I passed to Mike Neufeld during our meeting in early February in an effort to maintain a useful dialogue has even been cited out of context." Crouch responded that Hallion's supportive written remarks were "simple and straight-forward," and that there had been "no warnings . . . no 'red flags' in these comments. . . . If you are telling me that you simply wanted to be polite, I can only respond that we were looking for an honest reading—not polite chit-chat. If you really saw a problem, you should have indicated it. We might not be in this situation today." Hallion responded, "We trusted you, and believed that you would take our comments seriously. Since you did not, 'big trouble' naturally resulted."[49]

After the AFA publicly blasted the exhibition and the first angry media attacks followed, Harwit realized, belatedly, that there were serious problems ahead and did in fact turn to military historians. On April 13, 1994, the museum's exhibition team met with a number of military historians who had read the script: Edward Drea, chief, Research and Analysis Division, U.S. Army Center for Military History; Wayne Dzwonchyk, History Office, Joint Chiefs of Staff; Mark Jacobson, Marine Corps Command and Staff College; and Kathleen Lloyd, Naval Historical Center. It was a contentious meeting, as once again Harwit and the curators heard bitter complaints about the "balance" and "context" of their show, but what happened in the meeting was nothing compared with the political intrigue going on elsewhere.

On April 25, Commander Luanne Smith (U.S. Navy, retired), who was coordinating a series of discussions between military historians and the museum for the Pentagon's World War II Commemoration Committee, wrote a lengthy memorandum for the committee's executive director. "Behind the scenes," she reported, "Dr. Hallion has been orchestrating the various Service historical offices to not wait to see what changes the Air and Space Museum is prepared to make and to go on the record that they cannot support the exhibit. He knew about the April 13 meeting and was invited to attend, but chose instead to write a memo prior to the meeting to the Air Force Chief of Staff, attacking the Smithsonian and declaring that the Museum would not make any significant changes to its exhibit. The timing of the memo seems to demonstrate that he was bent on undermining any good will the Smithsonian would have received from holding the meeting. . . . Given Dr. Hallion's efforts to date in opposition to the exhibit and his personal predilections, it is unlikely that he will ever support the Smithsonian's exhibit, whatever major changes are made."[50]

The increasingly dangerous political situation moved Martin Harwit to reconsider his own favorable reaction to the script. Three days after meeting with the military historians, Harwit informed the curators, "Though I carefully read the exhibition script a month ago, I evidently paid greater attention to accuracy than balance. . . . A second reading shows that we do have a lack of balance and that much of the criticism that has been levied against us is understandable." Harwit soon appointed a second review group, the "Tiger Team," made up of Brigadier General William Constantine (U.S. Air Force, retired), a former executive officer to the chief of staff of the air force, and an NASM docent; Colonel Thomas Alison (U.S. Air Force, retired), a curator in charge of military aviation at NASM; historian Gregg Herken, chairman of NASM's Department of Space History; Colonel Donald Lopez (U.S. Air Force, retired), a fighter ace with the Flying

Tigers in World War II, former deputy director of NASM, and senior adviser emeritus; Kenneth Robert, an NASM volunteer docent; and Steven Soter, special assistant to the NASM director. The Tiger Team reviewed the script individually and then together for five nights, four hours each night. In their report, they found the script "too sympathetic to Japanese, too harsh on Americans," and judged the text on historical controversies "too speculative." They felt it "could lead the viewing public to conclude that the decision to drop the A-Bomb was questionable (perhaps unjustified?) rather than debatable (still open to question)." "Deletions" were suggested in the "redundant, horribly graphic close-up photographs of survivors as well as similarly redundant graphic quotations. Substitute mid-distance photographs which, in most cases, will adequately convey the devastation and the dazed, often helpless survivors." In conclusion, Constantine wrote, "however well-intentioned, the 'Crossroads' exhibit will not satisfy everyone, nor can it be all things to all people."[51]

A revised May 1994 script incorporated some of the changes sought by military historians and the Tiger Team. There was a new introductory section, "War in Asia and the Pacific: 1937–1945," which included photographs of Pearl Harbor and the Bataan Death March. After a description of the kamikaze raids, the script now pointed out in detail the heavy American losses they had caused (28 ships sunk, 176 damaged, 5,000 sailors killed) and said, "To the ships' crews, the experience seemed to confirm Japanese fanaticism and offer a grim foreboding of what they would face in future operations." The American home front was presented in a more sober manner, and a sentence from the first script that spoke of Americans yearning for the "realization of their deferred dreams of material prosperity" was deleted. The new text emphasized that "for all with loved ones in the Pacific, the cost of victory in American lives was devastating." Also included were a photograph of a mother who lost three sons, a telegram informing a family about their loss, a military letter of consolation, and a flag used in burial services. There was now more emphasis on the heavy losses expected in the event of an invasion of Japan, and on Japanese use of slave labor and misuse of prisoners of war, while the text in the historical controversy panels was even more cautious than before.

The museum's managers and curators reeled through the summer, facing attacks on various fronts—from journalists and media commentators, from Congress, from outraged veterans and citizens angered by news accounts. The script became an embattled text, attacked, defended, and endlessly revised in an increasingly embittered atmosphere that revealed more about American cultural politics in the 1990s than about the mission of the *Enola Gay* and the decision to drop the bomb. What emerged was not only a vitriolic conflict over a museum exhibition but a public relations disaster for the Smithsonian and a real threat to its budget, most of which came from congressionally appropriated funds. For many critics, the few sentences in the first script about why the two sides fought "proved" that the museum was, indeed, trying to rewrite history, by suggesting that Japan was the aggrieved party in World War II. Months after the passage had been excised from the script, it still appeared regularly in journalistic attacks. In an unreleased "draft statement for the media," the museum considered defending itself by pointing out that "this was obviously a clumsy and inaccurate attempt to portray how the American and Japanese people themselves saw the war after Pearl Harbor, not how the authors of the script saw it." Based on recommendations from the Tiger Team and others, Michael Neufeld rewrote the passage to read, "For most Americans, this war was different from the one waged against Germany and Italy: it was a war to defeat a vicious aggressor, but also a war to punish Japan for Pearl Harbor and for the brutal treatment of Allied prisoners. For most Japanese, what had begun as a war of imperial conquest had become a battle to save their nation from destruction. As the war approached its end in 1945, it appeared to both sides that it was a fight to the finish."[52]

Ironically, as attackers continued to blast away at the first script, the revision process went on. By August, for example, thirty of the forty-two Tiger Team recommendations had been fully implemented, seven had been implemented in part, and only five had not been addressed. Some military historians now thought the revised scripts acceptable. For instance, Brigadier General David A. Armstrong (U.S. Army, retired), the director for joint history, Office of the Chairman, Joint Chiefs of Staff, wrote Alfred Goldberg, historian at the Office of the Secretary of Defense, that "some attempt has been made to address virtually every criticism raised at the April 13 meeting . . . although in some cases, the fixes have been minor. . . . Revisionist interpretations no longer dominate discussion of the political and diplomatic issues surrounding the use of the Atomic Bomb. . . . The script no longer reads as a blanket indictment of the US casting the Japanese as helpless victims. . . . We will have to consider carefully how much farther the Smithsonian can be made to move before the law of diminishing returns takes over." On July 12, historian Edward Drea, a specialist on the Pacific war, wrote the World War II Commemoration Committee, "I find the script more balanced than its predecessor. I still have reservations about an imbalance of so many photographs of suffering Japanese women and children. Are there no photographs of Japanese males?" Alfred Goldberg proceeded to write Michael Neufeld that "the first three sections of this draft should dispose of most of the negative criticism. . . . The issues of racism, strategic bombing policy, decision to drop the bomb, and invasion casualties are handled with acceptable objectivity. . . . The section on the effects of the atomic bombs will no doubt continue to draw critical comment as being too long, too detailed, and too sympathetic to the Japanese, but the exhibit would be incomplete and much less meaningful without it." (Goldberg, however, suggested it be cut another 25 percent.) Also satisfied was historian Wayne Dzwonchyk. In conversation with Commander Luanne Smith, Dzwonchyk called the script "very good." It represented, he thought, a "total capitulation" by the museum to air force wishes. "He said," Smith reported, "he can find very little to complain about and that the script has gone a long way in addressing the complaints of the critics. . . . He said that his assessment of six months ago has been proven correct that some people will never accept the exhibit no matter the improvements made to it."[53]

Press reports consistently misinformed readers that the Smithsonian was ignoring its critics. The *Washington Post*'s Eugene Meyer informed readers that many of the Tiger Team's recommendations were not accepted, and a *Post* editorial stated that the museum had promised "extensive revisions, but it hasn't come through, and the conceptual gap between the museum and its critics remains wide." In one example of the enduring arrogance and ignorance of the many congresspeople who became involved in this controversy, twenty-four members of the House of Representatives wrote Secretary Adams that after review "we have found the revised script is still lacking in context, and therefore unacceptable. It seems that the planners of this exhibit ignored many of the constructive criticisms provided." They, too, claimed that few Tiger Team suggestions were "incorporated into the revised edition," and that Americans needed an "objective account . . . rather than the historically narrow, revisionist view contained in the revised script."[54]

Commander Luanne Smith directly contradicted such accusations. In August 1994 she observed that "the Air and Space Museum has been extremely accommodating to making changes to their script, contrary to what is being claimed by exhibit opponents. The NASM's opponents have gone out of their way to misrepresent the Museum's intentions, and to mobilize veteran opposition based on the first script, which has been greatly modified. The opposition is intent on canceling the exhibit as currently planned, and want to merely display the *Enola Gay* with a statement indicating that it was the aircraft that ended World War II." Smith was particularly sharp in her criticism of the Air Force Association. "I remain convinced that the Air Force Association's objections to the script had a good deal to do with Air Force fears of showing the horror of the use of nuclear weapons, which could revive strong anti-nuclear feelings among the public. The Air Force and the AFA wants the message to be 'the Air Force won the war.' Given the exhibit they wanted, I don't think *any* script would have met with their approval."[55]

In the ongoing campaign against the exhibition, *Air Force Magazine* published new articles almost monthly dissecting each new script revision. They called attention, for example, to the many photographs of Japanese victims and the few depicting the suffering of Americans and their allies at the hands of the Japanese, and argued that the scripts continued to be "soft" on the Japanese, failing to dramatize, for example, Japanese barbarism in China, the Bataan Death March, and related atrocities. They also called attention to internal NASM disagreements and contradictory statements about the purpose of the exhibition, which, they claimed, revealed the duplicity of the museum's staff.

The curators, of course, did not believe that their choice of photographs was unjustified, given that their show was not meant to be a history of the war in the Pacific, but rather to "freeze" a transformative moment in the twentieth century. Michael Neufeld also wondered why critics wanted the script to suggest that the United States "dropped the A-bombs as revenge for Pearl Harbor, Bataan, the Rape of Nanking? That is the equivalent of saying that one atrocity/war crime deserves another. . . . It is also bad history, because there is very little evidence that Truman, et al., made the bomb decision to get back at the Japanese. The primary motivations were casualties and [to] end the war early. . . . Trying to produce a 'balance' in the number of pictures therefore has the ironic effect of making the argument that the bombings were just the Truman administration's revenge on Japan."[56]

By mid-1994, other groups were also beginning to hold the museum's feet to the fire. As early as May 1994, the American Legion, for instance, went on record in opposition to the exhibit, and in a letter to President Bill Clinton, the legion's national commander, William M. Detweiler, said, "It prompts the unmistakable conclusion that America's enemy in the latter days of World War II was defeated and demoralized, ultimately the victim of racism and revenge, rather than a ruthless aggressor whose expansionist aims and war fervor yielded more than a decade of horror and deaths for millions of the world's people." At the legion's national convention in September, however, the legion agreed to withhold final judgment since the museum proved willing to "include representatives of the American Legion in all future script and exhibit reviews prior to release or final approval of the script, and . . . provide to the American Legion for its inspection and review copies of all material related to the exhibit, including but not limited to scripts, articles, videotapes, museum catalogues, translations and promotional materials."[57]

The Air Force Association also expended considerable energies in mobilizing Congress, other veterans' groups, and journalists, all of whom in turn shaped the public's perception of the nature and meaning of the exhibit. From the beginning, the Smithsonian's public response was virtually nonexistent, a fatal error. Jack Giese, chief of media relations at AFA, recalled, "There were certainly times when the museum could have mounted a defense, but they never did. At first we asked ourselves, 'what will they do?' After a while, we stopped worrying about it. They weren't going to do anything."[58]

In the spring, there had been scattered editorials in newspapers supporting the museum's attempt to show the devastation of Hiroshima and Nagasaki. But after the AFA put its clout behind a campaign against the exhibit, with the exception of several sympathetic editorials in the *New York Times*, influential editorial comment almost uniformly attacked the museum. Clearly, few of those writing about the exhibit had read the first script in its entirety, not to mention the following drafts; consequently, there was no serious attempt to help the public engage in thoughtful debate about the strengths and weaknesses of the evolving exhibit. Attack journalism simply fanned the flames. Calling the curators "politically correct pinheads," R. Emmett Tyrell, Jr., editor in chief of the *American Spectator*, wrote in the *Washington Times* of the casualties that would have resulted from an invasion and said that such casualties would have left "some of the present pinheads at the Smithsonian fatherless or even, oh bliss, unborn."

The *Boston Globe*'s Jeff Jacoby called the curators and historians involved in the exhibit people "who would warp history . . . slander the United States and merit the ridicule of honest men." *Time*'s Lance Morrow characterized the first script as an attempt "to transport a righteous '60s moral stance on Viet Nam . . . back in time to portray the Japanese as more or less innocent victims of American beastliness and lust for revenge." The *Wall Street Journal* insisted that the "scriptwriters disdain any belief that the decision to drop the bomb could have been inspired by something other than racism or blood lust." *Time*'s Charles Krauthammer called the exhibit a "disgrace" and demanded that "heads, and agencies, roll." The *Washington Times*'s Rowan Scarborough thought it important to inform his readers that curator Michael Neufeld was a "Canadian who is a former college professor" and said that curator Tom Crouch, who had been in charge of the Japanese-American internment exhibition at the National Museum of American History, was "enamored" of Japanese culture, which explained why the *Enola Gay* show "originally was sympathetic to Japan." Smaller newspapers inflamed public opinion as well. For example, an editor in North Carolina, also trying to prove that NASM was too sympathetic to the Japanese, misinformed his readers that "one Smithsonian exhibit is Japan's Hiroshima Memorial Peace Museum."[59]

Perhaps the most egregious examples of journalistic irresponsibility occurred at the *Wall Street Journal* and the *Washington Post*. The *Journal* attacked the "oozing romanticism with which the Enola show's writers describe the kamikaze pilots. . . . These were, the script elegiacally relates, 'youths, their bodies overflowing with life.' Of the youths and life of the Americans who fought and bled in the Pacific there is no mention." For this, the *Journal* editors took part of a quote from a kamikaze pilot that appeared in the script and attributed it to the curators. They also left out the sobering end of his statement, "and they were waiting their turn to die. It was no longer possible to refuse to go. It was impossible to escape." Ken Ringle of the *Washington Post* repeated the misattributed quote for his readers. (In both editorials and reporters' accounts, the *Post* was unsparing in its criticism of the exhibit and the motives of the curators.) In its unreleased "draft statement for the media," the museum noted that the quote was in the script "to show how the kamikazes saw themselves, to provide insight into their suicidal fanaticism, which many Americans would otherwise find incomprehensible. In any case, the quotation was later deleted."[60]

The media also almost uniformly ignored—or were ignorant of—the half-century-long controversy over the decision to drop the bomb. Since they had no idea of the rich and complex history of that controversy, they had no way of knowing that what struck them as unpatriotic, if not anti-American, criticism of Truman's decision had certainly not been construed that way in the late 1940s. If journalists had any sense of historical context, they might have wondered why it was easier shortly after World War II to talk openly about doubts connected with the decision to drop the bomb than it was fifty years later. Tony Capaccio, editor of *Defense Week*, and Uday Mohan, in a strong critique of the media for their *Enola Gay* coverage, concluded that "journalists did not do enough research and failed to hold the veterans' version of history to the same exacting standard they used in judging the curators' version. The initial exhibit had flaws of context and historical perspective—but not as serious and certainly not as ill-informed as the media coverage led the public to believe."[61]

By the time another revised script—now called "The Last Act"—was released in October, I. Michael Heyman, former chancellor of the University of California, Berkeley, had been installed as Smithsonian secretary. In a desperate attempt to save the exhibition, he invited representatives of the American Legion to meet with the exhibition team to review the script. The October script deleted the historical controversy panels, greatly expanded the introductory unit "War in Asia and the Pacific," reduced yet again the remaining photographs of Japanese victims, and shrank the section on the legacy of the bomb to just over a page. In a letter to an increasingly displeased Akira Iriye, Martin Harwit tried to explain these wrenching changes, including the removal of any serious mention of controversy regarding the decision to drop the bomb. That cut was justified, Harwit wrote, because while "postwar diplomacy and suspicion of Stalin's tactics played a role, it seemed to me, at least, that the evidence was equally clear on Truman's desire to end the war quickly to stop the killing and 'bring the boys' home." In a letter to the mayor of Hiroshima, Harwit justified the removal of many of the Japanese artifacts on the grounds that as the exhibit was originally planned, "we were giving the appearance that we were deliberately emphasizing the killing of children and the destruction of religious icons."[62]

Only in the latter months of 1994 did groups of scholars react angrily to what they perceived as the Smithsonian's caving in to various pressures. Informing Martin Harwit of his decision to resign from the advisory committee, historian of science Stanley Goldberg wrote that he was troubled the museum was willing to "cast aside fifty years of solid, hard-headed scholarship which clearly calls into question the immediate, post-war euphoric, self-serving judgement that the atomic bomb ended the war and saved hundred[s] of thousands of lives on both sides. . . . I simply cannot be a party to the exhibit which has now emerged from the Air Force Association's crusade."[63]

On November 17, a group of well-known scholars and writers—including Barton Bernstein, Gar Alperovitz, Kai Bird, and Robert Jay Lifton, whose writing challenged the official story of the decision to drop the bomb—met at the museum to argue for restoration of elements they thought inappropriately removed from the script. These included the statement that "the decision to drop the bomb will remain forever controversial," comments critical of the use of atomic weapons made by Admiral Leahy and President Eisenhower, and photographs of Japanese victims. They wanted "documentation of religious, moral, and political protest over the dropping of the bomb" and recognition that the "post-war nuclear arms race, five decades of nuclear weapons production and testing, radiation effects on both military personnel and civilians, [and] consequent environmental destruction" were important legacies of the bomb. They believed that the exhibit should also depict the "US and international disarmament movement, the post-war peace movement in Japan, and international commitments to the abolition of nuclear weapons."[64]

On November 16, forty historians signed a letter to Secretary Heyman objecting to what they characterized as the "historical cleansing" of the script. "It is unconscionable," the letter stated, "first, that as a result of pressures from outside the museum, the exhibit will no longer attempt to present a balanced range of the historical scholarship on the issue; second, that a large body of important archival evidence on the Hiroshima decision will not even be mentioned; and third, that the exhibit will contain assertions of fact which have long been challenged by careful historical scholarship." It urged Heyman to resist pressure from "what is perceived at the moment as 'patriotically correct' history."[65]

Compared with the tremendous political clout of veterans' groups, congresspeople, and the media, the historians' objections carried little weight, for the museum gained nothing politically by responding to their concerns. Yet despite the massive changes that prompted such angry responses from some historians, the revised scripts still did not satisfy the Air Force Association, the American Legion, or other veterans' organizations. The Veterans of Foreign Wars, for example, notified Harwit that even the October script "does not fairly commemorate and display the contributions made by American military forces in the Pacific theater of operations nor does it go far enough to cite the valor and sacrifice of individual Americans in combat." Some members of Congress wrote Heyman that there is "no excuse for an exhibit which addresses one of the most morally unambiguous events of the 20th century to need five revisions." William S. Anderson, a former POW of the Japanese, a retired chairman of the board of NCR Corporation, and a member of the Smithsonian national board, wrote Heyman in November that there was still overemphasis "on the suffering of the Japanese . . . including references to how they suffered long after the war. . . . I have already told you that many of the POW's from my camp never regained their eyesight, their ability to walk, work or lead a normal life, because of extreme malnutrition over three and ¾ years. . . . I don't think the Smithsonian realizes how much antagonism and anger has been generated by this controversy."[66]

Endgame

The exhibit now had been subjected, in the words of one NASM curator, to "death by a thousand cuts." Negotiations with the American Legion were Heyman's desperate attempt to salvage some shred of the former exhibit, satisfactory to veterans' groups and angry funders in Congress. Clearly, the Smithsonian's managers entered into deliberations with the legion because of threats of budget cuts unless they came up with a more "acceptable" script. For his part, the legion's Hubert Dagley felt his group's purpose in the meetings was "to achieve an exhibit that was historically accurate, with sufficient context in which the use of atomic weapons could be evaluated from all perspectives, including those who believed it saved their lives." However, argued Michael Neufeld, in the October script there was already little evidence of "all perspectives," and "the political pressure to have an exhibit that celebrated the dropping of the bomb was overwhelming." Perhaps, as Dagley would claim, the legion exercised no censorship over the exhibit, but whether or not the exhibit "lived" rested on its acceptance of the final product. The endgame demonstrated clearly just how fragile—indeed, illusory—was Martin Harwit's hope that seemingly endless compromise with powerful critics would result in a historically responsible and politically acceptable exhibit.[67]

The American Legion's national commander, William M. Detweiler, declared in November, "More than anything else, our disagreements center on the estimate of numbers of lives saved by the use of atomic weapons in 1945. . . . Does it matter? To the museum and historians, it seems to be of great importance in determining the morality of President Truman's decision. To the

American Legion, it matters less, if at all." In truth, to all concerned, it mattered a great deal.[68]

In their postwar memoirs, both President Truman and Secretary of War Henry L. Stimson had spoken of horrendously high numbers—hundreds of thousands, even one million casualties—in any invasion of Japan. Yet as military historian John Ray Skates notes in his book *The Invasion of Japan: Alternative to the Bomb,* "the source of the large numbers used after the war by Truman, Stimson, and Churchill to justify the use of the atomic bomb has yet to be discovered. Nor is there any record that Truman, [or] Stimson, or Churchill used such large casualty estimates in the weeks before or following the use of the bombs against Japan. The large estimates first appeared in their postwar memoirs." These numbers, however—particularly the one million figure—took on iconic significance over the years, much like the six million figure for the number of Jews killed in the Holocaust. Any attempt to question these numbers came to be construed as an attempt to belittle the horrendous reality that an invasion of Japan might have been, just as any attempt to adjust downward the six million of the Holocaust—even by several hundred thousand—was perceived as a murder of memory, akin to Holocaust denial.[69]

High projected casualty figures were useful for those who argued, as the American Legion did, that President Truman was concerned solely about American lives, and that the use of atomic weapons saved many of them. On any scale of suffering, these high numbers meant that the potential dead far outweighed the actual dead of Hiroshima and Nagasaki, thus justifying the use of the weapons. On the other hand, historians who called into question the numbers, on the grounds that they were not the ones Truman and his advisers operated from, believed lower numbers would provide additional support for the idea that atomic weapons were used for reasons other than, or in addition to, the desire to save lives. The museum's exhibit waded into these perilous waters from the beginning.

Under the label "Half a Million American Dead?" a text in the first script read: "After the war, estimates of the number of casualties to be expected in an invasion of Japan were as high as half a million or more American dead. . . . In fact, military staff studies in the spring of 1945 estimated thirty to fifty thousand casualties—dead and wounded—in 'Olympic,' the invasion of Kyushu. Based on the Okinawa campaign, that would have meant perhaps ten thousand American dead. Military planners made no firm estimates for 'Coronet,' the second invasion, but losses would clearly have been higher. . . . Early U.S. studies . . . underestimated Japanese defenses. . . . On June 18, 1945, Admiral Leahy pointed out that, if the 'Olympic' invasion force took casualties at the same rate as Okinawa [about 35 percent] that could mean 268,000 casualties (about 50,000 dead) on Kyushu. It nonetheless appears likely that post-war estimates of a half million American deaths were too high, but many tens of thousands of dead were a real possibility." The May 1994 revised script added information that a "June 1945 Joint Chiefs of Staff study also estimated about 40,000 American dead for the invasions of both Kyushu and Honshu," and added that tens of thousands of deaths were not only a real but a "frightening possibility." In a letter to Wayne Dzwonchyk of the History Office of the Joint Chiefs of Staff, Michael Neufeld said that he "looked for ways to . . . underline that casualties and a quicker end to the war were central to Truman's thinking. . . . I think that Truman would have been justified in making the same decision if he was confronted with 50,000 dead instead of 500,000 dead as his only alternative."[70]

The August 1994 revised script offered a new label, "Invasion of Japan—At What Cost?" and tried to balance lower and higher estimates ("from 30,000 to 500,000"). It noted that 40,000 Americans were killed during the Normandy invasion, and that the total killed in the Pacific theater was "about 90,000." It raised the figure of dead in the Leahy estimate from 50,000 to 67,000 and characterized estimates of expected American deaths as "horrendous." It said that "Japanese deaths, military and civilian, would have been many times greater, as they had been throughout the war." The October revised script reflected the results of the negotiated settlement with the American Legion. While it still noted that estimates "varied greatly," it said that casualties "conceivably could have risen to as many as a million (including up to a quarter of a million deaths)." The script declared that the Japanese would have suffered "five times" as many casualties. (In this formula, American and Japanese casualties came to six million, suggesting, perhaps, an unconscious reaching for an invasion-of-Japan "Holocaust.") The exhibit now endorsed—somewhat conditionally—the "worst case" casualty figures, and the labels had been written by the public relations director and an exhibit editor, not the curators.

After hearing complaints by historian Barton Bernstein and other critics of the museum's script revisions in November, Martin Harwit asked Michael Neufeld if there were factual criticisms that the museum could respond to. Neufeld replied that Bernstein had discovered the following sentence in Admiral Leahy's diary: "[Army chief of staff George] Marshall is of the opinion that such an effort [Operation Olympic] will not cost us in casualties more than 63,000 of the 190,000 troops estimated as necessary for the operation." Bernstein made the argument that when Leahy used the 35 percent casualty figure based on Okinawa casualty rates, it was not from the whole invasion force but from the combat force. Aware that lowering the figures was politically dangerous, Neufeld recommended a modest change in the label: "Admiral Leahy pointed out that the huge invasion force could sustain losses proportional to those on Okinawa—about 35 percent—which would make the operation much more costly than Marshall estimated."[71]

In mid-December, Neufeld was "stunned" to learn that Martin Harwit and Steven Soter had once again changed the second half of the invasion casualties text. "Although Martin later denied it," Neufeld said, "I remember him explicitly saying that we had to get away from us endorsing a potential worse-case scenario of a million American and five million Japanese dead . . . and put the responsibility back on Truman. . . . Martin later claimed that the 63,000 number had undermined his faith in the ultimate high numbers. I pushed him a little . . . by pointing out to him how politically dangerous this label was and I asked him whether he needed to clear this with the A.L. [American Legion] or others first. He said no." Neufeld later told colleagues, "This is suicidal."[72]

On January 9, 1995, Harwit wrote the legion's Hubert Dagley, informing him that as a result of the new interpretation of the Leahy diary entry, he had come to realize that the earlier text was based on a "misapprehension." Harwit enclosed the new text, which, he said, "does not alter the figures Truman cited after the war, but gives a different interpretation of what he might have had in mind." The label no longer was to say that Leahy estimated a "quarter of a million casualties," and "at least 50,000 dead," nor did it mention "perhaps five million" Japanese casualties. Rather it said, "Japan would also have lost many additional lives." It pointed out that Truman's high figures were made "after the war," and that "the origins of these figures is uncertain." Backing away from explicit endorsement of worst-case casualty figures, the text ended with an orthodox reading of Truman's motivation for using atomic weapons. "For Truman, even the lowest of the casualty estimates was unacceptable. To prevent an invasion and to save as many lives as possible, he chose to use the atomic bomb." Harwit asked Dagley to send any "concerns or comments."[73]

The legion reacted angrily. For them, Harwit's letter not only once again revised iconic numbers but reinforced a suspicion that, according to Dagley, "we could not rely on the assurances of either Smithsonian or [NASM] officials; in other words, we had no certainty that the exhibit to which we might attach our agreement would be the same exhibit finally mounted in May 1995."[74]

Harwit read the endgame differently, arguing that well before his letter to Dagley, the legion was looking for a way out of their relationship. Indeed, on January 4, 1995, five days *before* Harwit's letter to Dagley, National Commander William M. Detweiler informed his advisory committee that he believed the legion should "actively oppose" the exhibit, that Congress should investigate the museum's "role and intent in the controversy," and that the *"Enola Gay . . .* be immediately re-assembled and loaned, or ownership transferred, to an entity willing and able to display it without controversy." Detweiler specified the form of opposition, including meetings with members of Congress, a press conference in Washington, and "continued maximum exposure of the Legion's position in the public media."[75]

Given the evident importance of the politics of numbers, there was simply no way for the museum to satisfy all concerned parties except through the vaguest of formulations. Wilcomb Washburn, the director of American studies at the Smithsonian, wondered, in retrospect, if the curators could have indicated the "uncertainty" of casualties by plastering a wall "with such numbers, each with a question mark after it." Former chief of air force history Richard Kohn presented an even more commonsense solution and cautionary note to Martin Harwit in June 1994. "I've always thought," he wrote, "the casualty argument . . . simple-minded and lacking in context. The real issue was the campaign, not just the invasion. With Japan prepared to fight all-out indefinitely, and having stockpiled 9,000 aircraft, most for kamikaze use, the casualties would have been just tremendous on *both* sides, and everybody at the time knew it. That should be explained; planners put in numbers because that is necessary for logistical and other reasons, but to argue about them is utterly to miss the point, and that is what scholars have done. The controversy over numbers trivializes the business. If one were to project Iwo Jima and Okinawa onto Japan, the numbers are horrendous—and this whole dispute is in my judgment an embarrassment to the historical profession."[76]

Even before Heyman announced on January 30, 1995, that the exhibit would be canceled and replaced by a drastically scaled-back one, members of Congress had called for Harwit's resignation, and the AFA had joined with the American Legion in calling for a congressional investigation. Harwit resigned on May 2, writing Heyman, "I believe that nothing less than my stepping down from the directorship will satisfy the Museum's critics and allow the Museum to move forward."[77]

A Controversy for All Purposes

In the end, everyone believed that memory and history had been abused, and the controversy over the *Enola Gay* exhibit became a useful symbol for all sides in the history wars going on in America. For *U.S. News & World Report*'s John Leo, the proposed exhibit had been part of the "same dark vision of America as arrogant, oppressive, racist and destructive [that] increasingly runs through the Smithsonian complex." For presidential hopeful Patrick Buchanan, the conspiracy was wider than a "dark vision" at the Smithsonian. It was the result of a "sleepless campaign to inculcate in American youth a revulsion toward America's past. The Left's long march through our institutions is now complete. . . . They are now serving up, in our museums and colleges, a constant diet of the same poison of anti-Americanism upon which they themselves were fed." For Representative Sam Johnson, a Republican from Texas and air force veteran who was appointed to the Smithsonian Board of Regents by new Speaker of the House Newt Gingrich, the outpouring of anger at the Smithsonian indicated that "people" were taking back their history from elites. "We've got to get patriotism back into the Smithsonian," he declared. "We want the Smithsonian to reflect real America and not something that a historian dreamed up."[78]

For others, the opposition to and cancellation of the exhibition pointed to a poisonous reactionary populism, the heavy hand of governmental censorship, and a future in which controversial historical issues could not be addressed in public museums. Alfred F. Young, senior research fellow at the Newberry Library and a member of the executive board of the Organization of American Historians, warned that the "museum horrors of the previous few years raise questions that go to the heart of the enterprise of historical museums in the United States; their function in American society; the role of historians in museums; the role of interpretation and authorial responsibility in exhibits; scholarly peer review; and how museums should deal with those who have a stake in their exhibits and with public controversy in general—in short the entire decision making process." Young was not convinced that "balance" solved the problem. It could be a "recipe for blandness—the alleged professorial 'on the one hand' and 'on the other hand.' Curators should be free to take alternative paths to confront controversy . . . to question myths . . . to stir a passion for justice . . . to create empathy . . . or to challenge sacred cows." Many museum professionals both deplored the political pressures that led to the cancellation and spoke of a renewed conviction that historians involved in museum projects needed a much greater appreciation of the difference between an exhibit and a book. "Not everything you can write in a book is fair game for a museum exhibition," one Smithsonian curator told me. "The reality is, we must pay attention to those with political power as we plan exhibits. I'm not sure that Martin Harwit appreciated this enough with regard to this exhibition, nor do I think that the historians involved in the project appreciated enough what the political cost would be, given that they were so familiar and comfortable with these arguments."[79]

Historian and advisory board member Martin Sherwin thought that as a result of the controversy, Santayana's famous aphorism "Those who cannot remember the past are condemned to repeat it" would have to be restated as, "Those who insist only on their memories of the past are condemning the rest of us to avoid it." Michael Kammen, president of the Organization of American Historians and a member of the Smithsonian Council, called attention to a "vindictive partisanship that prompts elected officials to punish (or threaten to punish) their foes by withholding public funds. . . . Historians become controversial when they do not perpetuate myths, when they do not transmit the received and conventional wisdom, when they challenge the comforting presence of a stabilized past. Members of a society, and its politicians in particular, prefer that historians be quietly irenic rather than polemical, conservators rather than innovators."[80]

It is also true, however, that certain volatile stories can be told in some cultural moments and not others. In the early 1980s, a period of high nuclear anxiety, it was possible to turn to Hiroshima and Nagasaki for cautionary lessons. In 1980, for example, Republican senator Mark Hatfield of Oregon helped bring an exhibition of artifacts and graphic photographs from the Hiroshima Peace Memorial Museum to the rotunda of the Old Senate Office Building in Washington, D.C. Hatfield had been in Hiroshima a month after it was destroyed and recalled, "The bomb saved my life. . . . But to see the indiscriminate devastation and to think that now the world has one million times the nuclear explosive power of that one bomb—maybe this exhibit will give us pause." In this period, remembering the horror of Hiroshima and Nagasaki played a crucial role in the antinuclear fervor of the time. For increasing numbers of Americans in those years, this was the chosen narrative.[81]

The cultural climate of the 1990s, however, proved far less amenable to the telling of this darker narrative about atomic weaponry, especially in the "temple" of the National Air and Space Museum. In the wake of the collapse of the Soviet Union, as fears about global nuclear war eased, other kinds of fears—about the nature of America and its global role in a world without a superenemy—rose to the surface. In the overwhelming bitterness expressed toward the curators and historians involved in the Smithsonian show and in the invective that so often accompanied it, there were anxieties that could not be accounted for by any argument over the nature of the *Enola Gay*'s mission, how to portray Japanese civilian victims, or what casualty figures to settle on in a projected invasion of Japan.

That darker narrative—particularly when applied to the "Good War"—seemed to tap into deeper fears about whether or not the United States was a righteous and innocent nation. For many, even to allow mention of the ambiguities and darknesses in our country's history appeared a dangerous activity. Representative Peter Blute of Massachusetts, one of the leading congressional opponents of the *Enola Gay* show, struck this note in declaring, "I don't want 16-year-olds walking out of [that museum] thinking badly about the U.S." Testifying before the Senate Committee on

Rules and Administration, the American Legion's Herman G. Harrington intoned this new mantra of anxiety. "We believe," he said, "in passing a sense of America's unique role in world history, and a sense of its greatness, on to future generations. And we believe that the National Air and Space Museum consciously and intentionally violated every one of those principles by setting out to alter our citizens' views of themselves." Telling an "alien" story, the museum, in Harrington's eyes, "cease[d] to be an American museum and bec[ame] something else entirely."[82]

Embedded in such fear of the power of historians' words to shake the confidence of Americans was a sense that the whole nation was now in need of a dose of patriotic therapy; that history's purpose must be to bolster the self-esteem of a country of increasingly needy and vulnerable citizens. The irony that Americans have so harshly criticized other nations—notably Japan—for being unable to confront the complexities and ambiguities of their history was largely lost on those who opposed the Smithsonian and its exhibition. Also lost was the possibility that an American audience might be ready, willing, and able to face the complex past that the *Enola Gay* embodies.

Visitors to the United States Holocaust Memorial Museum just down the Mall from the National Air and Space Museum have, since 1993, had exactly that opportunity. There, they learn that Americans encountered and liberated the camps and that many Holocaust survivors found a home in the United States. They also learn, however, about official American anti-Semitism that kept thousands of European Jews from legally emigrating to this country. They find out that the SS *St. Louis* was turned away from American shores in 1939, resulting in the deaths of many passengers in the Holocaust. At that museum, visitors are judged to be mature enough to be able to confront a complex story. Sadly, they were not given a similar opportunity to engage the story of the end of the war and the use of the atomic bomb (as well as its various legacies) at the National Air and Space Museum.

2

THREE NARRATIVES
OF OUR HUMANITY

• JOHN W. DOWER •

Hiroshima as Victimization

For many years, American pundits and politicians have condemned the Japanese for failing to confront their role in World
War II honestly. Japan's "historical amnesia" has become a mantra in the media, and the Japanese are routinely castigated for
"sanitizing" the historical record of their aggression and atrocities.
There are solid grounds for such criticism. Until recently, textbooks approved by Japan's conservative Ministry of Education did
sanitize the treatment of Japan's aggressive actions in Asia and the
Pacific. For a while, even the term *shinryaku*, variously translated
as "aggression" or "invasion," was expunged from textbook accounts of the Japanese war against China that began in the 1930s.
Although the Education Ministry abandoned such blatant censorship in the 1990s, nationalistic Japanese, including conservative
politicians at the ministerial level, have continued with almost
metronomelike regularity to draw foreign scorn by publicly white-
washing their country's wartime behavior.

Even in 1995, the fiftieth anniversary of the end of the war, the
Japanese government found it difficult to acknowledge and apolo-
gize for imperial Japan's transgressions. Prime Minister Tomiichi
Murayama, the Socialist head of a fragile coalition government,

did indeed use August 15, the date of Japan's capitulation, as the occasion for a major speech condemning and apologizing for Japanese aggression and atrocities. His forthright statement was all the more notable because it followed the conspicuous failure of the lower house of the Diet, Japan's bicameral parliament, to agree on a similar apology. In a diluted resolution passed after great controversy on June 9, conservatives including Murayama's own coalition partners prevented the issuance of an unqualified apology (*shazai*) to Japan's war victims. Instead, they offered an expression of "deep remorse" (*fukai hansei*) for "inflicting pain and suffering upon the peoples of other countries, especially in Asia"—while simultaneously affirming that Japan's transgressions were not particularly unusual. In its final form, the brief Diet resolution emphasized that Japanese aggression and oppression abroad took place in the broader context of "many instances of colonial rule and acts of aggression (*shinryaku-teki kōi*) in the modern history of the world."[1]

Underlying this difficulty in confronting the past is the fact that many Japanese still recall the war experience primarily in terms of their own victimization. "Victim consciousness" (*higaisha ishiki*) is a familiar term in Japan, and the attitude itself finds expression at several levels. To old-guard nationalists, the wartime rationale for resorting to arms in the first place—to secure Japan's rightful place in the face of Western imperialism and Communist subversion in Asia (the "white" and "red" threats, as they used to be called)—still has validity. The pre–Pearl Harbor Asia they evoke is one in which Southeast Asia was controlled by European and American colonial powers, Japanese "treaty rights" in China were threatened by civil strife and Soviet-inspired radicalism, and the global political economy had been plunged into chaos by the collapse of a capitalist system centered in New York and London.

Japanese old enough to remember the war years are particularly sympathetic to this image of imperial Japan as a vulnerable nation struggling for security in a hostile world. Most Japanese, however, remember the war, or have been socialized to remember it, as it came home to them. For them, World War II calls to mind the deaths of family and acquaintances on distant battlefields and, more vividly, the prolonged, systematic bombing of their cities. Around three million Japanese were killed in what their government touted as the "Great East Asia War" (*Dai Tōa Sensō*), including more than four hundred thousand civilians who died in the air raids.

For a number of years after the war, moreover, most urban Japanese moved amid the rubble of bombed buildings and lived in a world of acute material scarcity. Until 1948 or even later, housewives cited food—where the next meal would come from—as their overwhelming source of concern. In most sectors of the economy, indexes of production did not begin to surpass the levels reached in the early 1930s until the mid-1950s, a full decade after Japan surrendered. Thus, the generation of Japanese who were children in the immediate postsurrender period, though too young to actually remember the killing years, nonetheless retains vivid memories of the war as a cause of personal deprivation and tribulation.

Such preoccupation with one's own suffering is natural and commonplace, but in Japan the narrative of victimization has assumed a unique dimension because of Hiroshima and Nagasaki. Over fifty million people were killed worldwide in World War II, many millions of them by the Japanese; but the trauma of nuclear destruction was experienced only in Japan. It is incorrect, of course, to say that only Japanese were killed by the atomic bombs, for the victims in Hiroshima and Nagasaki included thousands of Korean colonial subjects who had been conscripted for heavy labor, many hundreds of Japanese Americans who were stranded in Japan after Pearl Harbor, a dozen or more American prisoners of war, and small numbers of individuals from China, Southeast Asia, and Europe. In the popular Japanese consciousness, however, "the Japanese" tend to be regarded as the sole victims of the bombs (although this exclusivity—what might be called the reactive pride and possessiveness of victimization—is slowly diminishing).

More than battlefield casualties or the civilian deaths caused by conventional strategic bombing, these two cataclysmic moments of nuclear destruction solidified the Japanese sense of uniquely terrible victimization. The atomic bombs became the symbol of a special sort of suffering—much like the Holocaust for the Jews. The sixth and ninth days of August 1945 became detached from the ordinary calendar of World War II. Many Japanese still see themselves as having been chosen, almost in a religious sense, to bear witness to the apocalyptic vision of a world-destroying future that must not be allowed to happen.

The play of language in these matters is revealing. Even today, mainstream American commentary typically refers to the civilians killed in both the conventional and nuclear air raids against Japan as "casualties." Such leveling language—by making no distinction between combatants and noncombatants—helps legitimize the deliberate killing of enemy civilians. While the Japanese also refer to their collective "killed and injured" (*shishōsha*), it is more common to identify civilian fatalities and casualties as "victims" (*higaisha*, or even *giseisha*, a word connoting "sacrifices"). Victims of the atomic bombs, in turn, bear the special Japanese designation *hibakusha*. In its original and still most prevalent usage, this is written with three ideographs literally meaning "receive-explosion-person (or people)." The phonetic element *baku* is also occasionally rendered with an alternative ideograph meaning "exposure" (to radiation). This ambiguity of meaning is emblematic of a larger popular confusion regarding the victims of the atomic bombs, for the term *hibakusha* now legally applies to all Japanese who were within two kilometers of the epicenters of the bombs at the time they were dropped or during the days immediately following—regardless of their degree of exposure to radiation, or the severity of their atomic bomb–related injuries or illnesses. As the negative social stigma of being identified as an atomic bomb victim has been overridden by the medical or financial benefits to be gained from such an identity—benefits that have been extracted only belatedly from the Japanese government—this confusion has become greater.

Until recently, the somber Peace Memorial Museum in Hiroshima could be taken as an almost perfect example of the public enshrinement of such subjective recollection of the war's special horrors. Untutored visitors to the museum might easily have concluded that the war began for Japan on August 6, 1945, with the dropping of the first atomic bomb by the United States. In this Japanese war memorial, there was no Rape of Nanking, no Pearl Harbor, no Bataan Death March, no echo of the shrill voices of Emperor Hirohito's minions exhorting the "hundred million" to fight to the last man, woman, and child. There was no old photograph of the uniformed "god-emperor" himself, in whose name all the killing and dying had taken place.

In recent years, however, the victimization narrative has begun to lose its primacy. Japan's renewal of diplomatic relations with the People's Republic of China in the early 1970s prompted serious journalistic and academic treatment of Japanese atrocities against the Chinese as well as other Asians. And Hirohito's death in 1989, in the sixty-fourth year of his reign, removed the final taboo on discussion of Japan's war responsibility. Until the emperor died, forthright critical discussion of the war threatened to spill over into lèse-majesté, since it invariably raised questions about Hirohito's own moral as well as political responsibility for Japan's war crimes. The emperor's passing opened the door to critical engagement with the past.[2]

The Japanese themselves naturally bear primary responsibility for this long delay in addressing their war responsibility. Nevertheless, both the belated opening to China and the taboos associated with Hirohito's continued presence on the throne reveal the subtle and often perverse role the United States has played in shaping postwar Japanese discourse and practice. It is heretical but by no means excessive to argue that much of the "historical amnesia" Americans are fond of ascribing to the Japanese was for decades congruent with Washington's own objectives in Japan and Asia.

This is fairly obvious in the case of Japanese attitudes toward China. For more than two decades beginning in 1950, the Japanese government had no choice but to adhere to the U.S. Cold

War containment policy. In these circumstances—which coincided with intense U.S. pressure for Japanese rearmament—it served the purposes of both Japan's conservative leaders and their patrons in Washington to demonize the Chinese and downplay the aggressive nature of Japan's recent militaristic practices. In the heyday of the Cold War, that is, when in addition to promoting Japanese rearmament the United States was simultaneously touting Japan as an exemplary model of noncommunist "modernization," the soft-pedaling of Japan's war responsibility was an American *policy*, and not merely a peculiarly Japanese manifestation of nationalistic forgetfulness. Downplaying prewar Japanese militarism, sanitizing Japanese atrocities, minimizing the horror of war in general—including the horror of Hiroshima and Nagasaki—was a bilateral agenda.

Less well known is the manner in which the United States influenced Japanese reflections on war responsibility by its postwar policy toward Emperor Hirohito. Essentially for reasons of political expediency, American authorities in occupied Japan chose to absolve Hirohito from any taint of moral as well as legal responsibility for Japanese wartime actions. Doing so made it easier to administer the defeated nation. In practical terms, this entailed more than just exempting the emperor from the "Class-A" Tokyo war crimes trials that were conducted between mid-1946 and the end of 1948. On more than one occasion, occupation authorities also brushed aside high-level Japanese inquiries about whether Hirohito should abdicate as an acknowledgment of his moral responsibility for the war. With the supreme political and spiritual leader of the land absolved from any taint of juridical or moral responsibility for Japanese aggression, it was hardly surprising that the general populace saw little need for serious self-criticism. One could always just blame Japan's transgressions—as the Tokyo war crimes trials essentially did—on a cabal of conspiratorial militarists.

In these intricate and convoluted ways, the deep psychology of Japanese victim consciousness became entangled with political manipulation that reflected not merely the nationalism and

revanchism of conservative leaders but also the peculiar require-
ments of the postwar relationship between the United States and
Japan. At the same time, there have been conspicuous domestic
countercurrents to these attitudes ever since the end of the war.
Japanese leftists, including the Japan Communist Party and many
respected historians and social scientists, have consistently coupled a critique of the "emperor system" with strong emphasis on
Japan's particular *senso sekinin*, or "war responsibility."[3] Beginning in 1965, the judicial system became the venue for a protracted and highly publicized attack on the Ministry of
Education's sanitization of textbooks. The opening to China in
the early 1970s paved the way for detailed media treatments (as
well as predictable right-wing denials) of the Rape of Nanking and
other acts of atrocity. In recent years, scholars and the mass media
have devoted impressive energy to exposing such institutionalized
atrocities as lethal medical experiments on prisoners (centering on
the notorious Unit 731 in Manchuria) and the sexual enslavement
of huge numbers of non-Japanese "comfort women" who were
forced to serve the emperor's loyal soldiers and sailors.[4]

Public institutions have belatedly begun to reflect this changing consciousness. The Ministry of Education's watchmen, responding to domestic as well as foreign criticism, now condone
more forthright textbook treatment of Japanese aggression and
colonialism, including the Rape of Nanking and the oppression of
colonial subjects, especially Koreans.[5] Even the atomic bomb museum in Hiroshima (along with its counterpart in Nagasaki) has
made a gesture toward adding broader contextual material. Japan's aggression in Asia is now noted, Hiroshima is identified as a
city engaged in military activity, and at least passing attention is
paid to the presence of thousands of conscripted Korean laborers
in the city at the time the bomb fell.

With all this in mind, it is possible to draw several immediate
contrasts between Japanese and American recollections of the war.

In the Japanese milieu, the abiding sense of victimization has
contributed to a distinctive sort of nationalistic antimilitarism.
"Victim consciousness" may be subjective and nationalistic, but

the intense memories of individual suffering in World War II have fostered a strong popular strain of pacifist sentiment. Predictably, the atomic bombs occupy a central place in this antimilitarism, for the personal horrors of Hiroshima and Nagasaki provide a concrete, focused, unique, extraordinarily graphic and horrifying symbolic "epicenter" for prevailing antiwar sentiment. At the same time, and without real contradiction, a great many Japanese have undertaken to turn their "unique" experience of nuclear devastation into a universal message. The obvious "lesson of Hiroshima and Nagasaki," Japanese at all levels of society commonly declare, is that all peoples and nations must work for a world without nuclear weapons.

To most Americans, on the contrary, the abiding symbol of victimization in World War II is Pearl Harbor, which has succored an almost unassailable commitment to everlasting military preparedness and vigilance. And Hiroshima? The shattered, atomized, irradiated city remains largely a triumphal symbol—marking the end of a horrendous global conflict and the effective demonstration of a weapon that, by its "deterrence" effects, has prevented a third world war in the half century since World War II ended.[6]

In moving toward franker acknowledgment of their war crimes, the Japanese have begun to embrace a nuanced sort of war memory that is also quite alien to mainstream sentiments in the United States today. Japanese "victim consciousness" has become paired with a keener "victimizer consciousness" (*kagaisha ishiki* in the popular Japanese rendering). Whether actively or passively, most Japanese men and women who died abroad or were killed at home supported imperial Japan's rapacious war policy, as did those who survived the defeat.

That victims (*higaisha*) may simultaneously be victimizers (*kagaisha*) of others is the sort of notion we usually associate with ivory tower intellectualizing or works of tragedy. In Japan in recent years, however, this has been a subject of extended discussion in the country's several national newspapers, which reach tens of millions of readers daily. How seriously the general public has taken this issue is suggested by a 1994 opinion poll that found that 80 percent of Japanese believe their government has not adequately compensated the victimized peoples (as opposed to governments) in those Asian countries Japan colonized or invaded.[7] This is hardly the response of a people suffering from acute historical amnesia.

By contrast, as the fiasco of the *Enola Gay* exhibition at the Smithsonian Institution showed, American recollections of the war reveal a powerful emotional and ideological impulse to strip the historical record of all ambiguity, all contradiction, all moral complexity, and simply wrap it in the flag. Few developments in World War II were as momentous as the decision to develop and use the atomic bomb. Like few other moments in the war, August 6 and 9, 1945, epitomize graphically the ambiguous identities of victims and victimizers, an ambiguity inherent in Allied war policies—specifically, the Anglo-American decision to win the "Good War" against fascism and barbarism by identifying civilian men, women, and children as legitimate targets of strategic bombing. No serious chronicle of the horrors of our modern times can fail to mention Hiroshima and Nagasaki. None of the war's legacies have been more enduring and ominous than the nuclear one.

Yet in 1995—the fiftieth anniversary of the end of the war, a signal moment when people usually try to come to terms with the past—it became clear that federal institutions in the United States could not seriously address these issues. And it also became clear that citizens who raise intellectual and moral questions about the use of the bombs and the legacies of Hiroshima do so at the peril of being denounced as ideologues or even traitors.

Hiroshima as Triumph

If we think in terms of master narratives or "meta-narratives" of the war, the mainstream American counterpart to the victimization narrative that has preoccupied so many Japanese is obvious.

It is a heroic or triumphal narrative, in which the atomic bombs represent the final blow against an aggressive, fanatical, and savage foe. Hiroshima and Nagasaki become, as it were, a double exclamation point marking the end of the "Good War."

The title of a well-known essay by Paul Fussell, "Thank God for the Atom Bomb," perfectly captures in the plainest and most familiar capsule form the heroic rendering of the end of the war. This is a seductive phrase (doubly so, since it immediately brings God in on the American side, reminding us *pari passu* that the Japanese are pagans). And it invokes a simple, plausible argument: that the bombs were used to end the war against the last remaining Axis power quickly, thereby saving countless American lives. Fussell, a gritty and skillful writer about modern warfare, regards himself as one of those potentially saved, for he was among the young Americans scheduled to participate in the invasion of Japan.[8]

Many critics of the Smithsonian's original plans to mount an ambitious and nuanced exhibition argued that it was inappropriate for a public institution to go beyond the "simple fact" that the bomb was used to end the war and save American lives. As the intensely emotional attack on the museum's original plans revealed, however, the heroic narrative is much richer than a humble thank-you to God for deliverance. The bombs were not merely necessary. They also were just, in the biblical sense of righteous retribution against a savage enemy.

From this critical perspective, the bombs were "moral" and even humane. In August 1994, for example, Richard Hallion, the chief historian of the air force, publicly declared that the use of the bombs was "morally unambiguous" and that the Smithsonian curators' inability to get this straight was inexplicable. Four months later, seven members of the House of Representatives, led by Sam Johnson (who later chaired a House inquiry into the Smithsonian's conduct), wrote a denunciatory letter to the secretary of the Smithsonian that made Hallion's declaration pale by comparison. The nuclear bombing of Hiroshima and Nagasaki, these members of the lower house exclaimed, was "one of the most morally unambiguous events of the 20th century."[9] In the view of the Senate, the nuclear incineration of residents of the two Japanese cities was, indeed, "merciful." This stunning adjective, so alien to Japanese perceptions, appeared in a unanimously passed Senate resolution condemning the Smithsonian's original plans. In the Senate's words, "the role of the Enola Gay during World War II was momentous in helping to bring World War II to a merciful end, which resulted in saving the lives of Americans and Japanese."[10]

The Senate's resolution also made explicit the hitherto little-known fact that under federal law it is the duty of institutions such as the Smithsonian to commemorate "the valor and sacrificial service" of America's fighting forces, and to portray these forces as "an inspiration to the present and future generations of America." The proposed *Enola Gay* exhibition, it was stated, was "offensive to many World War II veterans" and would impugn "the memory of those who gave their lives for freedom." By official fiat, in other words, federally funded history in the United States, particularly where the country's military history is concerned, must be almost exclusively celebratory.

Veneration of one's war dead is hardly an exceptional sentiment, and in this regard the Senate resolution actually bears an interesting resemblance to the argument advanced by conservative Japanese who opposed any Diet resolution expressing "remorse" or "apology" for Japan's war. For obvious reasons, there can be no "heroic narrative" of the war itself in Japan. More agonizing for many Japanese, particularly those who lost family and friends on the battlefield, is the near impossibility of publicly praising those who died. Even if the nation's policies were misguided, and even if some elements of the imperial forces committed atrocities, these conservatives argue, it is still appropriate—and psychologically necessary—to acknowledge the valor and self-sacrifice of the roughly two million fighting men who gave their lives for their country. Thus, a petition opposing a Diet apology for the war, which reportedly attracted five million signatures, argued—much as the Senate condemnation of the proposed

Enola Gay exhibition did—that an unqualified, "one-sided" apology "harms the honor of our nation and race, desecrates our heroes who died for the nation at its time of crisis, and will become a grave source of trouble for the future of our country and people."[11]

In the Smithsonian imbroglio, intolerance for deviation from the heroic narrative found its most common expression in a blanket attack on "revisionism," seen as a perverse practice peculiar to anti-American left-wing ideologues. An uninformed observer of the conservative hue and cry of the mid-1990s could never have imagined that there had been a prior history of principled criticism of the bombs from across the political and religious spectrum, beginning from the moment Hiroshima and Nagasaki were devastated.[12] Thus, the Senate condemned the Smithsonian's plans for being "revisionist and offensive." John T. Correll, the editor in chief of *Air Force Magazine* who launched some of the earliest attacks on the National Air and Space Museum, denounced the original script as "historical revisionism at its worst."[13] Some two dozen congressional representatives wrote the secretary of the Smithsonian denouncing the "anti-American prejudice and imbalance of the exhibit."[14] The institution's job, it frequently was said, was "to tell history, not rewrite it."[15] Newt Gingrich, the new Republican leader of the House of Representatives, declared that the Smithsonian's proposed exhibition had become a "plaything for left-wing ideologies."[16]

Much of the media followed suit. The *Wall Street Journal* declared that the museum's curators were influenced by "academics unable to view American history as anything other than a woeful catalog of crimes and aggressions against the helpless peoples of the earth."[17] The *Washington Post*, not generally regarded as a clone of the *Wall Street Journal*, was in essential agreement on this issue. In an editorial, it condemned the museum's original scripts for their "tendentiously anti-nuclear and anti-American tone."[18] In the words of Jonathan Yardley, one of the *Post*'s columnists, the National Air and Space Museum was "seeking to engage in what can fairly be called anti-American propaganda." Yardley went on to use the controversy as a point of departure for an attack on "deconstructionist" critical theory in general. "Especially now," he wrote, "when the rank odor of deconstruction hangs over the scholarly community, it is easy for people to fabricate intellectual arguments for the triviality of facts and then to find whatever 'meaning' they choose in such facts, or non-facts, as they are willing to 'deconstruct' for their ideological convenience."[19]

Such fulmination trivialized the serious issues involved in the debate over use of the atomic bombs. At the same time, however, it made clear to many critics that the *Enola Gay* controversy was but the most recent—and perhaps most ominously contagious— eruption in the so-called culture wars. Where the Smithsonian's various museums were concerned, critics traced the virus of "politically correct curating" back to a precise origin: the exhibition dealing with the World War II incarceration of Japanese Americans titled "A More Perfect Union," which was installed in the National Museum of American History in 1987 and is still in place. In the same museum, the virus of "political correctness" was subsequently discerned in a 1991 installation titled "The West as America: Reinterpreting Images of the Frontier, 1820–1920," which offered critical commentaries on traditional romanticizations of the frontier experience. An exhibition called "Science in American Life" in the National Museum of American History drew similar fire for its attentiveness to such negative byproducts of scientific development as nuclear destruction and environmental degradation. In the National Air and Space Museum, the proposed *Enola Gay* exhibition was not the first undertaking to provoke the ire of conservative critics. A popular exhibition installed several years earlier, "Legend, Memory, and the Great War in the Air," which incisively debunks the "Hollywood" romanticization of pilots and planes in World War I, also has been denounced as left-wing propaganda. The "Great War in the Air" exhibition concludes with a video that conveys, in terse, shocking footage, the horrendously destructive legacy of strategic bombing that followed World War I: from World War II through the U.S. air war against Indochina to the high-tech air strikes by Americans in the Gulf War of 1991.[20]

None of these prior presentations, however, provoked criticism remotely comparable to that leveled at the Smithsonian's original plans for an *Enola Gay* exhibition. The visceral, seldom qualified attack on historical "revisionism" triggered by the attempt to treat the dropping of the bombs in a less than celebratory manner was a chilling broadside, for the lifeblood of serious intellectual inquiry in the humanities, social sciences, and natural sciences—and the lifeblood of democracy itself—lies in tolerance of principled criticism, a constant willingness to entertain serious challenges to entrenched and orthodox views. More specifically, the thwarting of this complex, probing exhibition amounted to a repudiation of what historians do. Serious historians are not mere scribes. They are not just entertaining storytellers or uncritical reciters of narratives handed down to them. They do not believe—as many of the Smithsonian's critics assumed—that "facts" (or artifacts, such as the *Enola Gay* B-29 Superfortress) "speak for themselves," or that "interpretation" is a vice, a luxury, an embellishment, an indulgence, rather than a necessity.

Serious historians do not define their task as one of celebration (such a task, by definition, is the province of propagandists), although certainly they may find occasions to celebrate—such as the victory over Nazism, fascism, and Japan's peculiar brand of fanatical emperor-centered aggression and oppression. Their primary task is to use the perspective of time, together with access to previously unavailable materials, to rethink the past. In the process, historians often embrace ambiguity (including the possibility that one might be both victim and victimizer). They believe, at least ideally, that one learns from controversy—indeed, that an expansive, detailed, controversial exhibition introducing the debates about the atomic bombs and their use that have unfolded among scholars and concerned citizens over the course of the last half century would have found an intelligent audience capable of forming its own judgments.

As a historian specializing in Japan and detached from the visceral emotions of half a century ago (I was seven years old when the war ended), I find much of the heroic American narrative compelling. The imperial Japanese war machine *was* aggressive, atrocious, and fanatical. The imperial high command, including Emperor Hirohito himself, was to virtually the very end inflexible, irrational, indifferent to atrocities committed by the imperial government and imperial forces, and immune to genuine sympathy for the suffering of ordinary Japanese. Japan at war's end, just as at war's beginning, was a formidable war machine headed by an intelligent but obtuse sovereign.

In retrospect, it seems clear that Japan was near the end of its tether by the time the bombs were dropped. A now-famous intelligence report made public by the U.S. Strategic Bombing Survey in July 1946, for instance, speculated that Japan would have been forced to surrender by the end of 1945, and possibly as early as November 1, without the atomic bombs, Soviet entry into the war (which occurred on August 8), or an invasion by U.S. forces.[21] At the same time, however, Japanese battle plans operative when the bombs were dropped still called for a massive, suicidal defense of the home islands, in which the imperial government would mobilize not only several million fighting men but also millions of ordinary citizens who had been trained and indoctrinated to resist to the end with primitive makeshift weapons.[22] Even to discuss capitulation was seditious (as well as psychologically impossible for the high command).

This said, it still remains to be asked: What does the heroic narrative omit? The answers to this question are numerous.

For example, the triumphal narrative commonly ignores materials that have become available since the war ended. For instance, Truman's fascinating, handwritten "Potsdam diary," in which the president recorded his immediate (and somewhat confused) response to learning about the successful "Trinity" test of the atomic bomb on July 16, did not become known to researchers until 1978.[23] Also, it was only belatedly that impeccably patriotic military leaders such as General Dwight D. Eisenhower and Admiral William D. Leahy made known their concerns about both the morality and necessity of using the bombs. Postwar researchers—Martin Sherwin, Barton Bernstein, Gar Alperovitz, Richard Rhodes, and Stanley Goldberg, among them—have drawn on a

vast array of declassified U.S. documents to offer closely anno-
tated reinterpretations of the "facts" Anglo-American political
leaders presented in 1945 and the years shortly thereafter to justify
dropping the bombs.[24]

The heroic narrative also tends to neglect Nagasaki. Even if it is
argued that the nuclear bombing of Hiroshima was necessary to
shock the Japanese into surrender, how does one justify the hasty
bombing of Nagasaki a mere three days later, before the Japanese
had time to investigate Hiroshima and formulate a responsive
policy? The American narrative almost invariably ends with Hiroshima, as the fixation on the *Enola Gay* reveals. (Who remembers
the name of the B-29 that dropped an atomic bomb on Nagasaki?)[25] Some years ago, a prominent Japanese conservative articulated a thesis shared by other Japanese: that the Hiroshima bomb
may have been necessary to shock Japan's fanatical militarist leaders into thinking about capitulation, but that the Nagasaki bomb
was unnecessary.[26] Needless to say, such ruminations have no
place in the heroic narrative.

Most serious Japanese accounts of the end of the war argue
that Japan's surrender was hastened by two cataclysmic developments: the atomic bombing of Hiroshima on August 6 and the
Soviet declaration of war against Japan two days later. U.S. officials at the highest level had long urged Stalin to enter the war
against Japan and had been assured by him at Potsdam that such
an entry was imminent. ("Fini Japs when that comes about,"
Truman wrote in his Potsdam diary on July 17.) The Soviet move,
so indisputably traumatic to the Japanese leadership at the time,
commonly receives little more than passing mention in the heroic
narrative. Usually ignored as well is a related, politically disruptive
question: Why did the United States hasten to atomize Hiroshima before the impact of the Soviet entry could be evaluated?

Historians of the decision to drop the bombs also pay close
attention to projected as well as actual chronologies. The "thank
God for the atom bomb" thesis—the very heart of the heroic
narrative, which emphasizes that it was essential to drop the
bombs quickly in order to save huge numbers of American lives—

must gloss over the now well-known timetables of the U.S. high command. No invasion of Japan was contemplated until November 1945, when an initial assault on the southern island of Kyushu was planned. The major invasion of the Japanese home islands, focusing on the Kanto Plain in the strategic Tokyo-Yokohama area, was to take place in March 1946. These timetables, projected in top-secret battle plans code-named Olympic and Coronet, are pertinent to the way "facts" are used, or misused, in the heroic narrative.

Most group-centered narratives, whether of triumph or victimization, involve an almost sacred numerology. In victimization narratives, for instance, there arises an almost irresistible impetus not only to maximize the quantification of one's own suffering but also to diminish countervailing or potentially "competitive" numbers pertaining to other victims. This can be seen in Jewish Holocaust studies, where the figures of six million Jews and five million "other" victims of Nazi extermination have assumed a status of almost scriptural unassailability.[27] The problem of "quantifying victimization" also marks the controversy over the Rape of Nanking, where right-wing Japanese revisionists have regularly challenged the figure of 300,000 Chinese victims that is literally carved in stone on the memorial in Nanking commemorating the victims. It may be mere coincidence, but in recent years Japanese textbooks have come to support extremely high figures for *hibakusha* deaths—some 300,000 to 350,000 for the two cities combined—that exceed China's claims for the Rape of Nanking.[28]

In the heroic American narrative of the war, the numbers game plays itself out in two ways. On the one hand, minimal attention is given to the number and nature of both immediate and long-term Japanese deaths from the bombs. Where "casualty" figures are given for the two cities, they usually reflect early estimates now regarded as low by most researchers. ("Tens of thousands of deaths" was the passing statement in the eventual Smithsonian exhibition.) On the other hand, as the Smithsonian controversy vividly revealed, the "thank God for the atom bomb" thesis is strongly fixated on *imagined* American deaths—that is, on the number of American fighting men who probably would have been killed in an invasion. No one disputes that the total number of casualties in the two projected invasions would have been extremely high, but a great deal of energy is expended in debating *how* high. In the most popular versions of the heroic narrative, the favored imagined numbers—ranging from a half million to one million—have gained an almost talismanic power.

The psychology that drives such sacred numerology on all sides is understandable. And the numbers themselves, whether of real or anticipated casualties, deserve careful analysis. While it is eminently reasonable to argue that any national leader would and should have done everything in his power to end the war quickly, as President Truman did, it is not possible to argue that by dropping the two atomic bombs so quickly he immediately saved countless tens or hundreds of thousands of American lives. The Olympic and Coronet timetables tell us otherwise.

Virtually by definition, the heroic narrative is also hostile to two notions that most historians take for granted: that controversy is inherent in any ongoing process of historical interpretation, and that policymaking is driven by multiple considerations and imperatives. As originally conceived, for example, the *Enola Gay* exhibition at the National Air and Space Museum would have included a number of wall-texts entitled "Historical Controversies," offering concise summaries of arguments that scholars, scientists, policymakers, and concerned citizens have made over the past five decades. Quite apart from specific points of disagreement, museum critics like the American Legion's spokesmen were unnerved by the notion of controversy itself and opposed such texts in principle. To them, this was the very antithesis of simply telling history "like it was," and obviously suggested that no single "truth" could be proclaimed regarding the decision to drop the bombs. Heroic narratives demand a simple, unilinear story line.

In popular tellings, that simple line often takes the form of an intimate human-interest story. Let the ordinary man (or, much less commonly, woman), the individual on the spot, tell his tale. In the case of the atomic bombs, the American narrative almost invariably gravitates to Colonel Paul W. Tibbets, Jr., who piloted the famous plane, and his crew—brave and loyal men, as they surely were. And the pilot and his crew tell us, truthfully, what we know they will: that they carried out their mission without a second thought in order to save their comrades and help end the war.

Such accounts by ordinary participants can reveal a great deal. They personalize our feeling for the past, make the temper of the times more palpable. But they tell us little if anything about how top-level decisions were made—about who moved these men, who gave them their orders, and why. To seriously ask these questions is to enter the realm of multiple imperatives.

Ending the war quickly and saving American lives was obviously of immense concern to President Truman and his close advisers, and the suicidal ferociousness of Japan's resistance made it all the more urgent to seek a dramatic way to do so without having to invade the enemy homeland. Everyone, including the curators and academics tarred and feathered as "revisionists," accepts this. At the same time, largely on the basis of previously classified documents, we now have a more detailed and dynamic picture of a complex synergy of bureaucratic, diplomatic, political, and scientific imperatives that also impelled the decision to use the bombs against Japanese cities. Psychological imperatives, it is clear, came into play as well. Saving lives was by no means the only consideration that drove the bombings.

We now know, for example, that although the Manhattan Project was created late in 1941 out of fear that Nazi Germany might develop its own nuclear weapon, as early as 1943—before the Americans learned that the Germans had never seriously embarked on such a project, before Germany's collapse was obvious, before the United States was even close to testing such a weapon, and at a time when the deadly advance on the Japanese home islands was still in the future—military planners were already anticipating that Japan would be the target of the fearsome new weapon.[29] The original rationale for its development was soon superseded by technocratic imperatives and a relentless bureaucratic momentum.

We also possess an abundance of primary documentation indicating that, by mid-1945, top American leaders regarded the atomic bomb as an important *card* (a word used by Secretary of War Henry L. Stimson) to be played against the Soviet Union in the tense diplomatic game that was already straining relations between the two allies. To engage in such an exercise in "atomic diplomacy" was perfectly compatible with using the bombs to end the war quickly. These were converging imperatives. At the same time, such a convergence meant that the decision to rush the use of the new weapons was not based exclusively on immediate war issues.

Domestic political considerations also came into play as the Truman administration finalized its policy. The new president and his secretary of state, James Byrnes, both savvy veterans of Congress, were keenly aware that once the war ended, bipartisan unity would end with it. Both men were deeply concerned that if the costly, ultrasecret Manhattan Project failed to show concrete results before war's end, it would inevitably become a target of "relentless investigation and criticism" (in Byrnes's words) in postwar Washington.[30]

While the scientists who actually developed the atomic bombs had scant influence on, or even knowledge of, the policymaking process, the Manhattan Project provides historians with a compelling case study of scientific and technological imperatives at work—particularly where these involve intellectually and technically seductive new weapons systems. Although most scientists joined the project in the belief that they were engaged in a race against the Nazis to make a nuclear weapon, virtually none left after Germany was defeated. On the contrary, they actually intensified their efforts, afraid that the war might end before they finished. "I don't think there was any time where we worked harder at the speed-up than in the period after the German surrender," Robert Oppenheimer, the charismatic head of the Manhattan Project, testified after the war. The bomb—to use an oft-repeated evocative phrase—was "technically sweet." Victor Weisskopf, a distinguished physicist on the Manhattan Project, for example, later used this phrase in expressing regret that neither he nor his colleagues considered quitting once the original anti-Nazi rationale for building the weapon disappeared. "It was the attraction of the task," he recalled. "It was impossible to quit at that time. I am ashamed that I did not even think of it." The scientists simply wanted to see their grand undertaking through to the very end. In Weisskopf's retrospective view, the fact that they were ultimately "attracted by the subject itself, not its applications," constituted a "dangerous lesson" for the future, albeit one not necessarily heeded.[31]

Other considerations also drove the decision to use the bombs on Japanese cities. High scientific advisers to the president such as Arthur Compton and James B. Conant, for example, argued that the new weapon's unprecedented destructiveness should be demonstrated not just to the Japanese or Soviet leaderships but to the world at large by actual use in combat. As Compton put it in an important secret report in June 1945, "If the bomb were not used in the present war the world would have no adequate warning as to what was to be expected if war should break out again." Postwar attempts to control nuclear weaponry would thereby become more difficult. This was one of the arguments used at the time in rejecting the suggestion that the bomb's destructiveness be demonstrated not by being dropped on Japanese cities but by being detonated on a noncombat target.[32]

Killing several hundred thousand civilians in Hiroshima and Nagasaki did not prevent the postwar nuclear arms race, of course, and retrospective appraisals of this particular rationalization for using the bombs vary greatly. Was it a peculiarly American example of what we might call—fully realizing the horror of the term—idealistic mass slaughter? Can the use of the new weapon against urban populations be seen as the inauguration of postwar deterrence policy—a concrete, graphic demonstration that there must be no more Hiroshimas in the wars of the future? Here, in any case, we encounter yet another explicit, but secret, rationale for using the bomb that had nothing to do with ending the war quickly.

Postwar considerations of a different sort came into play as the terrible endgame unfolded. Many contemporary American critics of the use of the bombs, for example, argue that the United States might have hastened Japan's surrender by abandoning the demand for "unconditional surrender" first articulated vis-à-vis both Germany and Japan by President Franklin D. Roosevelt and Prime Minister Winston Churchill in 1943. This would have entailed offering the Japanese leadership the prospect of a *conditional* surrender by assuring them that the Allied victors would demand no change in Japan's imperial "national polity."

This is a contentious issue indeed and provides an excellent example of the controversy that exists even among the so-called revisionist critics of the heroic narrative. Those who regard the Allied failure to guarantee the preservation of the Japanese throne as one of the great lost opportunities rest their argument on several observations that reflect our ex post facto knowledge of matters U.S. policymakers secretly considered at the time. By early 1945, for example, it was publicly known that guaranteeing the continuation of the imperial system had strong support in Washington from high State Department officials such as Joseph Grew, the urbane and conservative former ambassador to Japan. Grew had imbibed a heady dose of reverence for the chrysanthemum throne from his upper-class Japanese acquaintances in the 1930s. Shortly after the war it became known that Grew's advocacy of conditional surrender had received top-level consideration beginning in June 1945, only to be ultimately rejected. Through their ultrasecret code-breaking operations, we now know, the Americans had also been aware as early as June 1945 of secret Japanese overtures to the then-neutral Soviet Union in the vague hope of brokering some kind of peace settlement short of unconditional surrender. When Joseph Stalin informed President Truman and British prime minister Winston Churchill of these overtures at the Potsdam Conference in July 1945, all parties quickly dismissed them as unworthy of serious consideration.[33]

Perhaps an American guarantee of the imperial system might have prodded the Japanese militarists to capitulate before the bombs were dropped. We will never know, but we can learn a great deal about the war's violent denouement—and about crisis policymaking generally—by seriously considering such a hypothesis. In my own view, compromising the demand for unconditional surrender was not a viable policy option for many reasons. It would have been politically unfeasible in the United States and within the Allied camp. In all likelihood, Japan's floundering leaders would have seized on such an overture to press for additional clarifications and "conditions" beyond a vague guarantee to maintain the throne. Had a conditional surrender been agreed upon, moreover—and here is where concrete postwar considerations again enter the picture—it would have severely undermined the U.S. ability to impose extensive reforms in defeated and occupied Japan. Resorting to the bombs instead of pursuing a compromise Japanese surrender ensured that the United States would possess a virtually dictatorial hand in promoting "demilitarization and democratization" in postwar Japan.[34]

These numerous imperatives for using the bombs—often involving postwar rather than present-war considerations—are seldom mentioned in the heroic narrative; yet almost none of them were inconsistent with the objective of ending the war quickly and saving American lives. On the contrary, these additional arguments, or rationalizations, or psychological imperatives contributed greatly to creating a milieu in which alternative policies (such as demonstrating the new weapon on a noncombat or at least noncivilian target, or waiting to see the effect of the Soviet declaration of war against Japan) were brushed aside and Hiroshima and Nagasaki obliterated with hardly a second thought. Virtually every argument advanced said "Go!" Only a few marginal individuals questioned prevailing policy on practical grounds (by warning, for example, that attempting to maintain an Anglo-American monopoly on nuclear resources and technology would provoke an arms race with the USSR). Fewer still raised or seriously pursued basic questions about the morality of building and using on civilians a weapon of unprecedented destructiveness.

In the climate of the times, this seemed a natural thing to do, in part because by war's end the Japanese had been thoroughly dehumanized. Much of the outrage directed against the Smithsonian's original draft script focused on passing mention of the racist and retributive dimensions of the war. Clearly such references could only demean any celebration of the "valor and sacrificial service" of America's armed forces. Racial hatred and a thirst for vengeance could hardly serve as an admirable inspiration to present and future generations.

Yet vengeance and racism were powerful sentiments that shaped the conduct of the war on both sides, and to pretend otherwise is dishonest. Americans went to war against "the Japs" under such slogans as "Remember Pearl Harbor—Keep 'Em Dying." Home-front publications such as the monthly magazine of the American Legion (whose leaders were to play a major role in denouncing the Smithsonian and mobilizing political and media support against it) routinely portrayed the Japanese as monkeys or other subhuman species. In his Potsdam diary, President Truman rationalized the necessity of using the bombs by characterizing the Japanese as "savages, ruthless, merciless, and fanatic." On August 11, two days after the second bomb had been dropped on Nagasaki, he responded to a letter from a Protestant church official who criticized such "indiscriminate" killing by quoting the old canard that "when you have to deal with a beast you have to treat him as a beast. It is most regrettable but nevertheless true." Even after the Japanese government clearly indicated its intention to surrender, the United States chose to send a massive final bombing mission over Tokyo on August 14, killing and injuring additional thousands of civilians. The last planes were still in the air when the capitulation was finalized.[35]

Sheer visceral hatred drives people at war every bit as much as valor, every bit as much as rationality, every bit as much as patriotism, loyalty, or sense of duty. If we truly wish to understand the decision to drop the bombs on Japanese civilians, this, too, must be acknowledged.

Hiroshima as Tragedy

The heroic American narrative of World War II in Asia essentially ends where the Japanese narrative begins—with the crew of the *Enola Gay* turning sharply away from Hiroshima and gazing back at a towering column of smoke emerging out of an incredible flash of light. The minimalist exhibit ultimately offered at the Smithsonian conformed to this story line. Visitors remained with the crew. They stayed in the plane. They were completely detached from what took place at ground zero. They saw little more of the bomb's effects than a mushroom cloud.

Americans have rarely found it psychologically possible to look under that mushroom cloud. When they have—when photographs were offered or journalistic accounts presented—the emphasis has tended to be on physical destruction: panoramic photos of blasted cityscapes, close-ups of the iron-skeleton dome of Hiroshima's shattered city hall, left standing as a memorial when the city was rebuilt. When human figures appeared in the ruins, they were often seen from a distance. We encountered more survivors than corpses.

This has been the case from the beginning. Thousands of feet of film footage of Hiroshima and Nagasaki taken by Japanese cameramen between August and December 1945 were confiscated by U.S. authorities and suppressed for a quarter of a century. Journalistic accounts to the outside world about one of the most horrific scourges of the new weapon, radiation sickness, were carefully sanitized.[36]

If we do not turn away from the scene along with the *Enola Gay*—if we marshal the courage to look under the mushroom cloud—then, of course, we encounter not beasts and savages, but horribly mutilated men, women, and children; not "Japs," but individuals. As long as the mandate of public institutions in the United States is to celebrate the inspirational "valor and sacrificial service" of American armed forces, then—virtually by definition—such images of the other side can never be shown, or at least never shown in any extensive manner. The real nature of the nation's foreign killing fields must remain forever expunged from official places.

In the final analysis, more than anything else, the artifacts and images from ground zero that the National Air and Space Museum proposed to use in its ambitious *Enola Gay* exhibition spelled political doom; yet it is these concrete representations that best enable us to comprehend Hiroshima. What we ultimately see here is that the narrative transcending and indeed embracing the others is tragedy.

The visual representations speak, often in unanticipated ways. Critics of the institution's original script initially deplored the fact that representations of Japanese suffering greatly outnumbered those of the suffering the Japanese caused others. The exhibit essentially amounted, they claimed, to a replication of the Japanese victimization narrative; indeed, the artifacts and photographs at its emotional heart—the relatively small room in which "ground zero" would be presented—were to come primarily from the Peace Memorial Museum in Hiroshima.

Such criticism was not unreasonable, but it brought to the surface a dilemma incapable of resolution. For if one looks directly at the atomic bombs—not only at the events and imperatives and decisions that led to their use, but also at what took place beneath the mushroom cloud—then the near impossibility of mounting an exhibition that could be simultaneously "balanced" and "heroic" becomes obvious. Nothing exemplified this more dramatically than the juxtaposition of the Superfortress and the lunch box—an iconic confrontation that was peculiar to the Smithsonian controversy but far-reaching in its implications.

All narratives have their icons, and the heroic narrative of World War II has several. One stands at the beginning of the war and another at the end. The first symbolizes treacherous victimization and humiliation, the second triumph. The U.S. battleship *Arizona*, sunk with over two thousand American sailors on board in the Japanese surprise attack on Pearl Harbor, is the first of these icons, and the *Enola Gay* the second. Although the *Enola Gay* is clearly the more ambiguous, the veneration of both symbols in patriotic circles amounts to a civil religion.[37]

The love and reverence Colonel Tibbets held for his B-29 Superfortress, which he baptized with his mother's name on the eve of the Hiroshima mission, was unexceptional. Also unexceptional was his anguish a half century later at the prospect of the plane being dismembered—literally and figuratively mutilated—so that it might fit into the National Air and Space Museum's exhibition space. Writing in an American Legion publication in November 1994, Tibbets described the proposed display of the plane—"without wings, engines and propellers, landing gear and tail assembly"—as a "package of insults." This dismemberment struck him as blasphemy. To him, it revealed the true motives of the museum's curators. "If nothing else," he darkly observed, this mutilated presentation would enhance "the aura of evil in which the airplane is being cast."[38]

It is not surprising that these perceptions are couched in the language of sacrilege and blasphemy, for to most Americans who cherish the heroic narrative, the *Enola Gay* is a sacred icon. Even purportedly detached journalists fell into a cadence of adoration when writing of the plane. Thus, a *Washington Post* article critical of the Smithsonian opened with an evocation of desecration: "For years caretakers treated it like an outcast. First they locked it in a warehouse, then they parked it outside where it got rained on, vandalized and lived in by birds, bugs, and assorted vermin. They finally started working on it a decade ago, and now it's almost complete." Only after this reverent preface do readers learn that the subject is the *Enola Gay* and how it was restored in a labor of love.[39]

Such reverence for the machines of war is not strange. Sailors everywhere profess love for their ships, and airmen for their planes. One finds a similar reverence on the Japanese side, where one of the classic memoirs of the Pacific war is a requiem to the great battleship *Yamato*, which was sunk by American aircraft in the battle of Okinawa and took several thousand sailors with it to the ocean's depths.[40] What was distinctive about American agonizing over the mutilation of the *Enola Gay* was not that such agonizing occurred, but rather that it was accompanied by fury at the presentation of images of mutilated Japanese atomic bomb victims. This linkage of veneration for cataclysmic weapons of destruction and psychic denial of what they destroyed is a fit subject for students of social and cultural pathologies.

Even in its trimmed-down form, the *Enola Gay* was huge, well over fifty feet long. Refurbished and sparkling again after forty-four thousand hours of restoration work and the expenditure of $1 million (more time and money than the Smithsonian had ever lavished on a single object), the fuselage would dominate any exhibition in which it was placed. Or so it was assumed. In fact, it soon became clear that this would not be the case. On the contrary, the icons of the narrative of victimization—small objects intimately associated with individuals killed by the atomic bombs—threatened to overpower the great Superfortress in the eyes of visitors to the exhibition.

In their early scripts, the curators proposed displaying a number of such icons from the ashes of Hiroshima and Nagasaki, including such plain items as burned clothing, a twisted clock with its hands stopped at the time the Hiroshima bomb exploded, and Christian rosary beads fused in the heat of the Nagasaki blast. Critics responded with alarm not to the artifacts themselves but to mere descriptions of them in the museum's draft proposal, and nothing upset them more than the proposed inclusion of a school-girl's lunch box. This most humble of artifacts, containing carbonized rice and peas, had belonged to a seventh-grade student whose corpse was never found. To those who cherished the heroic narrative, it quickly became obvious that, for many visitors, this pathetic little container from near ground zero might carry far more emotional weight than the gigantic fuselage in the preceding room.

The lunch box certainly would weigh more than a Japanese soldier's helmet, or a similarly martial artifact, and for obvious reasons. It was all that remained of a noncombatant, a schoolgirl denied a future. The precise nature of her extermination was left to the viewer's imagination. The girl's mother, still living when the Smithsonian's first plans were drafted, was reportedly fearful that American visitors to such an exhibition might somehow desecrate the lunch box. This never became public, but the contrast—a mother's fear of her daughter's memory being despoiled set against the umbrage of nationalistic Americans at the possible demeaning of the airplane that dropped the bomb that killed the child—captures the inherently inequitable play of imagery in any exhibition that attempted to portray not only the bombers but also the bombed.

Here resided the insurmountable contradiction of a celebratory exhibition focusing on the atomic bombs and the end of the war. The heroes of the triumphal American narrative who physically dropped the bombs, Colonel Tibbets and his crew, were vigorous and confident young men in the armed forces, possessed of the most advanced technology the world had ever known, flying a solo mission that did not even require protective escort planes (since by this date the Japanese could barely muster the most tokenistic of anti-aircraft defenses)—and their target was a dense concentration of civilian men, women, and children. Encountering the *Enola Gay* and the lunch box in juxtaposition, only the most fervent American patriot could still marshal an unalloyed and unambiguous passion for heroism, triumphalism, valor, and self-sacrifice. In Japanese fiftieth-anniversary commemorations, it was of course the intimate icons of the two bombed cities—which simply have no American counterpart—that received greatest attention.[41]

This unnerving clash of icons extended to photographs. Critics of the Smithsonian's original plans argued—in the standard leveling language that sought to equate Japanese civilian deaths with combat deaths—that "photos of Japanese casualties" should be fairly counterbalanced by "photos of American casualties."[42] The sentiment behind this desire was reasonable. In qualitative terms, the Japanese had proved themselves undisputed masters of sadism in the war in Asia. Quantitatively, they had built a higher mountain of corpses. In practice, however, it was not possible to convey such a balance without appearing to place American war conduct in the same zone of behavior.

It did not work, for example, to place the visual representations of ground zero "in context" by filling preceding museum rooms with photographs depicting the valor and self-sacrifice of American servicemen. Photographs of dead soldiers and sailors rarely carry the same weight as those of civilian war fatalities, and the graphic image of a suffering fighting man touches the heart differently than that of a brutalized woman or child. In interim stages of the dispute between the museum and its critics, when some sort of compromise was still being considered, it was proposed that the number of photos of atomic bomb "casualties" be drastically reduced and more graphics depicting such subjects as Allied prisoners of war celebrating the Japanese surrender be added. Again, no true "balance" could come of this, for a photo of captured servicemen, no matter how maltreated they may have been, still fails to carry the emotional impact of a photo of a mother and infant burned by the bomb (to give an example that greatly upset the museum's critics).

It was also not feasible to place the artifacts and photographs associated with the atomic bomb experience "in perspective" by including more illustrations dealing with Japanese atrocities. Finding such illustrations posed no problem. The visual record of Japanese brutality is extensive, ranging from a notorious photograph of a Japanese soldier beheading a blond prisoner to shocking film footage of Chinese victims of the Rape of Nanking in 1937 to the camera's ghastly pan of bound and slaughtered men, women, and infants in Manila in 1945. From the beginning of their war to its end, Emperor Hirohito's soldiers and sailors behaved horrifically—but what would be accomplished by including exhibits depicting this as a prelude to an exhibition on the atomic bombs and the end of the war? It would simply suggest, by the very nature of such an attempted balancing act, that the atomic bombings of the two Japanese cities were on a par with—or at least in the same comparative universe with—Japan's own war crimes.

Were they?

Two terrible observations, or terrible questions perhaps, arise at this point: the first concerns the essential character of the bombings; the second, the broader historical context in which American policymakers agreed, almost casually, to exterminate the civilian residents of two cities. We confront at this point not just an American or Japanese tragedy, but a tragedy of our modern times.

Imagine this: if Colonel Tibbets and his crew had been ordered to infiltrate Hiroshima and, one by one, incinerate, irradiate, and mutilate tens upon tens of thousands of the men, women, and children living there, would they have done so? *Could* they have done so psychologically—even if told this might hasten the end of the war? And would we have looked upon their mission differently? And if so, why? In what way morally is the instantaneous infliction of immense and grotesque suffering on a civilian population from a great height, where human targets are invisible, and with a single devastating weapon, different from doing this one on one, eye to eye, hand to throat?

In fact, almost no one would argue that the crew of the *Enola Gay* were immoral. Through this controversy, they have retained their images as brave and patriotic men. Those who have argued that the killing of civilians in Hiroshima and Nagasaki was substantially the same as the atrocities committed by Emperor Hirohito's war machine, or even was comparable to the Nazi Holocaust, constitute a tiny minority—led, most conspicuously, by the Indian justice Radhabinod Pal, who offered this opinion in his dissent to the verdict of the war crimes trials conducted by the Allied powers in Tokyo after World War II.[43]

Yet we are left with these great numbers of dead and mutilated civilians, and with the recognition that Hiroshima and Nagasaki, though unique in the technological nature of their devastation, were not regarded by Americans or other members of the Allied camp as posing any particularly acute moral dilemma. The American decision to exterminate as many Japanese as possible in the two cities was arrived at without great soul-searching and certainly without significant internal debate, for by this point in the war, combatants on all sides had identified civilian populations as legitimate and indeed primary targets. In the new world of "total war," enemy morale—and thus every man, woman, and child in the enemy camp—became a potential target for "terror bombing."

As Native Americans, combatants on both sides of the Civil War, and Filipinos at the turn of the century well knew, mass slaughter was not alien to the American military tradition. Until the closing stages of World War II, however, the wholesale killing of noncombatants was not embraced, or at least not trumpeted, as official policy. When Japan and Germany began employing such tactics in the late 1930s, the United States denounced the deliberate slaughter of civilians by aerial bombardment as an act beyond the pale of civilized societies.

This condemnation was unequivocal. The "ruthless bombing of unfortified localities with the resultant slaughter of civilian populations, and in particular of women and children," the U.S. government declared in a typical statement in 1937, in response to Japanese bombings in China, was "barbarous" and "in violation of the most elementary principles of those standards of humane conduct which have been developed as an essential part of modern civilization." Similarly, in June 1938 the Senate denounced the "inhuman bombing of civilian populations" as a "crime against humanity" that was "reminiscent of the cruelties perpetuated by primitive and barbarous nations upon inoffensive people." Great Britain as well as the League of Nations made similar public denunciations of such policies. Much of the early Anglo-American identification of the Axis powers as savages operating in a different moral universe rested on a genuinely horrified reaction against the wanton and indiscriminate use of airpower by the Japanese and Germans.[44]

Great Britain led the way in abandoning this moral high ground in the summer of 1942 by turning to the obliteration of German cities with incendiary bombs. By 1945 the United States had openly accepted the firebombing of enemy cities as basic and appropriate strategy. Residents of Dresden learned this in February of that year, when a joint British and American air raid killed forty thousand citizens in what Prime Minister Churchill frankly and unapologetically called terror bombing. Soon afterward, the policy of deliberately targeting urban populations was introduced to Japan with the great Tokyo air raid of March 8–9, which destroyed roughly sixteen square miles of the capital city and killed as many as one hundred thousand civilians.

A few highly placed Americans privately expressed dismay at these developments. In mid-June 1945, six weeks before Hiroshima and Nagasaki were destroyed, Brigadier General Bonner Fellers, one of General Douglas MacArthur's closest aides, confidentially characterized the saturation bombing of Japanese cities with napalm incendiaries as "one of the most ruthless and barbaric killings of noncombatants in all history." In the high Washington circles that made the decision to use the atomic bombs, individuals such as Secretary of War Henry Stimson and General George Marshall, the chief of staff, briefly sighed at the changing moral tenor of the times. When all was said and done, however, no one seriously challenged on moral grounds this crossing of a great divide regarding the legitimate targets of war.[45]

By failing to do this, genuine heroes in the war against fascism denied themselves a firm and morally unambiguous place in history. They became heroes with the blood of women and children on their hands, and in this regard protagonists in a tragic rather than a triumphal narrative. The tragedy of their acts was compounded, moreover, when it became apparent—as soon happened—that the decision to develop and use atomic bombs had ushered in not a new age of peace and security, but rather an age—our postwar world—of mistrust and everlasting insecurity.

Even President Truman, who maintained until his death that he had never had second thoughts about the decision to drop the bombs, and who generally is esteemed as one of the stalwarts of the heroic narrative, was not insensitive to the tragic nature of his acts. In the brief interim between the bombing of Nagasaki and the Japanese surrender, he gave orders that no further atomic bombs be used without his specific authorization. From all we can tell, he did so on the grounds that he did not wish to sanction more killing of women and children. Henry Wallace, who was present on this occasion, summarized the president's rationale with a notation in his diary that "the thought of wiping out another 100,000 people was too horrible. He didn't like the idea of

killing 'all those kids.' " The "savages" and "beasts" that the president said he was incinerating had somehow, however momentarily, been restored to their humanity in his mind.[46]

Years later, in Truman's private library, a researcher discovered
that the former president had collected most of the books written
on the atomic bombings and had underlined portions of a post-
script in one of them. It was Horatio's famous soliloquy in
Hamlet:

> . . . let me speak to the yet unknowing world
> How these things came about: So shall you hear
> Of carnal, bloody, and unnatural acts,
> Of accidental judgments, casual slaughters,
> Of deaths put on by cunning and forced cause,
> And, in this upshot, purposes mistook
> Fall'n on the inventors' heads. . . .
> But let this same be presently perform'd
> Even while men's minds are wild; lest more mischance,
> On plots and errors, happen.[47]

As with so many other things, we never will really know
whether President Truman had second thoughts about his decision to kill huge numbers of civilian men, women, and children
with the new weapon available to him. At the very least, however,
we can say that his modest, private underlinings help remind us of
the tragic nature of this decision. In the strident, jingoistic milieu
of present-day, end-of-the-century America, such a perspective—
and such eloquence—is officially taboo. We can calculate from
this how greatly we have failed in comprehending our humanity.

3

PATRIOTIC ORTHODOXY
AND AMERICAN DECLINE

• MICHAEL S. SHERRY •

Historic changes in America's patriotic culture emerged in sharp relief during the 1990s, especially in the debate over the National Air and Space Museum's *Enola Gay* exhibit. In that debate, as in similar contests, self-proclaimed patriots—the Air Force Association (AFA), the American Legion, and their corporate and congressional allies—sought victory at home, not the extension of U.S. military power abroad. As such, the *Enola Gay* controversy signaled the waning of American global power and highlighted the evolution of patriotic culture into a brittle, nostalgic, and inward-looking orthodoxy.

In the 1930s and 1940s, patriotic culture had been capacious, loosely defined, and outward looking. Liberals like Franklin D. Roosevelt worked its symbols and themes more successfully than mainstream conservatives like Senator Robert Taft or idiosyncratic ones like aviator Charles Lindbergh. Dissent from national policies in those years often came from conservatives: many criticized the use of the atomic bomb, for example, while Taft inveighed against the nascent imperialism of American Cold War policies.

Closely tied to the celebration of the United States as a "melting pot," patriotic culture was also widely inclusive. It welcomed European ethnics like New York's Mayor Fiorello La Guardia. African Americans could plausibly, if less easily, align themselves with it: "Are you for Hitler's Way or the American Way?" asked the placards of demonstrators against Washington, D.C.'s racial segregation in 1944.[1] Shaped by perceptions of totalitarian and technological menace, patriotic culture was expansive. Focusing on global conditions, it helped mobilize Americans to exercise extraordinary power abroad. The creation of a huge military force during World War II allowed a diverse, though hardly complete, range of Americans to acquire patriotic credentials. Although nearly all Japanese Americans had earlier been forced into concentration camps by American authorities, by late in the war, even Japanese-American soldiers found their combat service for the United States widely hailed.

To be sure, as the fate of Japanese Americans early in the war indicated, this patriotic culture had its coercive, exclusionary, and hard-edged qualities. As Walter Millis, a popular journalist and military historian, bitingly wrote of Americans on the eve of World War II: "Since the great mobilization of the First War, a quasi-religious nationalism had been sedulously cultivated in the United States. It had acquired its creed (the oath of allegiance), its icons (the Flag), its ritual observances [promoted by] patriotic societies like the American Legion." As a result, a once unimaginable "degree of regimentation and centralization . . . had by 1941 become no more than a normal and patently necessary order of affairs."[2] Misogyny, homophobia, religious intolerance, and racial and ethnic hatreds waxed and waned in post-1941 patriotic culture; peace activism, leftist radicalism, left liberalism, and at times even far-right agitation were extruded from it at moments of crisis. As always, patriotic culture served to assert power by some and deny it to others. Still, closely linked as it was to the expansion of American power abroad, it prized an inclusive and varied domestic unity over a divisive, purified order. President Harry Truman's famous 1948 ban on segregation in the armed forces powerfully illustrated that inclusive impulse.

Increasingly under strain, however, patriotic culture split apart during the Vietnam War. Diminishing faith in the necessity and practicality of enforcing U.S. hegemony abroad was the overarching cause; detached from a widely shared vision of American power, patriotic culture had to change. Some antiwar protesters angrily opted out of it, equating patriotism with conservatism; while, with more effect, many conservatives began a quarter-century-long campaign to use patriotism to regain power and defeat their real and imagined enemies at home. Subordinate elements of patriotic culture in an earlier era—its exclusionary thrust and brittle edge—now became dominant.

In the wake of Vietnam, patriotic culture devolved into a rigid patriotic orthodoxy—tightly linked with political and cultural conservatism, baldly insistent on a singular version of the American past, crudely celebratory of the United States' history of war making. When patriotic culture had been more inclusive, it had at least partially embraced the idea that many visions of the past were possible. Patriotic orthodoxy embraced a past which, its proponents claimed, had only one true and unchanging meaning. In that view, the turmoil and radicalism of the Vietnam era disrupted an otherwise stable American history. As Speaker of the House Newt Gingrich put it, "From the Jamestown colony and the Pilgrims . . . up to the Norman Rockwell paintings of the 1940s and 1950s, there was a clear sense of what it meant to be an American."[3]

In one sense Gingrich was right. Since the United States had never before so clearly lost a war, patriotic orthodoxy after Vietnam was driven by something new, the determination to redeem a lost cause (as had been true in the white South after the Civil War) and to erase the sting of defeat. Yet in the 1970s and 1980s, few patriotic conservatives—certainly not Ronald Reagan, their symbolic leader—sought redemption through major war making. Instead, they sought it through largely symbolic military actions abroad in places like Grenada and Panama, and through the discrediting of foes at home, who presumably had caused defeat in Vietnam and later resisted martial renewal. As their relentless reliance on POW/MIA mythology indicated, they leaned heavily on symbols of (or substitutes for) redemption. In this, they extended the politics of Richard Nixon (and some of the antiwar left as well), who had argued that America's greatest enemy was in its midst, not in Hanoi. As Nixon put it in 1967, "The war in Asia is a limited one with limited means and limited goals. The war at home is a war for survival of a free society."[4] Given such reasoning, patriotic orthodoxy turned inward, its focus on American power abroad gradually, though never fully, yielding to its quest for victory at home.

The *Enola Gay* debate dramatized that process. Adherents of patriotic orthodoxy sought not just a voice in the exhibit but total victory over their domestic foes, as if they were symbolically replaying the total U.S. victory over Japan in 1945. While the Air Force Association's *Air Force Magazine* acknowledged as early as April 1994 what it called "major concessions to balance" by the museum in its revised script for the exhibit, AFA spokesman Jack Giese commented months later, after even more museum concessions, "We welcome their changes, but they are by no means close to what we've asked for." Indeed, each new concession emboldened veterans' groups to demand more, including finally the resignation of Martin Harwit as the museum's director.[5]

Underlying their demands was an insistence that only veterans could divine the meaning of the atomic attacks. "All we want is for the museum to tell history the way it happened," Giese declared, not how museum curators "thought it should have happened. We're vets, we've actually been in the Cold War—they haven't."[6] Giese here echoed a demand on the rise since the mid-1970s and loudly made by critic and World War II veteran Paul Fussell, among others, in the 1980s: the history of World War II belonged solely to those who fought it (although, of course, not all present-day veterans did duty in World War II, as Giese's careful reference to the Cold War implicitly acknowledged, and many of the AFA's allies in Congress and elsewhere had done no military duty at all).

Patriotic orthodoxy also sought the virtual silencing of views and voices once heard within patriotic culture. Before Hiroshima, most military leaders, in secret deliberations on the atomic bomb, had questioned the wisdom or necessity of its use on Japan's cities, although they eventually acquiesced in that use. Army generals like George Marshall and Dwight D. Eisenhower had expressed major reservations. So, too, had navy admirals, convinced that *their* fleet had already crippled Japan, fearful of air force aggrandizement, or, like Admiral William D. Leahy, troubled by the barbaric nature of atomic bombing. Even air force generals like Curtis LeMay, though hardly opposed to the bomb's use, had insisted that their campaign of firebombing was about to end the war anyway. Among civilian officials informed about secret Japanese diplomatic feelers (including Joseph Grew, acting secretary of state until James Byrnes took over in July 1945, and Secretary of War Henry L. Stimson), the expectation had been widespread that modification of America's surrender terms and/or the Soviet Union's entry into the war (or even its mere signature on the Potsdam Declaration) might suffice to end the war quickly. But President Harry Truman and Secretary of State Byrnes, at least in part for reasons of "atomic diplomacy" against the Soviets, pressed ahead with the atomic attacks. Moreover, after the war a number of these leaders stated—boldly and publicly in some cases—their reservations about the bomb's use, and they did so without suffering condemnation as traitors to a patriotic cause.[7]

But in 1994, orthodox patriots all but obliterated such reservations from their otherwise lengthy accounts, as if embarrassed by them, and assailed as "revisionist" those who highlighted the doubts of an earlier generation's leaders. Although the *New York Times* claimed that the *Enola Gay* debate pitted "revisionist historians" against "veterans groups protecting their heritage," in truth, the latter were drastically revising that heritage rather than receiving it as an unchanged bequest from 1945. In their new mythology, not only was the decision to use atomic bombs beyond questioning in retrospect, it had not been questioned at the time.[8]

Indeed, new truths were invented to sustain that mythology. For historians, according to one account of the museum fracas, "the atomic bomb has acquired political and emotional baggage in the intervening half century" as "the opening event of the nuclear age" rather than as the climax of World War II. But in fact, that supposedly "academic view of history" had weighed heavily on scientists and policymakers in the summer of 1945, on the air force before and after Hiroshima, and on pundits assaying the meaning of the event at the time. For many officials, the future implications of the bomb had often consumed more attention that summer than its consequences for the war against Japan. Byrnes pursued its apparent potential to intimidate the Soviets; Stimson urged that it "not be considered simply in terms of military weapons, but a new relationship of man to the universe"; physicist Robert Oppenheimer hoped that showing the bomb's power might avert a future arms race; air force general Henry H. "Hap" Arnold probed the bomb's consequences for interservice rivalries and global peacekeeping. Public commentary after Hiroshima often showed the same emphasis: "[One] forgets the effect [of the bomb] on Japan," according to the *New York Herald Tribune*, "as one senses the foundations of one's own universe trembling."[9]

Thus it was veterans' groups, not historians, who were adding new baggage to the events of 1945—and stripping them of the load they had once carried. Seeing only a morally simple decision to end the war and save American lives, they wrote off much of what had shaped that decision: the passion for retribution against Japan, the desire to overawe the Soviet Union, the hope for nuclear mastery, and the fear of a titanic arms race. Taking the invention of new truths even further, Colonel Paul W. Tibbets, Jr., the *Enola Gay*'s commander, now claimed that "the urgency of the situation demanded that we use the weapons first—before the technology could be used against us." Apparently, unbeknownst to anyone in 1945 or since, Japan was about to get its own bomb.[10]

Defenders of patriotic orthodoxy revealed their new priorities by directing their greatest animus and contempt at the Americans who planned or supported the museum's exhibit. Triumphal and hostile sentiments toward Japan did appear—especially in the indignant, unwarranted claim that the museum treated Japan as America's wartime moral equal—but played a distinctly subordinate role. The case against Japan was short and perfunctory compared with the lengthy, bitter denunciations of the museum, its curators and historians, and its director. Those attacking the museum showed little interest in what Japanese authorities or historians now said about the use of the atomic bomb. They wanted to force their view of the war not on the Japanese but on fellow Americans. Just as the once-common rhetoric of a U.S.-Japanese "trade war" had generally receded by the mid-1990s, so orthodox patriots rarely linked their views of 1945 closely to present-day tensions between the two countries. American virtue and victory *were* to be celebrated; that they were revealed in the defeat of Japan was a secondary matter. The diminishing attention paid to Japan was a sign that the enemy at home, not American power abroad, was what now consumed the orthodox patriots.

Likewise, their celebratory version of America's military past was now largely detached from a coherent vision of its military future. In earlier moments of patriotic revival, such a linkage had been strong. On the eve of World War II, for instance, films like *Sergeant York* got official endorsement as part of efforts to mobilize patriotic sentiment against the Axis powers. And in the 1950s, "under God" was inserted in the Pledge of Allegiance and the new Iwo Jima Memorial at the Arlington National Cemetery was celebrated in the effort to generate indignation against godless communism and support for stockpiling American weapons to guard against it. Again in the 1970s and 1980s, patriotic revitalization was closely tied to efforts to expand and update the U.S. nuclear arsenal.[11] To be sure, at every such moment advocates of revitalization were also jockeying for cultural and political power at home, but that power was at least plausibly linked to plans for exercising military might abroad. In the mid-1990s, the link between the two had all but disappeared. And so had anxieties about and ambitions for nuclear weapons. Earlier controversies about the remembrance of 1945 had been yoked to sharp debate over what the United States and other nations might do with their nuclear arsenals. With the end of the Cold War—and of intense nuclear anxiety focused on a superpower enemy—debate about the bomb's use in 1945 was stripped of the resonance that its link with global problems had once given it.

Revealingly, the allies of veterans' groups in Congress and other political circles now charted no plausible course for using American military power. Defense policy was of minor concern to ascendant Republicans like Speaker of the House Newt Gingrich; his "revolution" was to be carried out against domestic foes and in pursuit of a new domestic order. Statements like the GOP's 1994 Contract with America did demand greater military spending and specific programs like a revived antimissile defense system. But this was a call to arms with no identified purpose—no particular enemies to fight or threats to counter, only vague talk of a world still troublesome and of the problems second-rate powers like Iraq or North Korea might pose. Like preparedness advocates before World War I, those of the mid-1990s seemed "more interested in polishing the fire engines than finding the blaze."[12] In fact, their primary mode was to carp at nearly every use of military power that President Bill Clinton pondered or tried—primarily, "peacekeeping" missions of various sorts—and to bemoan the actual or prospective loss of *any* American lives in such operations. As the *New York Times* observed, the October 1993 firefight in Somalia, which left eighteen American soldiers dead, "in many respects had a bigger impact on military thinking than the entire 1991 Persian Gulf war," and that impact enhanced reluctance to deploy American military power anywhere.[13]

Championing that reluctance, the forces of patriotic orthodoxy also borrowed their rhetoric and concerns, largely unwittingly, from the antiwar culture of the Vietnam era. While anti–Vietnam War protest had embraced many themes, revulsion at the loss of American lives in a needless war had been its most broadly sustained impulse. The response of patriotic forces to the Vietnam War Memorial in Washington, D.C., revealed how much they had come to endorse that impulse by the early 1980s. By starkly naming the American dead while avoiding any other explicit message about the Vietnam War, the memorial, at least as it was commonly understood, left the loss of American lives as the war's only widely accepted meaning. Despite scattered protests against the memorial before its completion, conservative patriots in the end embraced that meaning. Their role in the long POW/MIA controversy reflected a similar emphasis: however fanciful its premises, indignation that some Americans remained alive in Vietnam, like various Ramboesque cinematic fantasies of their rescue, demonstrated that patriotic conservatives valued the saving of American lives above all else. By the same token, most patriots celebrated the Gulf War for its remarkably low death rate among Americans more than for any American geopolitical or moral gains. Indeed, by the mid-1990s, the saving of American soldiers' lives, rather than their expenditure in a valued cause, had become a mantra for nearly all U.S. politicians: the dramatic rescue from Bosnia of downed airman Scott O'Grady in June 1995, insisted Bill Clinton, revealed not military failure in a mission but what is "best" about Americans; O'Grady should never have been in harm's way in the first place, responded his critics.

That self-proclaimed patriots would stress the avoidance of American deaths as their supreme priority—when earlier they had touted the need for sacrifice and excoriated antiwar activists as cowards for refusing to risk their lives in Vietnam—was a striking development. Such a stance, though, left them in no position to entertain the major use of U.S. forces abroad, except in a scenario similar to that of the Gulf War, an anomalous conflict that forecast no pattern for the future.

This revulsion over possible American casualties in any military action fit precisely with the view of 1945 expressed by those attacking the proposed *Enola Gay* exhibit. There were many ways to valorize the use of the atomic bomb: it presumably ended a terrible war, punished a bestial foe, demonstrated American might, avoided a prolonged Soviet role in the Pacific war, squeezed Stalin out of a share in the occupation of Japan, and showed the Soviets just how formidable U.S. power would be in the postwar period. But among orthodox patriots, those claims were barely noted, brushed aside, angrily rejected, or, at best, subordinated to an insistence that, above all, the atomic bomb had saved American lives. Contemporary patriots stressed for 1945 precisely the theme they were sounding for 1995: the necessity of avoiding American deaths in war.

The focal points of their fury drove home that theme. They were outraged at historians' claims that the Truman administration had not expected half a million (or more) casualties in an invasion of Japan, and that Japan's surrender had been imminent in August anyway, making moot the question of the administration's expectations. Indeed, as we have seen, it was over the issue of invasion casualty estimates that the final breach between the museum and its critics occurred in January 1995. The museum's opponents insisted that various revised, lower figures offered by historians for what U.S. officials had expected in 1945 constituted a final insult warranting the cancellation of the planned *Enola Gay* exhibit. An earlier object of opponents' fury—the museum's plans to display photographs and artifacts dramatizing the carnage wrought in Japan—was also linked to the emphasis on the saving of American lives. Evidence of that carnage might, after all, raise troublesome questions about what it cost to save those lives. Thus veterans' spokesmen scrupulously counted the museum's planned photographs of Japanese casualties, as if each such image somehow diminished the value of the American lives saved. To be sure, their preferences also replicated those of 1945, when photographs of Japanese dead were few and visual culture was dominated by images of American technological supremacy and the lives it had saved. But while insistence on the virtue of saving American lives was an old theme, in 1995 it was a singularly overriding one, congruent with a newly dominant view of a military future free of American deaths.

Ostensibly, such insistence honored the sacrifices that American veterans of World War II had made and the value of those lives the bomb had presumably saved. Yet this way of honoring them was, as Robert Jay Lifton and Greg Mitchell have noted, oddly "self-diminishing for the veterans, because it shift[ed] the credit for defeating the Japanese from the military personnel in the Pacific to a small group of bomb makers in New Mexico, and decision makers in Washington." Since Japan was defeated and suing (if ineptly) for peace in July, it was strange that veterans would "accept, even promote, the bomb as necessary to end the war when they could, with justification, claim that *they* had already completed the job."[14]

The saving-lives theme came to bear enormous moral weight for some, even allowing them to lay claim to the high moral ground of the Holocaust. In words and images, the Nazi Holocaust and the atomic "holocaust" (as it was sometimes called in the 1940s) had been linked by American commentators from August 1945 on. But in the *Enola Gay* debate, some proponents of patriotic orthodoxy reconfigured that old linkage by suggesting that the use of the bomb had averted a holocaust on the scale of Nazi genocide. In August 1994, a commentator in *USA Today* "established a new high for American lives saved [by the bomb]— six million—and claimed that this was 'the consensus view,' " while in 1995 a crewman of the B-29 that had attacked Nagasaki offered the same number (one million Americans and five million Japanese). Thus absurd claims about lives saved in the past emerged just when willingness to risk American lives in the future diminished to nothing.[15]

If their only vision of the future lay in its risk-free nature, what were the exhibit's attackers fighting for? Primarily, they sought immediate victory over cultural and political foes at home. As Irving Kristol, one of their intellectual godfathers, put it in 1993: "There is no 'after the Cold War' for me. So far from having ended, my cold war has increased in intensity, as sector after sector of American life has been ruthlessly corrupted by the liberal ethos. . . . Now that the other 'Cold War' is over, the real cold war has begun," one for which "we are far less prepared" and "far more vulnerable."[16] With the end of the Cold War abroad, it was time to win that "real" cold war, the one that Pat Buchanan kept championing, against enemies now deemed far more dangerous than those in Moscow and Beijing had been. The *Enola Gay* exhibit provided an important arena in which to pursue that victory. As one political cartoon had it, replaying the famous scene of surrender on the deck of the battleship *Missouri*, "the Smithsonian"—humbled and professorial—capitulated to military force, with Japanese diplomats (bucktoothed and caricatured) playing only a background role.[17]

On the most general level, the *Enola Gay* contest echoed earlier struggles over who controlled American culture, who valued the American past, who deserved mention within it, and who controlled any federal action that touched on such matters. Bitter controversies had already erupted, for example, over a federal amendment against flag burning, over funding by the National Endowment for the Arts of "dirty" pictures, over the museums that displayed such work, over battle sites like Pearl Harbor supervised by the National Park Service, and over earlier Smithsonian exhibits on airpower and the settlement of the West. Rehashing those exhibits while mounting its case against the *Enola Gay* display, *Air Force Magazine* heightened its adherents' sense that there were powerful and dangerous connections among these controversies. Avid historians in their own way, patriotic conservatives felt themselves facing the same domestic enemies—liberals, America-bashing scholars, feminists, gays, racial and ethnic minorities, antinuclear and antiwar activists—in all these battles, as well as in the lopsided contest over U.S. entry into the Gulf War. The nitpicker could point out that the political coalitions in these struggles were complex and shifting: unilateralist queer baiters like Pat Buchanan had railed against the American war in the Gulf, libertarian conservatives had inveighed against the flag amendment, and most historians associated with the museum's exhibit were indifferent to the cultural politics of queers and feminists. But there was enough stability in these coalitions for the defenders of patriotic orthodoxy to imagine themselves besieged by the same forces in every contest.

Those struggles also prepared the way for the *Enola Gay* debate by shaping the orthodox patriots' attack on "political correctness," the loose phrase already much employed by conservatives claiming to face a rigid, ruthless, ever-growing assault from radical academics and their allies. The historians' and curators' "academic arrogance is beyond belief," insisted the AFA's Jack Giese, and indeed arrogance is hardly unknown among academics.[18] But as in many preceding struggles, outrage at such arrogance was largely a posture calculated to disguise the grip on cultural power sought by many conservatives, whose claim that only veterans could assess the war's meaning was itself remarkably arrogant. Moreover, those outraged over political correctness conveniently overlooked the fact that much initial criticism of the bomb's use had come from conservatives, Republicans, and military figures. Herbert Hoover, John Foster Dulles, and William D. Leahy, among others, had weighed in, while Fulton J. Sheen, the prominent Catholic monsignor and Cold Warrior, had asserted that defending the bomb's use as a way to save lives "was precisely the argument Hitler used in bombing Holland."[19] In any event, quarrelsome leftists and liberals had long been unable and unwilling to impose "political correctness" on their own ranks, much less the nation. Instead, cultural conservatives (though their cohesiveness, too, was sometimes exaggerated both by them and their opponents) were the ascendant force in this regard.

The noisiest of those earlier contests was the one in 1993 about gays in the military. There, as in the *Enola Gay* struggle, the use of American power in the world was hardly the real issue. Instead, "patriotic" forces momentarily defeated their perceived foes at home while pursuing a vision of purity rooted in a mythology about military manhood in the past. At the same time, however, they revealed how fragile their notions of military manhood had become and how disconnected they were from the exercise of American power. Military officials reluctantly had to admit what secret Pentagon studies had long made clear—that lesbians and gay men were wholly fit to serve and that they had long done so. Defenders of the gay "ban" did claim that the presence of openly homosexual men would damage military fitness and "unit cohesion," but only because frightened or offended straight soldiers would resign, fail to enlist, or panic in the showers: in short, be unwilling or unable to fight. However, the orthodox patriots' specter of straight soldiers fleeing in terror from the sexual lust of gay comrades, as women might do in the face of male sexual lust, unwittingly feminized the (straight) American fighting man. Implicitly, it called into question whether he had the courage and fortitude that war presumably requires, and whether the ban's defenders really even cared about America's war-making ability.

Indeed, the 1993 debate was largely about citizenship, not marksmanship. Advocates of the ban on gays feared that the military's acceptance of homosexuals would underwrite their fuller citizenship—a fear with foundation, since African Americans and other social groups had successfully used military service to that end. Ominously in the background was the notorious Tailhook affair, in which male servicemen celebrating victory in the Gulf War had sexually assaulted female personnel. The Tailhook affair played into the gay debate because patriotic conservatives also feared expanding numbers of and roles for women in the armed forces, against which a formidable weapon had long been the lesbian-baiting that the ban made possible. Had the ban's defenders been seriously worried about military readiness, they could have accepted, even demanded, that the military recruit as widely as possible for the best personnel, as some patriotic dissenters like retired senator Barry Goldwater argued. "You don't have to be straight to shoot straight," he insisted.[20] That a substantial pool of Americans would be excluded from service underlined how much a vision of sexual and cultural purity at home, rather than power abroad, was the goal of most conservatives, with whom Goldwater, far more interested in an older vision of martial virtue, was now badly out of step.

This debate foreshadowed the position of the "patriotic" forces in the *Enola Gay* controversy, with their insistence that military veterans alone (though only straight ones) could judge such things. President Clinton's claim as a nonveteran to have a voice in the debate was widely ridiculed, as was his right to be commander in chief. Sailors openly mocked him during a presidential visit to one ship, and Congress insisted on legislating, for the first time, in this matter. Indeed, expelling the nonveteran from this arena, as from the *Enola Gay* debate, was another way to attain a new kind of purity at home.

The connection between the gay debate of 1993 and the bomb debate of 1994 was more than temporal and political. It was also imaginative and intuitive. One article on the bomb debate was, for instance, devilishly titled "Enola Gay Baiting," while political cartoonists had a field day with the connection. One cartoon featured the name Enola Gay with *"Gay"* crossed out and replaced by *"Heterosexual,"* while another rendered the bomber sitting at the Smithsonian with "Enola Sexually Undifferentiated" emblazoned on it. Other cartoons added to the mix an incident in which GOP congressman Richard Armey called gay Democratic representative Barney Frank "Barney Fag": one pictured a TV reporter "at the Smithsonian to unveil the controversial exhibit of the Enola Frank—I mean GAY!"; another showed Armey commenting "on the proposed commemoration of the Enola Fag."[21] If such material did not trace a precise path connecting the gay and museum debates, it did powerfully evoke a sense of connection. The name of Tibbets's mother, Enola Gay, probably had long sounded odd to many Americans, too feminine for such a mighty deed (though American crews often named their bombers after women) and lacking the ring of an authentic American name. In the wake of the gays-in-the-military debate, that name seemed to tap visceral fears that the America of patriotic memory was succumbing to the dark forces of a feminine, feminized, and homosexualized post-Vietnam era, or to a "culture of appeasement," as Norman Podhoretz had complained in the 1970s, cultivated by the "kind of women who do not want to be women and . . . men who do not want to be men."[22] To restore that imagined pre-Vietnam America, guardians of patriotic orthodoxy felt they had to defeat first Clinton's effort to alter the Pentagon's antigay policy and later the museum's exhibit.

Their subsequent initiatives indicated a similar impulse to defeat foes at home. Emboldened by apparent victory in the *Enola Gay* fracas, the American Legion, backed by 170 House members and 29 senators, launched a new campaign for an amendment banning flag burning. "Nothing disgusts me more than liberals who hide behind the 1st Amendment and want to support people who desecrate Old Glory," commented Van Hilleary, a Republican representative from Tennessee and Gulf War veteran.[23] His language directly echoed earlier charges that liberals hid behind the First Amendment to defend dirty pictures, just as "disgust" captured the feeling of many orthodox patriots toward advocates of the museum's exhibit.

Thus self-proclaimed defenders of the flag, like foes of the museum's exhibit, revealed how much the new patriotic orthodoxy was both inward and backward looking, far more focused than midcentury patriotic culture on enemies at home and long-ago triumphs abroad. The fact that it drew so heavily on a half-century-old event suggested as much, for its dependence on that event cannot simply be attributed to some mysterious alchemy produced by fiftieth-year anniversaries. Such moments never just carry intrinsic power and resonance but instead derive much of their meaning from current circumstances. In 1968, for instance, no great hubbub among Americans characterized the fiftieth anniversary of victory in World War I; disarray in patriotic culture and anti–Vietnam War fervor made this impossible. Champions of patriotic orthodoxy drew on 1945 because after that date, there was little for them to tap. Korea and Vietnam were useless for such purposes. The most recent case of patriotic glory, the Gulf War, offered little of value; it had been too lacking in gravity of sacrifice, too easy to win, and too ambiguous in outcome—with Saddam Hussein still in power—to establish a new reservoir of patriotic memory.

In part because the reservoir was so dry, victory in the *Enola Gay* debate rang a bit hollow. The forces of orthodoxy defeated the planned exhibit but got only a puny alternative (to be sure, perhaps all some of them wanted), just as they had achieved, at best, only limited success in other recent struggles over how to memorialize America's military past.[24] They did not prevent withdrawal of a proposed atomic bomb postage stamp that embodied (if in trivial fashion) their celebratory view of the bomb's use. They did not stop ABC-TV from showing in July 1995 a biting prime-time documentary (*Hiroshima: Why the Bomb Was Dropped*) embracing historians' arguments, condemning the exhibit's opponents, and challenging the celebratory view. In addition, erasing all signs of the bomb's destructive power had ambiguous consequences; for that destructiveness, above all, gave visual proof of the magnitude of American triumph. How were Americans to celebrate an event whose effects they could not see, and how long could the celebration go on if entrusted only to the war's aging veterans?

Wounded and reviled in the *Enola Gay* fracas, many curators and historians understandably had trouble grasping the ambiguity of its outcome. Some perceived an "unprecedented" assault on intellectuals, on historians' expertise, and on truth itself, carried out by patriotic bullies who used words like *liberal* a bit the way Nazis had once used *Jew*.[25] They were hardly wrong to sense defeat, but little in the assault was unprecedented, as historians of the McCarthy era could have told them. What also made the ambiguity hard to grasp was that challenges to patriotic culture were, in the context of public institutions, relatively recent. The National Air and Space Museum itself had largely been founded and long maintained as a celebratory showcase for U.S. technology.[26] Stopping the *Enola Gay* exhibit marked an attempt to turn back the clock, but without re-creating the global conditions and American power that had given patriotic culture its meaning in the 1940s and 1950s.

The backward and inward focus of the new patriotic orthodoxy can be exaggerated. Success in such cultural struggles also shapes the future: bearing down on defense policy, influencing how textbooks and the media teach Americans to perceive both past and future, and strengthening political and cultural conservatism. The failure of the exhibit's supporters indicated what a free rein patriotic orthodoxy now had. By the same token, the tight links of the AFA with the aerospace industry and other allies involved a real political and budgetary agenda. As has long been true, airpower patriots were less "isolationists" averse to the use of American power than "unilateralists" insistent on its unfettered application. (Their version of the atomic bomb's use, for instance, conveniently erased the role of the Soviet Union and other Allies in ending the Pacific war.) As they saw it, the bomb's use embodied unilateral action, supremely destructive power, and the total absence of risk to American lives—an ideal combination they believed had been realized again in the Gulf War, and which they yearned to replicate in a new crisis. After all, it might be hard to keep "polishing the fire engines" without finding a blaze to justify their existence.

But among most guardians of patriotic orthodoxy, neither the fear of crisis abroad nor the will to use American power in any such crisis was apparent, in part because patriotic culture also had absorbed key themes from antiwar culture, especially the horror of losing American lives in war. At least for the foreseeable future, the thrust of patriotic orthodoxy would be to defeat perceived foes at home and advance its vision of American cultural purity, not to do battle with enemies abroad. Its proponents seemed intent on entombing patriotic culture in museums—and making a museum of it—not on projecting it into the world. For them, the proper exhibit was to be a monument to the past, not a beacon to the future. Far from anticipating new glory for U.S. military power, they seemed more like Englishmen in the early post–World War II years, fondly remembering or angrily defending the lost imperial glory of the pre–World War I era. Ironically, the *Enola Gay* debate, and the partial triumph by "patriots" in it, showed that America's great age of military hegemony was drawing to a close.

4

WHOSE HISTORY IS IT ANYWAY?
MEMORY, POLITICS, AND
HISTORICAL SCHOLARSHIP

• PAUL BOYER •

"**A**s soon as you bring historians in, you run into problems. You get distortions." This comment might well have been made by one of the Washington politicians or veterans' organizations that in 1994 attacked the Smithsonian Institution's plans for an exhibit observing the fiftieth anniversary of the atomic bombings of Hiroshima and Nagasaki. In fact, a Shinto priest at Japan's Yasukuni shrine to the nation's war dead made it while criticizing proposals to add an educational component to the shrine's commemorative functions.[1] The priest's comment reminds us of the universality of the suspicions and hostility that historians (who like to think of themselves as fairly inoffensive and harmless folks) can arouse when they become involved in matters about which great numbers of citizens feel passionate emotion.

With the fiftieth anniversary of World War II's final events behind us, we can perhaps begin to gain some perspective on the remarkable rancor the commemorative effort unleashed. The storm center of the controversy was, of course, the proposed *Enola Gay* exhibit at the Smithsonian's National Air and Space Museum, which was to feature extensive treatment of the current state of historical scholarship on the decision to drop the atomic bomb and the ending of the world war, as well as the bombs' immediate effects on the people of Hiroshima and Nagasaki and the long-term implications of the development and use of nuclear weapons.

As early drafts of the exhibit text became known, the Air Force Association, the American Legion, and conservative members of Congress, sensing the issue's demagogic potential, denounced the exhibit as "anti-American," insensitive to veterans, and too sympathetic to the bomb victims. Numerous meetings and extensive modifications in the text did no good. When the smoke cleared, the original exhibit had been scrapped; the museum director had been forced out; and Republicans in Congress (joined by a few Democrats) were gearing up for hearings that, for a time, threatened to turn into a McCarthyite witch-hunt for the sinister and disloyal persons responsible for the shameful exhibit. When the Senate hearings began in May 1995, Chairman Ted Stevens, a Republican from Alaska, asked ominously, "What went wrong with [the Smithsonian's] management practices, and what steps have been taken to correct the revisionist and 'politically correct' bias that was contained in the original script?"[2] (Though marked by senatorial rancor and ill temper, the hearings actually proved fairly tepid and inconclusive.)

Reeling and shell-shocked, the Smithsonian mounted a cautious, scaled-back exhibit that simply portrayed the fuselage of the *Enola Gay* and videos of the crew, with minimal historical context on President Harry Truman's decision, the bomb's human toll, or the long-term consequences of its use. Air force historian Richard Hallion dismissed the new exhibit as "a beer can with a label." Historian Kai Bird, modifying the chilling term *ethnic cleansing* coined by the genocidal Bosnian Serbs, spoke of a "historical cleansing" of the museum. A cartoon in the *Boston Globe* pictured an empty museum with an official announcing, "We're returning to our original mission as the air and space museum." An ironic outcome of the episode was that far more Americans undoubtedly became aware of the scholarly debate over the atomic bomb decision than would otherwise have been the case.

While the Smithsonian flap attracted the most public attention, the fiftieth-anniversary cultural struggle over the meaning of

Hiroshima and Nagasaki erupted on other fronts as well, even in the arcane realm of postage stamp design. Because of their ubiquity, lowly postage stamps represent a significant visual means by which a nation's historical perception can be shaped, hence the controversy over a proposed stamp commemorating the atomic bomb. The original Postal Service plan was to issue an atomic bomb stamp as part of an ongoing series recalling the major landmarks of World War II. Those planned for 1995 release were to note the principal events of 1945, including the atomic bombings—certainly the most notable war events of that year apart from the actual capitulation of Germany and Japan.

Planning went forward in the recesses of the postal bureaucracy. At one point I received a telephone call from a historian friend who had been asked to evaluate an early draft of the proposed stamp. (I had not realized until then how carefully the proposed textual and visual content of stamps is reviewed and evaluated. The Citizens Stamp Advisory Committee oversees the process, consulting specialists in various fields.) In this version, the mushroom cloud appeared to float in space, with no hint that a city lay below; the historical tag line read (as I recall), "Atomic Bombs Level Hiroshima and Nagasaki." I immediately agreed with my friend that some geographic features should be included to link the bomb to its target, and that the word *Level*—with its bland and even positive connotations ("This is absolutely on the level")—be dropped in favor of a more accurate phrase: perhaps "Atomic Bombs *Destroy* Hiroshima and Nagasaki." In fact, the message was softened, rather than made more precise, eventually evolving into "Atomic Bombs Hasten War's End."

But the entire issue soon became moot. In December 1994, under protest from the Japanese government, with whom the Clinton administration was already embroiled in trade conflicts, President Bill Clinton canceled the much-revised stamp, relegating it to the limbo reserved for postage stamps that never actually reach the nation's post offices.[3]

In one way or another, across the United States, journalists, pundits, and ordinary citizens found themselves unexpectedly wrestling with the historical meaning of Hiroshima and Nagasaki in the angry months leading up to the fiftieth anniversary of the bombings. A Gallup Poll jointly commissioned by *USA Today* and CNN found that 59 percent of Americans expressed approval of Truman's decision and 35 percent disapproved. Fifty years after the event, Americans remained uncertain and deeply divided about its meaning.

The Bomb and the "Good War"

Why do Hiroshima and Nagasaki stir so restlessly in our national psyche after the passage of half a century? Why do we have such trouble not only reaching consensus about how we should view these events, but even discussing them calmly and rationally? Whereas the fiftieth anniversaries of Pearl Harbor, D day, Germany's surrender, and other World War II landmarks were observed by public ceremonies and general agreement about their significance, Hiroshima and Nagasaki generated only recrimination and angry debate.

One reason Americans have had so much trouble coming to terms with Hiroshima and Nagasaki surely lies in the fact that what our atomic bombs did to those cities has never been easily assimilable to the prevailing public view of World War II as the "Good War"—a noble struggle against forces that threatened not only Western values but the survival of civilization itself. Particularly in the aftermath of the bitterly divisive Vietnam conflict, Americans looked back nostalgically to the 1941–45 period as a time when the nation's aims were clear and just, a time when nearly all citizens had rallied behind the government. This show of unanimity was sharply at variance with the turmoil of the 1960s. No campus protesters in 1944 had accused Franklin Roosevelt of being a baby killer; no one had dubbed the conflict "Stimson's War." On the contrary, World War II symbolized a moment of shared national purpose and unity in a righteous cause. Studs

Terkel's decision to call his 1984 oral history of World War II *The "Good War"* helped fix this image in the public mind. (Though Terkel's ironic quotation marks suggested certain reservations about the appropriateness of the popular label.)

Of course, even without the atomic bomb, this version of the war elided some awkward realities. The Roosevelt administration's grudging response to the plight of European Jewry, the arrest and internment of Japanese-American citizens, the flourishing of black-market chiselers and wartime profiteers, the persistence of racism in the military and on the home front, the incineration of Dresden and other German cities, and the firebombing of Tokyo on the night of March 10–11, 1945 (in which more people may have died than initially perished at Hiroshima) all complicate the Norman Rockwell image of the war. While historians have explored these darker facets of the conflict, and while some history textbooks deal with them, they have not loomed large in either the public memory or the media's treatment of the war.

But if the popular image of the "Good War" involved selective memory and the downplaying of certain awkward facts, it also contained much truth. By and large—and certainly in contrast to the Vietnam era—1941–45 *did* mark a time of national unity and moral clarity. The bombings of Hiroshima and Nagasaki, however, have long complicated this picture of a crusade pursued by a unified nation employing wholly justifiable means. They are the misshapen pieces that prevent us from completing the picture puzzle in an entirely satisfactory fashion. While some of the awkward realities noted above were partially redressed as the years passed—survivors of the internment camps were belatedly compensated; a Holocaust Memorial was erected on the Mall in Washington, D.C.; the civil rights movement erased the more blatant forms of racial segregation—the issues posed by the atomic annihilation of two cities remained contested terrain. As the semicentennial approached in 1995, the subject seemed farther from closure than ever. Now that the anniversary has passed, the controversy has receded from the front pages, but the wounds and animosities remain.

Opinion Manipulation, Ethical Discourse,
Antinuclear Activism: The Symbolic Functions
of "Hiroshima" and "Nagasaki"

The inability to fit the destruction of Hiroshima and Nagasaki comfortably into the "Good War" paradigm did not prevent those events from figuring prominently in the polemics of the Cold War years. Indeed, the very uncertainty that surrounded the meaning of those acts made them available for a variety of polemical uses. President Truman initially presented the Manhattan Project as the greatest scientific achievement in all history and defended his decision to drop the bomb as a fully justifiable action that had ended the war, saved untold thousands of American lives, and repaid Japan for Pearl Harbor, the Bataan Death March, and other atrocities.[4] As the wartime enemy became the postwar ally, the argument that the bomb "saved American lives" was sometimes expanded to encompass the contention that it had also ensured the survival of multiple thousands of *Japanese* who would otherwise have been killed in the invasion that supposedly would have been inevitable had the bombs not been dropped. At a 1984 conference at the Woodrow Wilson International Center for Scholars, on the centennial of Harry Truman's birth, Truman adviser Clark Clifford expatiated on this humanitarian theme with a considerable show of emotion. On the evidence of public opinion polls, a vast majority of Americans initially accepted the official justification for the atomic destruction of Hiroshima and Nagasaki,[5] and a majority—though a steadily dwindling one—has continued to do so ever since.

This public endorsement of the government's rationale for the dropping of two atomic bombs in 1945 may in part reflect the public's insulation from the actual human consequences of that action. From the first, Washington officialdom, often with the complaisant support of much of the media, offered for public consumption a selective and sanitized version of these events. In

Japan, U.S. occupation authorities strictly censored photographs and films showing bomb victims. Medical data on both the bomb's short-term blast-and-fire effects and the long-term consequences of radiation exposure (not only at Hiroshima and Nagasaki but also at later nuclear test sites in the Marshall Islands and the American Southwest) were kept from the public or discussed in bland and general terms.

In "The Decision to Use the Atomic Bomb," a highly influential—and artfully misleading—article published in the February 1947 issue of *Harper's* magazine, former secretary of war Henry L. Stimson justified and rationalized the U.S. action. In the behind-the-scenes discussions that led to this seminally important essay, Stimson, his wartime aide Harvey Bundy, Harvard president James B. Conant, and Bundy's son McGeorge Bundy made their purpose crystal clear: to influence the larger public by reaching teachers and other opinion molders and, in Conant's words, by combating the "sentimentalism" that, if not resisted, could "have a great deal of influence on the next generation." Continued Conant in a September 1946 letter to Harvey Bundy, "A small minority, if it represents the type of person who is both sentimental and verbally minded and in contact with youth, may result in a distortion of history."[6] From such concerns the Stimson essay took shape, and in the years to follow it would play a significant role in sustaining the official version of events and warding off the inroads of "sentimentality" that Conant so feared.

Hollywood films such as *The Beginning or the End* (1947), a ludicrously fictionalized version of the Manhattan Project and the decision to drop the bomb, and *Above and Beyond* (1952), a formulaic tale of marital discord and reconciliation supposedly based on the life of Paul W. Tibbets, Jr., the pilot for the Hiroshima mission, further served to shore up the official government version.[7] Since most Americans very much wanted to believe the fundamental message of all this propaganda—that dropping the bomb was essential, wholly justified, and fully in keeping with the nation's high war aims—the opinion-molding effort proved highly effective. The subtle process of creating a dominant hegemonic discourse unfolded in almost textbook fashion in the shaping of postwar American attitudes about the atomic bombing of Japan.

The campaign to forestall criticism of Truman's decision was part of a larger government and media effort throughout the early postwar period to soothe atomic fears and play down the true effects of nuclear weapons. In its August 11, 1951 issue, to cite only one of hundreds of examples, *Collier's* magazine published "Patty, the Atomic Pig." The article was based on an actual incident in which a piglet that was part of the Noah's Ark of goats, pigs, rats, and other animals assembled for the July 1946 Operations Crossroads nuclear test at Bikini Atoll was later found swimming in the radioactive waters of Bikini lagoon. The *Collier's* story, presented as a whimsical fairy tale, began, "Once upon a time, there was a great group of generals, admirals, scientists, newsmen and curious people who wanted to know more about atomic explosions." Illustrated with cute drawings, the story imagined Patty's thoughts before the blast (" 'My, oh, my,' thought the little piglet, 'What will become of us all?' ") and her adventures afterward ("Patricia swam as fast as she could thrash her little legs, holding her nose high out of the water"). Patty not only survives (no long-term radiation-exposure hazards here!) but grows to be a six-hundred-pound porker under the benevolent care of kindly scientists at the Naval Medical Research Institute at Bethesda, Maryland, and ends her days as a coddled exhibit in a zoo.[8] Sugarcoated propaganda like this, part of a mountain of material in the media that reinforced the government's version of both the 1945 bombings and of Washington's subsequent nuclear program, served to deflect and neutralize serious scrutiny of the meaning and implications of atomic weaponry, past or future.

For all its power and pervasiveness, however, the official justification for the atomic bombing of Hiroshima and Nagasaki never achieved absolute dominance; a "counterhegemonic discourse" was present from the beginning. The announcement that a new atomic weapon had been dropped on Hiroshima immediately seized the attention of theologians, ethicists, pacifists, religious leaders, and other Americans concerned about the moral implications of war. Many pointed to the instantaneous annihilation of that city, and then of Nagasaki, as the logical and chilling culmination of a long process by which the rhetoric of "total war" undermined the centuries-old "just war" doctrine (most fully articulated by Roman Catholic theologians) that sought to shield civilian populations from the worst horrors of wartime.[9]

The distinction between civilians and combatants had broken down badly in the course of World War II. The leaders of all the belligerent nations, including President Roosevelt, spoke the language of "total war," insisting that every citizen, not just the military forces, must share in the struggle. Wartime vegetable plots became "victory gardens"; the sale of government bonds became "victory drives." Even children were militarized. I vividly recall the pressures in my third- and fourth-grade classes at Fairview Elementary School in Dayton, Ohio, to buy war stamps, collect scrap metal, and turn in pencil stubs for the graphite they contained. (Worried about what my pacifist parents might think of these efforts, I once asked my teacher to return a pencil stub I had contributed, leading her to ridicule me before the class as an "Indian giver.") If an entire society is mobilized for war, the entire society also becomes a legitimate target of war. President Truman, justifying the atomic bombing, accurately pointed out that Hiroshima and Nagasaki were centers of military production—just as were Seattle, Los Angeles, and countless other U.S. cities.

The atomic bombing was only the culminating act in the breaking down of a never wholly effective ethical barrier—already breached in World War I by Germany's U-boat attacks on passenger ships; at Guernica and Nanking in the 1930s; in the Nazi V-2 raids on London, Antwerp, and other Allied cities; and in the Allied firebombings of Hamburg, Dresden, Tokyo, and other crowded urban centers. But the technological gift that the physicists presented to President Truman in 1945 rendered the mass extermination of civilians vastly more efficient, radically raising the stakes of the larger postwar debate over the viability of the "just war" doctrine and the ethical implications of the "total war" language so enthusiastically embraced by wartime leaders.

Hiroshima and Nagasaki also naturally came to loom large in

the discourse of antinuclear campaigners. As the Cold War deepened, and as waves of nuclear fear periodically swept the nation,
activists regularly invoked the two cities as symbols of what must
never happen again. "No More Hiroshimas" became a rallying cry
of the antinuclear cause.

Indeed, the degree of attention accorded to Hiroshima and
Nagasaki as symbols of a future to be avoided can be correlated
closely over time with the pervasiveness and intensity of anxiety
about nuclear war. In 1946, with fear of the new weapon still raw
in America and a campaign for the international control of atomic
energy at full throttle, John Hersey's journalistic account of six
A-bomb survivors, entitled simply *Hiroshima*, became a best-
seller. In the mid- and late 1950s and early 1960s, as public fears
of radioactive fallout from nuclear tests fueled a test-ban movement that won broad support, iconic images of Hiroshima and
Nagasaki abounded. Survivors of the 1945 bombings addressed
rallies; test-ban activists marked the anniversaries each August. In
1955, Ralph Edwards's popular TV show *This Is Your Life* featured
a Hiroshima survivor in a staged "reconciliation" with a crew
member of the *Enola Gay*. The survivor solicited contributions for
the "Hiroshima Maidens," a group of bomb-disfigured young
women brought to the United States for plastic surgery by the
magazine editor and antinuclear campaigner Norman Cousins.[10]

In the early 1980s, as the Reagan administration's military
buildup and belligerent rhetoric inspired a nuclear-weapons freeze
campaign, allusions to Hiroshima and Nagasaki were again commonplace. In 1985, on the fortieth anniversary of the bombings,
Time magazine, both reflecting and contributing to the fears of
nuclear war so pervasive at that moment, featured on its cover the
nuclear age's instantly recognizable logo: the mushroom cloud
ascending over Hiroshima. In short, in every period of heightened
nuclear anxiety and antinuclear activism from 1945 on, Hiroshima
and Nagasaki did polemical duty as emblems of a global fate to be
avoided at all costs.[11]

Historians Confront the Bomb

Despite the use of "Hiroshima" and "Nagasaki" as points of reference in various public discourses, the actual events of August 6–9, 1945, and their devastating consequences, obscured from the very beginning by official censorship and deception, grew steadily dimmer in public memory with the passing years. In the early 1960s, however, historians and other scholars turned a fresh eye on those events, and especially on President Truman's decision to authorize the military use of two atomic bombs at a moment when Japan's war-making capability was near collapse. Their findings made it increasingly hard for informed observers to continue to view this decision from the uncritical perspective of 1945.

In fact, from the earliest moments of the atomic age, a few critics had challenged the official rationale for dropping the bomb, but not until the 1960s did this dissident viewpoint gain a significant scholarly hearing. In his 1961 book *Japan Subdued: The Atomic Bomb and the End of World War II*, historian Herbert Feis, while generally supportive of Truman's action, became the first major American historian to suggest that the calculations underlying it might have been more complex than official dogma conceded.

Only in 1965, though, with the publication of historian and political scientist Gar Alperovitz's *Atomic Diplomacy* did an American academic offer a radical frontal challenge to the received interpretation. Why the rush to deploy the new weapon when leaders of Tokyo's wartime government were urgently signaling a desire to end the fighting? asked Alperovitz. Why did Washington so vehemently insist on "unconditional surrender" prior to August 6, only to do an abrupt about-face and accept a whopping condition—Emperor Hirohito could remain on his throne—as soon as the bombs were dropped?

Any meaningful response to these questions, Alperovitz concluded, required attention to broader strategic and economic considerations. A dramatic demonstration of the atomic bomb's destructive power, he suggested, promised to introduce a potent new factor into U.S. dealings with the Soviet Union, a wartime ally already shaping up as a postwar adversary. Doubtless the passions of war, the impulse to avenge Pearl Harbor, Japanese atrocities, and the appeal of ending the war with a fantastic display of American firepower rather than by painstaking negotiations (which would later have to be explained to a restive public) all played their role—especially after the desperate and bloody Okinawa campaign of March–June 1945. But other considerations entered the picture too, considerations that scholars began to probe with increasing insistence.

Despite Truman's later claims, suggested Alperovitz (and soon other scholars as well), the grim prospect of a land invasion of the Japanese main islands, tentatively scheduled to begin November 1, was not necessarily paramount in the president's mind in late July and early August 1945. He was, they argued, more concerned with the precise way the war might be ended in the coming few weeks or even days. At the Yalta Conference in February 1945, Stalin had pledged to declare war on Japan "two or three months" after Germany's surrender; in other words, as it turned out, by early August at the latest. If a spectacular American blow demonstrating an awesome new secret weapon, not Russia's impending declaration of war, were seen as having forced Japan's capitulation, America's role in postwar Japan and the Far East, as well as Washington's bargaining posture vis-à-vis the Soviet Union in shaping the politics and economy of postwar Europe, might be vastly enhanced.

Combing the primary sources, Alperovitz—and an impressive group of historians that eventually included Martin Sherwin of Tufts University (later of Dartmouth); Barton Bernstein of Stanford University; Robert Messer of the University of Illinois-Chicago; Michael Sherry of Northwestern University; J. Samuel Walker, historian of the U.S. Nuclear Regulatory Commission; James S. Hershberg, director of the Cold War History Project at the Woodrow Wilson International Center; independent scholars such as Stanley Goldberg and Kai Bird; and a number of others—

documented a variety of considerations that clearly seemed relevant to a full understanding of Truman's decision. Stanley Goldberg, for example, emphasized that Truman and his inner circle of atomic advisers, including General Leslie R. Groves, majordomo of the Manhattan Project, feared an angry public and congressional reaction if they failed to use the new weapon that they had secretly spent billions to develop. Hershberg, in a massively researched biography of James B. Conant, a member of the Interim Committee that advised Truman on atomic matters, revealed that the high-minded university president favored demonstrating the bomb's power in the most awesome possible way—by destroying a city—as the best hope of rallying world support for the postwar international control of atomic energy.[12]

Meanwhile, historian John W. Dower's book *War Without Mercy: Race and Power in the Pacific War*, published in 1986, documented the racism that pervaded America's anti-Japanese wartime propaganda (as well as Japan's anti-American wartime propaganda). *Eagle Against the Sun: The American War with Japan* (1985) by historian Ronald Spector (a Vietnam veteran and member of the U.S. Marine Corps Reserves) similarly emphasized the centrality of racism on both sides. This, too, it seemed, must be factored into the equation when evaluating Truman's readiness to drop two atomic bombs on a defeated Japan.

Yale psychiatrist Robert Jay Lifton had earlier contributed to this surge of scholarly attention to the bomb with his important 1967 study *Death in Life: Survivors of Hiroshima*. His book moved under the mushroom cloud to explore the psychological responses of bomb survivors as well as the deep psychic effects of living with the fear of future thermonuclear war. Transcending the limits of diplomatic history (sometimes, it seemed, almost transcending history altogether), Lifton added a new perspective to the debate, along with a powerful new set of analytic terms, notably *psychic numbing*, that would prove enormously influential.[13]

Washington's original justification for the A-bomb decision had arisen in the specific context of the immediate postwar years, when wartime passions still ran high, and the Cold War and the nuclear arms race were just taking shape. The post-1965 wave of critical scholarship about the bomb was shaped by a very different historical moment. Alperovitz, born in 1936, represented a younger generation of historians who came of age in Cold War America, when the bomb (now called a "thermonuclear weapon") evoked not so much victory over Japan as nuclear tests, radioactive fallout, a grim struggle with the Soviet Union, and the threat of a world-destroying thermonuclear holocaust. As an undergraduate in history at the University of Wisconsin in 1958, Alperovitz encountered William Appleman Williams, who was radically revising conventional diplomatic history by insisting on the primacy of economic factors—especially the influence of corporate capitalism—in shaping U.S. foreign policy.

After a stint as legislative assistant to Robert Kastenmeier, a Wisconsin congressman known for his strongly antimilitarist views, Alperovitz entered a doctoral program in political economy at Cambridge University, where he read with economist Joan Robinson. She, like Williams, stressed the interplay of politics, economics, and diplomacy. Alperovitz's 1963 Ph.D. dissertation (published two years later by Simon and Schuster) was a product of these experiences. Reflecting Joan Robinson's influence, his initial thesis topic had not been "the atomic bomb decision" but the economic and political planning for postwar Eastern Europe that went on in wartime Washington. This, in turn, led him to the larger topic of how Washington policymakers viewed the Soviet Union, and ultimately to how these postwar calculations influenced the Truman administration's strategy for ending the Pacific war. The specific issue of the atomic bomb was initially quite peripheral to his research focus.[14]

When *Atomic Diplomacy* appeared in 1965 (timed by the publisher to coincide with the twentieth anniversary of the Hiroshima and Nagasaki bombings), reviewers and scholars at once recognized it as a thoroughgoing challenge to a version of the atomic bomb story that for two decades had enjoyed broad public assent and minimal critical scrutiny. The book and the times were made for each other. Early in 1965, President Lyndon Johnson massively escalated the Vietnam War—and he did so with a decision to launch an intensive bombing campaign against North Vietnam (after running as a peace candidate against Barry Goldwater a few months earlier). That year saw the first major stirrings of an antiwar movement that would soon come to question the official version of the war and the bombing campaign against the North Vietnamese. It was a propitious moment, indeed, to probe the motives that led an earlier American president to call tremendous destructive power down upon an Asian people.

Not surprisingly, the critical reassessment of the A-bomb decision launched by Alperovitz steadily gained ground after 1965 within academia, especially among younger scholars, as a succession of events eroded the credibility of public officials and their pronouncements: the optimistic bulletins that flowed from Vietnam as the body bags and the shocking TV images multiplied; the New Left's ideological assault on "the Establishment"; Henry Kissinger's secret bombing of Cambodia and wiretapping of his own staff; and, of course, the tangle of official crimes collectively known as Watergate that ended with a discredited Richard Nixon driven from office.

Like *Atomic Diplomacy*, Martin Sherwin's *A World Destroyed: The Atomic Bomb and the Grand Alliance* (1975), a major contribution to the scholarly reassessment of the A-bomb decision, was based on his Ph.D. thesis—completed in 1971 as the controversy over the Vietnam War raged, and revised for publication as newspaper headlines screamed of secret Cambodia bombings, the Pentagon Papers, the Watergate hearings, and a president's forced resignation. These were not times that fostered the uncritical acceptance of official versions of public events. Indeed, the political-cultural climate of 1965–75 almost demanded the skeptical reassessment of accepted historical interpretations and even of the fundamental assumption—a legacy of World War II, really—that the government's version of the truth was ipso facto trustworthy, disinterested, and reliable.[15]

All this unfolded just as new methodological approaches and new areas of research transformed the history profession. The rethinking of the Hiroshima/Nagasaki bombings was, in fact, only part of a much broader process whereby an older historiography that had focused mainly on elites—whether political, military, social, intellectual, or cultural—gave way to a "new social history" more attuned to the experiences of ordinary people, particularly the underclass, and more critical of the actions of policymakers, statesmen, corporate leaders, generals, and other power wielders. In diplomatic history, focus shifted from treaties and conferences to the larger economic, cultural, and ideological framework within which foreign-policy processes unfolded.

These new historiographical emphases, coupled with the broader political and cultural currents that flowed across America in the wake of Vietnam and Watergate, encouraged the skeptical reassessment of received wisdom on many topics. Inevitably, this reassessment included attention to the events of August 6–9, 1945, that had taken the lives of well over two hundred thousand human beings (including long-term deaths related to radiation exposure) and laid the groundwork for an ever more dangerous nuclear arms race between the United States and the Soviet Union.

Atomic Bomb Scholarship
in the Arena of Public Opinion

By around 1980, the reassessment of the A-bomb decision launched by Alperovitz and others, while still a subject of lively debate among historians, had generally been welcomed as stimulating and provocative. Within the guild, it was widely viewed as another manifestation of the familiar process by which historians continually reassess the past and question received interpretations. Debated at scholarly conferences and dissected in journal articles, the new analytic hypotheses were beginning to make their appearance in college textbooks as well as classroom lectures.

For most Americans, however, the debates of historians on this topic remained arcane and remote, a matter of no concern. When nonhistorians did encounter the new scholarship, many rejected it contemptuously; the received wisdom about the justice of the atomic bomb decision generally retained its sway over grassroots America. For those who had embraced the "Good War" paradigm, any questioning of Truman's oft-repeated justification of his action challenged an image of World War II that had become a cornerstone of national identity. If the motives for dropping the atomic bomb could be probed and problematized by historians, what part of the American past was safe from skeptical critical scrutiny? As historian Michael Kammen would write in the aftermath of the Smithsonian debacle and other cultural battles involving conflicting interpretations of the American past: "Historians become notably controversial when they do not perpetuate myths, when they do not transmit the received and conventional wisdom, when they challenge the comforting presence of a stabilized past"—and, it may be added, when news of what they are up to finally gets out.[16] Perhaps no issue of the postwar era confirmed this generalization more dramatically than the angry struggle over who would finally determine the meaning of Hiroshima and Nagasaki: historians or "the people."

Exacerbating the populist (or pseudopopulist) reaction against the scholarship of the atomic bomb historians was the widespread practice (adopted by many historians as well as nonhistorians) of attaching to them the blanket label "revisionists." They *were* engaged in a process of historical revision, of course, but when the term was applied exclusively to this one group, it suggested that they were deviants who had departed from the accepted norms of professional practice. In fact, these scholars were "revisionists" only in the sense that all good scholars are "revisionists," continually questioning and revising standard interpretations on the basis of new evidence, deeper analysis, or the fresh perspectives offered by the passage of time.

The allusions to *"the* revisionist school" of atomic bomb historians also conveyed a certain conspiratorial implication, as though these scholars had colluded, presumably with sinister or subversive motives, to concoct and foist upon an unsuspecting public a single, agreed-upon new version of history. In fact "the revisionists" were a diverse and contentious crew, representing a wide range of often conflicting viewpoints, based on different research findings and different weighings of the facts. Barton Bernstein, for example, sharply criticized Gar Alperovitz for talking of Truman's "decision" to drop the bomb when, in Bernstein's view, Truman inherited from the Roosevelt administration both the *assumption* that the bomb would be used and a tolerance for destroying entire cities. As a new president in office for only a few months, Bernstein argued, Truman had simply fallen back on these inherited assumptions and practices when news of the successful Alamogordo test reached him at the Potsdam Conference in mid-July 1945. Bernstein also took both Alperovitz and Sherwin to task for treating as a virtual certainty the possibility that the war could have been ended long before the planned invasion date of November 1, 1945, without the atomic bomb. While agreeing that other alternatives were available and should have been tried, he remained agnostic as to whether they would have succeeded in forcing Tokyo's surrender.[17]

Certainly, most historians who addressed the question agreed that the factors shaping Truman's actions in the war's climactic days were too complex to be summed up in a single, easily recited formula ("The atomic bomb saved American lives, ended the war, and repaid Japan for Pearl Harbor")—a formula that, if not demonstrably false, was demonstrably inadequate. But beyond this, one would be hard put, despite accusations to the contrary, to identify a monolithic "revisionist" position on the A-bomb decision. The process of historical reassessment on this subject is continually evolving, as it is on every topic of sufficient complexity to warrant historians' interest, with a variety of arguments and hypotheses in play at any given moment.

That the fury over historians' examination of the Hiroshima/Nagasaki bombings exploded so spectacularly in 1994–95 was linked, I think, not only to the fiftieth-anniversary observances but also to the fact that American society was racked by new kinds of cultural conflicts and political turmoil. Conditioned by four decades of black-and-white Cold War thinking, many Americans in the aftermath of the Soviet Union's collapse seemed to transfer the same "us-*versus*-them" outlook willy-nilly to the domestic sphere. From this perspective, the angry denunciations of "the revisionists" as unpatriotic and contemptible, and the refusal to grant their findings any shred of legitimacy, became simply another manifestation of a political climate marked by inflammatory, polarizing rhetoric.

In this climate, the low-level irritation felt by many ordinary citizens, especially older Americans and World War II veterans, at historians who questioned an article of national faith was exacerbated and amplified by a braying army of jingoistic politicians, editorial writers, and radio talk-show hosts who saw this as another emotion-laden "wedge" issue—like attacking the National Endowment for the Arts for "promoting obscenity" or advocating constitutional amendments permitting school prayer, requiring a balanced budget, and banning flag desecration. By such issues, the New Right defined itself, rallied the faithful, and demonized its enemies.

Conservative presidential aspirants made sure the issue would remain divisive. Senator Bob Dole, in a red-meat speech to the American Legion in September 1995, denounced the Smithsonians' original *Enola Gay* exhibit as another example of the insidious work of "intellectual elites" and other "arbiters of political correctness" who were contemptuous of patriotism, scornful of veterans and their sacrifices, and intent on waging "war on traditional American values."[18]

But even in this volatile climate, popular attitudes toward the atomic bomb decision resisted easy generalization. Over the decades, different groups had diverged markedly in their judgments about Truman's action, and this remained true in the 1990s. In a 1995 Gallup Poll, for example, the aggregate results concealed important variations in opinion on the basis of gender, race, and age. The rate of approval of Truman's action, for instance, was notably higher for men than for women. (A similar gap emerges in almost every poll dealing with military issues, including defense spending, the use of force to achieve U.S. aims, armed interventions such as the Persian Gulf war, and so forth.) As to race and ethnicity—no surprise here—a significantly higher percentage of whites approved the atomic bomb decision than did African Americans, Hispanics, or Asian Americans. From the first, non-white groups had raised the issue of racism in the A-bomb context and posed awkward questions about whether President Truman would have been ready to drop the bomb on Germans, had the European war continued into the summer of 1945.[19] Given the firebombing attacks that turned German cities into raging crematoria, it is by no means clear that Truman would have refrained from using the atomic bomb on white Europeans, but the nagging "what if" question can never be answered with certainty.

Another key division that showed up in public opinion data as early as the 1960s—and again quite sharply in the 1995 poll—is a generational one. Broadly speaking, the older generation that remembers World War II and that initially associated the atomic bomb with Japan's surrender and frenzied celebrations of V-J day tends to be strongest in the conviction that dropping the bomb was justified. By the same token, succeeding generations, having very different associations with nuclear weapons and no direct memories of the war, tend to be more critical of Truman's action.

As a result, it was misleading to frame the *Enola Gay* controversy as a simple, straightforward conflict between historians (or academics) on the one hand, and the general public on the other. Some historians continue to accept the Truman administration's justification for dropping the bomb as sufficient; a few have attacked "the revisionists" as scornfully as any conservative politician or professional veteran.[20] Nevertheless, broadly speaking, the controversy of 1994–95 did expose a considerable chasm between the methodology of historians and the way many Americans think about the past, especially the portion of the past encompassed by their own experiences and memories. Historians are constantly challenging the received wisdom and established interpretations of events. This is what they do. Usually this process unfolds in scholarly journals or at professional gatherings out of the public eye. As new interpretations filter into textbooks and classrooms, they may eventually modify the general public's historical understanding, but the shift is typically gradual, almost imperceptible.

Occasionally, however, the disjunction between the scholarly approach to history and the public's personal, even semimythic view of the past is exposed with stark clarity, usually when the ongoing process of historical revision and reassessment focuses on an issue about which many citizens feel passionately, or that has great patriotic resonance. Such a moment occurred in 1913, for example, when Charles A. Beard argued in his *Economic Interpretation of the Constitution of the United States* that the Founding Fathers had in fact pursued public policies that served their pecuniary interests. Beard was roundly vilified; he had questioned the motives of patriots revered by every schoolchild! This controversy over an issue of historical interpretation also unfolded at a moment of highly charged ideological conflict, as conservatives and reformers battled over the government's role in regulating industrial capitalism.

A similar phenomenon, I suspect, underlay the reaction, ranging from annoyance to rage, roused by the historical profession's ongoing examination of the atomic bomb decision—a long-term scholarly project that the *Enola Gay* controversy suddenly thrust into public view. As the Air Force Association demanded in one of its many press releases aimed at discrediting the Smithsonian exhibit, "All revisionist speculation should be eliminated."[21] The Shinto priest at Japan's Yasukuni war shrine could not have put it better.

This reaction was undoubtedly intensified by the fact that August 1945 remained a part of many Americans' living memory. As Edward T. Linenthal has pointed out, the tension between the commemorative impulse and critical historical scholarship can be profound, and fiftieth anniversaries, the "last hurrah" for most survivors, highlight this tension in a particularly volatile way.[22]

The First Thing We Do,
Let's Kill All the Historians

In the early 1980s, as the nuclear-weapons-freeze campaign unfolded and I pursued research of my own on the atomic bomb's
cultural fallout, I often lectured to community groups. When
asked about Truman's A-bomb decision (as I almost invariably
was), I would discuss the work of Alperovitz, Sherwin, and others
as an interpretive approach that merited consideration. But often
the questioner would have none of it, especially if he (usually it
was a male) remembered World War II, and most especially if he
was a veteran convinced beyond all argument that the atomic
bomb had saved his life.

I recalled these exchanges in 1988 when Paul Fussell, in *Thank
God for the Atomic Bomb*, argued that his personal status as an
infantryman in Europe fearing transfer to the Pacific in the spring
of 1945 granted him special insight into the decision to use the
bomb that far transcended what he lampooned as historians' "tidy
hindsight." Professor Fussell ridiculed scholars like Michael
Walzer and Michael S. Sherry, too young to have fought in the
war, who presumed to offer interpretations of Truman's actions.[23]
Whatever the solipsism and anti-intellectualism of Fussell's position, his views are far from unique and are easy enough to understand. They have, however, more recently been adopted by many
who were not themselves participants in World War II, as the
battle over the *Enola Gay* exhibit made only too clear.

In August 1995, when I published an essay in the *Chronicle of
Higher Education* reviewing the controversy over the A-bomb decision and (as I thought) offering a fairly balanced, uncontrover-
sial assessment of the cultural issues and fault lines it had
exposed, the response was revealing.[24] While fellow historians and
other scholars reacted positively, the scattered responses from
outside academia proved uniformly hostile. An early-morning
telephone call, for example, came from a gentleman in North

Carolina who, though born after the war, was the son of a veteran who had fought in the Pacific. My caller therefore insisted that he also owed *his* life to the atomic bomb, since if his future father had died in an invasion of Japan, he, the son, would never have been conceived.

The larger implications of my caller's argument were fairly breathtaking: the bomb saved not only the lives of untold thousands of American soldiers who might have perished in the invasion, had it occurred, but also the lives of all the children they subsequently fathered, and by now presumably their grandchildren and even great-grandchildren. If we project into the infinite future the potential descendants of all the men who did not die in the invasion of Japan that was never launched, the atomic bombs that destroyed Hiroshima and Nagasaki must surely be ranked among the most beneficent and life-giving forces in all human history!

Shortly after this call, a Louisiana investment counselor wrote a sarcasm-filled letter that attacked me as a typical "off-the-wall," anti-American academic eager to besmirch the United States while glossing over all of Japan's misdeeds. He concluded with this final thrust: "I await your political comments on the justification of the war between Athens and Sparta. I am sure that you have an opinion on this and I welcome your comments."

Those who articulate such responses are not interested in debate; for them, unquestioning support for Truman's atomic bomb decision becomes a litmus test of patriotism. Indeed, they reject the legitimacy of the historical enterprise itself. What right have you, a mere academic, such critics are really asking, to publish dissenting views on matters about which true patriots cannot possibly hold differing opinions? As my Louisiana correspondent put it, *"No one can doubt* that this horrible weapon saved American lives." That precisely this assertion is, in fact, a matter of considerable doubt, and certainly open to historical inquiry and discussion, was a position whose legitimacy he simply could not acknowledge. He was left, therefore, with no alternative but to impugn the character and integrity of those who do hold it. The confrontation between popular memory and patriotic affirmation on the one hand, and the norms of historical research and argument on the other, could hardly be more starkly revealed.

•   •   •

Like "Waterloo" and "Verdun," Hiroshima and Nagasaki in the half century since 1945 have often functioned as a kind of rhetorical shorthand in a variety of public discourses. For some, these two cities, set apart forever by history, served as emblems of America's scientific and technical prowess; for others, as places on a map whose obliteration allowed the nation's just purposes to be attained and countless American (and even Japanese) lives to be saved. They were invoked by moralists as symbols of modern warfare's transgression of all ethical bounds; and seized upon by antinuclear activists as cautionary reminders of what the world must never again permit to happen.

In the fiftieth-anniversary year, however, with the public mood both retrospective and ideologically charged, attention focused once again on the original events in all their jagged immediacy. In the process, many citizens grasped—perhaps for the first time—that for several decades, scholars had been questioning the official justifications originally advanced for the atomic bombing of Japan. The result was not thoughtful discussion and the search for a new, more historically defensible consensus, but high-decibel contention, inconclusive recrimination, and accusations of bad faith and disloyalty. The Smithsonian exhibit did not cause the controversy; it merely provided the occasion for it and guaranteed that it would be played out amid shameless political opportunism and in a glare of media publicity.

The emotional debate will probably continue so long as politicians see political capital in it, and so long as vast numbers of Americans remain convinced that the atomic bomb was an essential and wholly justifiable means to end a righteous war. It will most certainly continue so long as significant numbers of World War II veterans remain among us, many forever convinced that without the bomb they would have died on Japanese soil.

Even Smithsonian secretary I. Michael Heyman, in a post-mortem on the canceled exhibit, gave the back of his hand to the historians who had helped plan it and ignored his institution's mandate to promote "the increase and diffusion of knowledge," as he abjectly capitulated to the exhibit's detractors: "In this important anniversary year, veterans and their families were expecting, and rightly so, that the nation would honor and commemorate their valor and sacrifice. They were not looking for analysis, and, frankly, we did not give enough thought to the intense feelings such an analysis would evoke."[25] Whether the "intense feelings" aroused by thoughtful analysis might in the long run have been more helpful than not to Americans who continue to struggle with the meaning of Hiroshima and Nagasaki, Heyman did not consider.

In the face of assumptions like this—that "analysis" and "feelings" are mutually exclusive, that when passions run high, analysis must give way to feelings—it is understandable that historians, with their insistence on research and their readiness to question established interpretations and mythic versions of the past, should be viewed as a threat.

But historians, too, have their convictions and commitments, and we should not underestimate the long-term power of critical historical inquiry, even on emotion-laden topics. For better or worse, it is the historians, at the end of the day, to whom society delegates custodianship of the past.

Whatever the long-term resolution of this divisive and unhappy controversy, Hiroshima and Nagasaki are likely for the foreseeable future to remain the Banquo's ghost of World War II, perennially challenging comfortable generalizations about the conflict and underscoring the disparity between the mythic past inscribed in popular memory and the past that is the raw material of historical scholarship.

5

HISTORY AT RISK:
THE CASE OF THE *ENOLA GAY*

• RICHARD H. KOHN •

The cancellation of the National Air and Space Museum's original *Enola Gay* exhibition in January 1995 was one of the worst tragedies to befall the public presentation of history in the United States in this generation. In displaying the *Enola Gay* without analysis of the event that gave the B-29 airplane its significance, the Smithsonian Institution forfeited an opportunity to educate a worldwide audience of millions about one of this century's defining experiences. An exhibition that explored the dropping of the atomic bombs on Japan—an event historians view as significant in itself and symbolic of the end of World War II, the beginning of the Cold War, and the dawn of the nuclear age—would have been a truly important museum presentation. The secretary and the Board of Regents of the Smithsonian abandoned this major exhibition for political reasons: veterans' groups, political commentators, social critics, and politicians had charged that the exhibition script dishonored the Americans who fought the war by questioning the motives for using the bombs, by portraying the bombs as unnecessary to end the war, and by sympathizing too much with the Japanese killed by the bombs and, by implication, with the Japanese cause. Thus one of the premier cultural institutions of the United States and its foremost museum system surrendered its scholarly independence and a significant amount of its authority in American intellectual life to accommodate to a political perspective.

The full implications of the cancellation are still far from clear, but an interpretation deeply disturbing to historians and museum professionals has begun to emerge. Smithsonian secretary I. Michael Heyman has suggested that the institution should perhaps eschew such controversial exhibitions and that its exhibitions cannot combine commemoration and celebration with scholarship. He has put on hold several projects, including a National Air and Space Museum (NASM) exhibit on airpower in the Vietnam War that avoided almost every controversy about that divisive war. He has promised to revise exhibits that have angered viewers, one by treating science and technology negatively, others by criticizing or seeming to disparage American character, society, or behavior. Anecdotal evidence suggests that elsewhere, planned commemorations of the end of World War II—even scholarly events—were modified or abandoned.[1] These troubling developments have led some observers to label the cancellation political censorship. If such a famous and prestigious cultural institution cannot present scholarship to the public, they ask, can there be any displays, exhibitions, or programs that offend politically powerful or vocal groups? American museums and other publicly—and even privately—funded organizations may find it intimidating to offer anything controversial for public consumption, no matter how significant or sensitively portrayed. If the idea that everything is politics now colors American cultural life, civic discourse could begin to succumb to the suppression characteristic of the totalitarian regimes Americans have fought and died to defeat. Unable to explore their past openly or critically, Americans might endanger their political system and damage the liberty on which that system is based and which it is designed to preserve. George Orwell's warning—that those who control the past control the future and those who control the present control the past—could, according to the critics, come to pass.[2]

Before history and museum professionals conclude that responsible scholarship and the pursuit of truth on controversial topics are too dangerous to attempt in public forums, we need to subject the *Enola Gay* exhibit episode to historical examination. It is early to attempt an investigation, the evidence being fragmentary and our perspectives hardly impartial. But little can be learned, and similar experiences cannot be averted, until we reconstruct exactly what happened. Without that reconstruction, we may draw mistaken lessons and act to the detriment of the historical profession and the public.

◆ ◆ ◆

The *Enola Gay* conflict began at least two decades ago. The controversy comprised at least five separate stories; they came together in 1994 to set off the national explosion that resulted in cancellation of the exhibition. The first story traces planning for the exhibition in a museum whose staff was increasingly determined to apply professional, scholarly standards in a previously celebratory institution. The second concerns the uneasy relationship between the museum and many in the military aviation community. The third, of course, tells of the larger culture wars and the reaction of the museum to its critics. The fourth and fifth concern the appointment of a new secretary of the Smithsonian Institution just when political power in Congress shifted, for the first time in almost two generations, from Democrats to Republicans. Although the following discussion treats some of these stories at far greater length than others, each was crucial to the character and timing of the outcome.

◆ ◆ ◆

The first and most basic ingredient was the exhibition script itself, a product of the National Air and Space Museum and its history over the last twenty years. Since its opening in the mid-1970s, the museum had gained a worldwide reputation for breathtaking artifacts, huge and laudatory crowds of visitors (the highest numbers in the world, as many as ten million in some years), but little intellectual or scholarly content. Indeed, Congress appropriated money to construct the building on the Mall largely on the promise of what historian Alex Roland has called "good, old-fashioned celebration of American achievement . . . enshrinement, pure and simple." Five years after the building opened, an observer characterized the museum as "largely a giant advertisement for air and space technology." NASM was criticized for memorializing individual inventive genius and the corporations that create the machines, "equat[ing] technological advance with social progress," and "desir[ing] to promote aerospace activities"—all of which cost it respect in the Smithsonian community. When NASM's director was forced out in the mid-1980s, the criticism of his leadership included charges of hostility to historians and to analytical scholarship. Even the museum's displays and exhibits seemed to command less respect among aerospace museum professionals than did the size and comprehensiveness of its collection of air- and spacecraft and associated artifacts. "Give me that collection and a building on the Mall and I could have ten million visitors easy," the chief curator of another museum told me in the late 1980s.[3]

The appointment in 1987 of Martin Harwit, a respected astrophysicist from Cornell University with a long-standing interest in the history of science, seemed to promise a solution to many of the problems. The first academic and scholar to head the museum (his predecessors had been scientists, engineers, or aviators), Harwit was selected by Robert McCormick Adams, secretary of the Smithsonian from 1984 to 1994. Very much an academic, Adams eschewed such Washington power folkways as dark suits and the trappings of office. He managed the institution in a style that Smithsonian insiders characterized as "laissez-faire in a funny way . . . like academia," "collegial," and intended "to stimulate more independence." But his management was also criticized, from within and without. Adams's priority was research. He aimed to put the institution on the cutting edge of scholarship, or at least to modernize exhibits and programs where the institution had fallen behind—in Adams's words, "deepening the intellectual structure of the place." He wanted to encourage critical scholarship in an institution whose reputation for scholarly leadership had waned as its reputation for uninspired establishmentarianism flourished. One role of the Smithsonian, as Adams saw it, was to "put on exhibits that make people uncomfortable," so it was no

accident that in recent years at least four Smithsonian exhibits—
"The West as America," "A More Perfect Union," "Science in
American Life," and the planned *Enola Gay* exhibition—were
criticized for "counterculture" "political correctness." Adams
showed little respect for military history, at least as he saw it
practiced. He allowed the Eisenhower Institute, a Smithsonian
military history research institute, to fold by not replacing its director, Forrest Pogue, when he retired. In 1987 Adams told a reporter, "We have lots of artifacts, but [military history is] a field
that involves strategy, human suffering. . . . Somehow we
haven't picked that up and run with it. That's an opportunity,
among many, which we ought to seize." "Take the Air and Space
Museum," he said. "What are the responsibilities of a museum to
deal with the destruction caused by air power?"[4]

Martin Harwit, whom Adams chose over a distinguished retired
four-star U.S. Air Force general with a graduate history degree,
embraced Adams's agenda of scholarship and apparently shared
his views of military affairs and airpower. Harwit set out to encourage the curators to extend their historical research and writ-
ings, to hire bright young scholars, to help staff members finish
graduate degrees, to increase the intellectual content of displays
and exhibitions, and to foster scientific as well as historical study,
but not to lessen either the appeal of the museum or its service to
public, professional, industrial, and military constituencies. He
even confronted two nagging problems of long standing: the con-
servation of precious but deteriorating artifacts and the size of the
collection, which had been built by the legendary chief curator
Paul Garber. (For over fifty years, Garber had collected anything
valuable, regardless of whether the Smithsonian had the storage
space or the resources to care for the object.) Patient and consul-
tative, open to ideas, considerate of staff while insisting on high
standards, Harwit made many difficult choices. Although he did
not please everyone or solve every problem, under his constant
and consistent prodding, the museum made steady progress. By
the early 1990s, NASM had progressed to a standard of excellence
appropriate for the Smithsonian's most popular museum, located

on the Mall in the nation's capital and possessed of the world's greatest collection of air- and spacecraft.[5]

The *Enola Gay* exhibition would advance Harwit's agenda of promoting scholarship and exploring the social contexts and human implications of the aviation and space experiences, while avoiding the uncritical celebration of technology. Restoration of the famous airplane began under his predecessor. From the outset the museum staff recognized how controversial the airplane would be, even if it were displayed with only an identifying label. For years, veterans had badgered the museum to restore the *Enola Gay* and display it or to loan or transfer it to a site or institution where it would receive the honor they felt its historic flight deserved. During the 1980s, NASM's Research Advisory Committee several times debated whether the aircraft should be restored and displayed. Members of the committee favored restoration and exhibition because of the plane's educational value in an exhibition. The only dissenter was the outspokenly antinuclear retired admiral and former commander of U.S. armed forces in the Pacific, Noel Gayler, who argued forcefully against any act that could be interpreted as a celebration of destruction or a memorialization of the killing of so many innocent civilians. Thus, well before the museum began mounting an exhibition, even before it began the expensive restoration of the aircraft, the Hiroshima bomber had already come to symbolize both conflicting perspectives on American war making—emphasizing either innovative technological achievement or the mass death of enemy civilians—and, more widely, positive and negative judgments on the American past. The airplane had come to be understood within the museum as a flash point of profound, often emotional disagreement about how to observe, or even whether to observe, the event that had made this most famous of military aircraft significant. When, in 1989 and 1990, in preparation for the exhibit, the museum undertook a sixteen-month program of lectures, films, panel discussions, and scholarly symposia about strategic bombing, argument was often intense. Disagreement even broke out in the planning committee over who should be invited to participate. During the events, participants and people in the audience disagreed among themselves, often radically, particularly over the motives for, and the effects of, the bombing campaigns during World War II and over the use of nuclear weapons both in 1945 and, during the Cold War, for deterrence.[6]

In keeping with the goals of scholarship and education and in spite of the conflict any exhibition was sure to provoke, the museum embedded in the exhibit a didactic objective that exacerbated the potential for controversy. According to the 1993 planning document, the exhibition's "primary goal" was "to encourage visitors to make a thoughtful and balanced re-examination of the atomic bombings in the light of the political and military factors leading to the decision to use the bomb, the human suffering experienced by the people of Hiroshima and Nagasaki and the long-term implications of the events of August 6 and 9, 1945." In other words, the chief purpose was not simply to present a historical investigation of what happened, why, and what it meant, but to revisit the American decision to use the bomb in 1945, to ask whether the bomb was needed or justified, and to suggest "an uncertain, potentially dangerous future for all of civilization." The exhibition would conclude, as it began, by "noting the debatable character of the atomic bombings," read an earlier document.

Secretary Adams expressed worry about the contentious nature of the proposal. In response, the chairman of the Aeronautics Department, Tom Crouch, who would oversee production of the exhibit script, told Harwit: "Do you want to do an exhibition intended to make veterans feel good, or do you want an exhibition that will lead our visitors to think about the consequences of the atomic bombing of Japan? Frankly, I don't think we can do both."[7] From the beginning, then, the *Enola Gay* exhibit was designed to provoke its audience; in the mind of the chief supervising curator, the museum faced an unbridgeable chasm between scholarship and commemoration. Harwit insisted that the museum could do both, impartially and responsibly, and he offered Crouch and Michael Neufeld, the lead curator, the option to withdraw if work on the exhibit would violate their professional ethics. Both agreed that it would not, and they continued.[8]

The first script, finished in January 1994, titled the exhibition "The Crossroads: The End of World War II, the Atomic Bomb and the Origins of the Cold War," and it combined patriotic commemoration with serious scholarship. The 303 pages of text, comprising narrative explanation and labels to connect and identify dozens of photographs, paintings, maps, charts, documents, videos, and artifacts, including the fuselage of the *Enola Gay*, was a sophisticated historical collage. The exhibition told the story with a clarity and completeness designed to appeal to varied audiences, while compromising none of the complexity. The first of five sections set the scene by describing the war in the Pacific during 1945, focusing on the mounting casualties in the island campaigns, the strategic bombing of Japan, and the two home fronts at war. The second investigated the decision to drop the bomb, beginning with the Manhattan Project and ending with an exegesis of the factors that influenced President Harry Truman and his senior advisers. The third and longest (92 pages) recounted the history of the B-29, its use against Japan in 1945, the formation and training of the 509th Composite Group (which dropped the bombs), the history of the *Enola Gay* airplane, and the details of the two missions on August 6 and 9, 1945. The fourth described the effect of the bombs on Hiroshima and Nagasaki, emphasizing the human suffering. The fifth, the shortest and most superficial, devoted 10 pages to Japan's decision to surrender and 14 to the Cold War and the nuclear arms race.[9]

The story was told in context, frequently with rich detail. The themes of risk, bravery, and struggles to overcome unprecedented technical and operational problems underlay the third section. The script thus celebrated American ingenuity and technical prowess. The two longest subsections in the exhibition script, nearly 20 percent of the entire text, reconstructed with respect and sensitivity the experiences of the *Enola Gay*'s aviators: their selection, training, life in the United States and in the Pacific, and challenges in flying the two missions. The museum consulted and worked with veterans, and it arranged for loans of documents and artifacts, most notably from museums in Japan.

In presenting historical interpretations, the texts were cautious and balanced, choosing words precisely so as to treat controversial subjects with a tone of distance and detachment. On the cause of the war, the script said, "Japanese expansionism was marked by naked aggression and extreme brutality. The slaughter of tens of thousands of Chinese in Nanking in 1937 shocked the world. Atrocities by Japanese troops included brutal mistreatment of civilians, forced laborers and prisoners of war, and biological experiments on human victims." On the decision to use the bomb, the script portrayed the president rather sympathetically.

> According to British Prime Minister Winston Churchill . . . "the decision whether or not to use the atomic bomb . . . was never even an issue." Upon becoming President in April 1945, Harry Truman inherited a very expensive bomb project that had always aimed at producing a military weapon. Furthermore he was faced with the prospect of an invasion and he was told that the bomb would be useful for impressing the Soviet Union. He therefore saw no reason to avoid using the bomb. Alternatives for ending the Pacific war other than an invasion or atomic-bombing were available, but are more obvious in hindsight than they were at the time.

Churchill observed that "Truman and his advisers could not know how the war would actually end." On projected American casualties in the planned invasion of Japan, perhaps the greatest bone of contention between the museum and its critics, the original script was fair. "To many on the Allied side, the suicidal resistance of the Japanese military justified the harshest possible measures. The appalling casualties suffered by both sides seemed to foreshadow what could be expected during an invasion of Japan. Allied victory was assured, but its final cost in lives remained disturbingly uncertain." On Japanese resistance to surrender, the script characterized the Japanese government as "dominated" by "hawkish Army generals" and "die-hard military leaders who wished to fight a last battle in Japan." The Japanese peace feeler in the spring of 1945 was therefore "weak and indecisive." "As a result, opportunities to end the war early were greatly limited." NASM's exhibit advisory committee, composed of ten scholars from the government, academe, and the literary community who were charged with critiquing this first script, praised the curators for a "sound" approach and "a careful and professional job," which required only "a little refining." Individual committee members disagreed with parts of the script, but, according to one participant, "these concerns were a matter of emphasis." All agreed that the exhibit "would inform, challenge and commemorate" and was "solid and . . . rooted in the latest historical scholarship."[10]

What most bothered the critics, including some historians, and led to the public campaign of opposition by the Air Force Association, other veterans' groups, politicians, and commentators were not the carefully crafted statements of interpretation, virtually all of which were consensus scholarship. (A very few statements, mostly taken out of context, were used publicly to accuse the museum of an anti-American and pro-Japanese portrayal.)[11] The problems with the script lay in the omission of material, the emphasis on particular material, the order and placement of facts and analysis, and the tone and the mood. Taken as a whole and read with the emotional impact on viewers in mind, the exhibition *was* in fact unbalanced; it possessed a very clear and potent point of view. On a level of feeling that could be reached more powerfully through the senses of sight and sound than through the reading of words, the exhibit appealed to viewers' emotions, and its message could be read to be tendentious and moralizing; the exhibition script could be read to condemn American behavior at the end of World War II.[12]

On the first panel of text at the entry to the exhibition, in the second sentence mentioning the atomic bomb, visitors would learn that "to this day, controversy has raged about whether dropping this weapon on Japan was necessary to end the war quickly."[13] Nearly every section of the exhibit that followed would contribute, directly or by its placement in the narration of events, to doubts not only about the necessity and appropriateness of the bomb but also about American motives, honor, decency, and moral integrity in wreaking such destruction on what the script portrayed as a defeated (but not surrendering) enemy.

The first of the five sections, "A Fight to the Finish," characterized combat in the Pacific as a bitter contest of racial hatreds that by 1945 had escalated to unprecedented ferocity; thus it implied that racism was an important impulse for using the atomic bombs. The script seemed sympathetic to both sides, but it contained an inherent imbalance of sympathies: the Japanese fought out of fear "that unconditional surrender would mean the annihilation of their culture," the Americans out of vengeance, although "the suicidal resistance of the Japanese military justified the harshest possible measures." The next part treated the kamikazes with sensitivity and sadness. What followed detailed the vast destruction wrought by the B-29 firebombing of Japanese cities; condemned strategic bombing by saying that "during World War II civilians themselves had become the target"; equivalently quoted Franklin D. Roosevelt, Adolf Hitler, and Neville Chamberlain in 1939 eschewing the bombing of civilians, and a few pages later George Marshall threatening the firebombing of Japanese civilians in November 1941; and generally sympathized with the Japanese victims of the 1945 bombing campaign. The comparison between the American and Japanese home fronts—one description emphasizing dedication, unity of purpose, material production, and prosperity (and mentioning the internment of Japanese Americans), the other focusing on increasing deprivation and suffering ("on the brink of collapse")—completed the contrast and could be read to swing the weight of sympathy clearly to the Japanese side.[14]

The second section, "The Decision to Drop the Bomb," offered in its concluding analyses consensus interpretations that avoided criticizing the U.S. action. But the text also took every opportunity to pose alternatives and raise doubts. Viewers of the exhibition could not help but walk away believing, as the planning document promised, that a different outcome would have been not just preferable but possible. The titles of some parts of this section indicated a line of interpretation that visitors could read as skeptical of the necessity of using the bomb. In seven sidebar "Historical Controversies," the curators emphasized disagreements among scholars:

"Would the Bomb Have Been Dropped on the Germans?"
"Did the United States Ignore the Japanese Peace Initiative?"
"Would the War Have Ended Sooner if the United States Had Guaranteed the Emperor's Position?"
"How Important Was the Soviet Factor in the 'Decision to Drop the Bomb'?"
"Was a Warning or Demonstration Possible?"
"Was the Invasion Inevitable if the Atomic Bomb Had Not Been Dropped?"
"Was the Decision to Drop the Bomb Justified?"

While the texts always identified what was counterfactual or speculative and emphasized what decision makers knew or how they reasoned in 1945, the script as a whole emphasized the idea that hindsight could offer different perspectives. On the Japanese peace feeler in spring 1945:

It is nonetheless possible to assert, at least in hindsight, that the United States should have paid closer attention to these signals from Japan. Like so many aspects of the "decision to drop the bomb," this matter will remain forever speculative and controversial.

It is possible that there was a lost opportunity to end the war without either atomic bombings or an invasion of Japan.

Some combination of blockade, firebombing, an Emperor guarantee, and a Soviet declaration of war would probably have forced a Japanese surrender, but to President Truman an invasion appeared to be a real possibility. Matters were not as clear in 1945 as they are in hindsight, because Truman and his advisers could not know how the war would actually end.

> It is . . . clear that there were alternatives to both an invasion and dropping atomic bombs without warning—for example guaranteeing the Emperor's position, staging a demonstration of the bomb's power, or waiting for blockade, firebombing and a Soviet declaration of war to take their toll on Japan. Since these alternatives are clearer in hindsight and it is speculative whether they would have induced the Japanese government to surrender quickly, the debate over "the decision to drop the bomb" will remain forever controversial.[15]

The third and longest section, "Delivering the Bomb," celebrated American technological and operational ingenuity and the bravery of the American aviators. Its texts and its titles, however, were admiring but matter-of-fact, especially in comparison with the sections preceding and following:

"The B-29: A Three-Billion-Dollar Gamble"
"The B-29 and the Bombing of Japan"
"The World's First Atomic Strike Force"
"The B-29 Superfortress 'Enola Gay' "
"The Missions"

Sandwiched between the long second section, questioning the use of the bomb, and the fourth section, depicting what happened when the bombs killed tens of thousands of Japanese civilians, this careful, laudatory reconstruction of airplanes and fliers might have had very little emotional impact. And once visitors moved on to the next viewing area, they would have confronted scenes that made any impulse to memorialization utterly inappropriate.

Section four possessed no ambivalence whatsoever. "When visitors go from Unit 3 to Unit 4," predicted the 1993 planning document, "they will be immediately hit by a drastic change of mood and perspective: from well-lit and airy to gloomy and oppressive. The aim will be to put visitors on the ground during the

atomic bombings of the two cities." "Ground Zero: Hiroshima,
8:15 A.M., August 6, 1945[;] Nagasaki, 11:02 A.M., August 9, 1945"
was designed to shock. "If Unit 2 [the decision to drop the bomb]
is the intellectual heart of the exhibit, Unit 4 is its emotional
center. Photos of victims, enlarged to life-size, stare out at the
visitor. . . . The emphasis will be on the personal tragedy of this
experience."[16] The four parts—"Before the Bomb: Two Cities at
War," "The Incredible Avalanche of Light," "Two Cities in
Chaos," and "A Deadly New Threat: Radioactivity"—were horrifying. Relentlessly, repetitively, redundantly, in excruciating detail, returning again and again to the death and mutilation of
women and children, this section of the exhibit succeeded even in
text form in eliciting shock and disgust. The many pictures of
human pain and suffering, the heartrending quotations from observers and victims, all appealed to the emotions of viewers. Such
scenes not only would have reinforced anxieties about whether
the United States needed to use the bomb, but might well have
provoked feelings of guilt and shame among American visitors,
including veterans. In the ensuing controversy, no part of the
exhibit angered veterans more.[17]

The final section, "The Legacy of Hiroshima and Nagasaki,"
told two stories: "Japan Surrenders" and "The Cold War and the
Nuclear Arms Race."

> For Japan, the United States, and its Allies, a horrific war was
> brought to an abrupt end, although at a cost debated to this
> day; for the world, a nuclear arms race unfolded that still
> threatens unimaginable devastation. The bombings of Hiro-
> shima and Nagasaki cannot be said to have simply caused
> either the end of the war or the nuclear arms race, but they
> have exercised a profound influence as military and political
> acts, as symbols of the arrival of the nuclear age, and as a
> glimpse of the realities of nuclear war.

Although the first part of this section concluded that "the surrender of Japan was doubtlessly a critical legacy of Hiroshima and
Nagasaki," that statement grudgingly followed 162 words focusing

once again on the controversy over whether the bombs were needed to shock Japan into surrender, whether the United States should have moderated its demand for unconditional surrender, and whether the Soviet intervention was equally responsible for the surrender. The brief discussion of the Cold War depicted the nuclear arms race ("A World Gone 'M.A.D.'") in starkly simplistic terms; an entire page examined the 1954 nuclear test accident that killed one crewman and sickened others on the Japanese fishing boat *Lucky Dragon*—emphasizing once more the personal, human tragedy of atomic and nuclear power.[18]

Read in this fashion with the probable reaction of visitors imagined, the entire exhibition cast a wholly negative interpretation on the development, use, and impact of atomic bombs. It was thus possible, looking beyond the careful wording of each individual panel or label, to detect in the five sections of the exhibit an interpretation that was in today's parlance revisionist, countercultural, and condemnatory of the United States: the war was a racist conflict waged by Americans for vengeance, a war essentially won by mid-1945. The bombings were unnecessary acts, growing out of bureaucratic, diplomatic, and political as well as military impulses, that wreaked an atrocity upon a defeated Japanese population. The bombings made an uncertain contribution to ending the conflict but an unquestionable one to a more dangerous, depressing world that still troubles us today.

To be fair to the curators, few readers saw such extremes in the first draft or voiced strong objections, at least before the controversy over the script burst into public view. The exhibit followed recent innovations in the museological community: to explore the broad contexts of important events, particularly their human dimensions; to include complexity; to stimulate viewer interest and evoke controversy; to educate as well as to commemorate; and to combine the best recent scholarship with artifacts and other materials in multimedia, interactive "shows" that draw in audiences in powerful ways, intellectually and emotionally.[19] The exhibit contained a balance of techniques and approaches. The first section, on 1945, provided context, and it was strongly interpretative.

The second, on the decision to use the bomb, emphasized recent historical scholarship. The third—on the bomb, the airplanes, and the mission—memorialized American science, technology, industry, and fighting men. The fourth roused powerful emotions in viewers, while memorializing people the museum perceived as among the major stakeholders, the Japanese. The fifth, on Japan's surrender and the nuclear age, explored implications and meanings. If the story featured civilian death, a case could be made that the most enduring significance of strategic bombing and of the atomic bombs, perhaps even of World War II, was to spread destruction to civilian populations in ways and with results heretofore unknown in the history of war.[20]

Knowing that the exhibit was meant to provoke and that it addressed hot-button issues, the museum administration consulted a distinguished group of scholars, balanced to include a range of expertise. The museum's leaders emerged from the meeting with this exhibit advisory committee in February 1994 believing that the product was sound and that the necessary modifications were not major. Apparently the discussion at that meeting and the written critiques that grew out of it did not give sufficient warning about the imbalances in the script to prepare the museum for what followed. Military historians who scrutinized the script later would flag the problems, of detail and conception, and criticize the script in much stronger terms, a few questioning its scholarship and interpretations as well as its balance. But by then it was too late.[21]

◆ ◆ ◆

The second story that helps to explain why the exhibition was canceled involves the reaction of the Air Force Association and its public attack on the exhibition, undertaken either to force a revision or to stop it altogether. The association, formed immediately after World War II by Army Air Forces veterans to promote airpower and the air force, had evolved over two generations into a large, powerful advocate for a strong national defense and a chief connecting link between the air force and its industrial suppliers.

A private organization with an elected leadership and professional staff, it is separate from the United States Air Force, although the association's membership includes many active-duty and reserve servicemen and -women and many veterans—overwhelmingly of the air forces—of World War II and the Cold War. Some of the association's Washington staff had come to view the Smithsonian in general and NASM in particular with suspicion; the exhibit script confirmed their worst fears. This was the fourth planning document for the *Enola Gay* exhibition that they had seen. They had detected hidden political messages in all those documents. Especially offensive to people who viewed their organization as representing tens of thousands of Army Air Forces veterans of World War II, living and dead, were the hints of doubt about the ethics and morality of the way the United States fought Japan and, by implication, about the honor of those who did the fighting. From the association's perspective, this "emotionally charged program," which "was fundamentally lacking in balance and context," was all the more suspect because the museum had been assuring veterans for years that the exhibition would honor their service.[22] Association staff members believed their objections were disregarded, although NASM officials believed they were consulting and listening (if not exactly responding) to a primary stakeholder and an important potential opponent. Having shared its plans, the museum leadership was therefore shocked when the association's journal, *Air Force Magazine*, published a virulent attack on the exhibit script, the curators, the director, and the museum, less than two months after the exhibit advisory committee had seemingly approved the script.[23]

The violence of the Air Force Association's public assault—the personal attacks on Smithsonian secretary Robert Adams and NASM director Martin Harwit, the accusation that the museum had been neglecting its primary task of preserving its priceless artifacts, the charges of political correctness—indicated something deeper at work.[24] Just as that first script cannot be understood apart from the museum's history of the previous ten years, so the Air Force Association's public blast, which brought the controversy over the exhibit to the nation's attention, cannot be understood apart from the unhappiness with the museum felt by some in the air force community. They believed that the Smithsonian as a whole and NASM curators in particular were antimilitary, that displays downplayed military as opposed to commercial or general aviation, that the museum sometimes took a skeptical or disparaging attitude toward aviation, flight, airpower, space exploration, even science and technology per se. Such perceptions were all the more irritating because Army Air Forces chief Henry H. "Hap" Arnold had been instrumental in founding the museum and had donated many aircraft (including the *Enola Gay*) to the Smithsonian, and Senator Barry Goldwater, a pilot in World War II and a general in the air force reserve, had provided the final push to get the museum built, citing the need to celebrate aviation's achievements. A permanent exhibition on World War I airpower that opened at the museum in 1991 drew special ire, not only because it emphasized the carnage of the war, the airplane as an instrument of death, and the invalidity of popular myths about "knights of the air" but also because the exhibit relegated the airplanes to a secondary role, hanging them from the ceiling virtually out of sight. The exhibit labeled the effect of aviation in that war both limited and a failure. Most infuriating, that exhibit ended with a video on strategic bombing in the seventy-plus years *after* World War I, including the atomic bombings and controversially high estimates of Iraqi casualties in the Gulf War, all of which air force people interpreted as biased, gratuitous, and indicative of the anti-airpower attitudes pervading the museum. The aspirations of the aviation community for the museum were revealed in the association's first published attack on the *Enola Gay* exhibition, in the caption to the full-page illustration opposite the first page: "To aviation enthusiasts, the National Air and Space Museum is a special place, where priceless artifacts are held in trust, to be displayed with understanding and pride."[25]

A further irritant lay in the lack of public monuments or national memorials to airpower and the air force in Washington when compared with those of the army, navy, and marines. There may have been a subtle resentment that the most public reminder of aviation's contribution to American life and the nation's security was left by default to the Smithsonian. The marines have the Iwo Jima Memorial across the Potomac River in Arlington; the navy's is on Pennsylvania Avenue halfway between the White House and the Capitol. Both those services have national museums in the Washington Navy Yard, with historic residences for their ranking officers nearby. (The air force's national museum is at Wright-Patterson Air Force Base in Dayton, Ohio.) The army lacks a national museum in Washington, but statues of famous generals dot the Washington landscape, which also includes Civil War fortifications, Arlington National Cemetery with its Tomb of the Unknown Soldier, and many other reminders of army history. Even the merchant seamen of World War II have a memorial, near the Pentagon along the George Washington Parkway. The air force began only recently to raise money and seek a site for an air force memorial in the nation's capital.[26]

Nor can air battles be commemorated like those on land or sea by setting aside battlefields or large vessels, which become sacred ground (or decks) where people can walk, visualizing a two-dimensional clash of arms that moved in relatively slow, understandable terms. Air battles have been sudden, confusing three-dimensional melees difficult to depict adequately even in videos. Historically, airpower has been memorialized almost exclusively by means of the machines themselves, displayed alone with labels describing what they did or what they represent. The more famous the aircraft, the more symbolic an emblem to be venerated, not only for the aviators who risked their lives but for all who contributed to creating and supporting the machines in the sky.[27] For the military aviation community, the *Enola Gay* was an icon. Perhaps from the beginning, some wanted to abort any exhibition beyond the display of that icon, perhaps with some brief celebration of the achievements of the crew, the designers, and the builders, the U.S. war effort, and the contribution of the Army Air Forces to victory in the war. It may well be, as one historian has charged, that the association's campaign "was designed, in part, to embarrass the Smithsonian and force the resignation of Harwit" so that the museum would revert to a "strictly celebratory" orientation.[28]

In other words, the willingness of the Air Force Association to initiate and lead a public campaign against the exhibit must be understood within two contexts beyond the content of the exhibit: resentment of the National Air and Space Museum and the churning culture wars that surfaced during the 1980s and had risen to a crescendo in 1994.

◆　◆　◆

These culture wars are the third ingredient that helps explain the calamity of the *Enola Gay* controversy. The Air Force Association's attack of April 1994 landed like a match on dry tinder. There exploded over the summer and fall of 1994, among veterans' groups and in the speeches of politicians, a rising chorus of criticism, almost all of it directed at the museum. Some, indeed, came from the liberal press and columnists as well as from conservatives. A good deal of the outcry was almost certainly spontaneous, but the Air Force Association and veterans' groups did much to plan and manage the public criticism. "Changing the exhibit was no small task," according to one reporter in *Air Force Times*. "It took 18 months of relentless effort from dozens of groups, especially the Air Force Association and the American Legion, which mobilized their members to pressure Capitol Hill lawmakers to stop the exhibit."[29]

Historians and other scholars will need to locate the *Enola Gay* exhibit battle in the wider culture wars. From the initial attack by *Air Force Magazine* to the postmortems after the exhibit was canceled, those involved in the battle connected the exhibition and the argument over it to the campaigns over political correctness, provocative art, multiculturalism, equal-opportunity programs, gender and sexual orientation, the national history standards, revisionist history, and just about every other divisive social or cultural issue rending American society, save abortion and prayer in the schools.[30] "What can't be altered," opined the *Wall Street*

Journal, "is the clear impression given by the Smithsonian that the American museum whose business it is to tell the nation's story is now in the hands of academics unable to view American history as anything other than a woeful catalog of crimes and aggressions against the helpless peoples of the earth."[31]

The museum responded in a number of ways. Harwit, in a letter to *Air Force Magazine* and in short essays, appealed to verifiable history and to recent scholarship, acknowledging the differing views of the function of the museum and the differing perspectives of the World War II and Cold War generations on the atomic bombings.[32] During the spring and summer of 1994, museum officials also undertook to defuse the criticism by changing the exhibit. Harwit gave the script another careful reading to judge its balance, and he found "much of the criticism . . . understandable."[33] Having circulated the draft script with the intention of consulting widely, listening to responses, and altering the exhibit where appropriate, the museum changed the script, making use of criticism from Department of Defense historians and from a team inside the museum consisting chiefly of senior retired military aviators. The museum leadership also began to negotiate content with groups outside the museum with political agendas and no claim to scholarly knowledge, museum expertise, or a balanced perspective. Museums customarily consult, consider, react, and modify their products according to the best advice they can gather, but to negotiate a rendering of the past in exchange for acquiescence posed special dangers.[34] To negotiate an exhibition on the U.S. labor movement with the American Federation of Labor–Congress of Industrial Organizations (AFL-CIO) or one on medicine with the American Medical Association would potentially make the exhibition hostage to a constituent group that could then wield a veto over fact or interpretation. That was exactly what happened to the National Air and Space Museum during the last six months of 1994.[35]

By the end of October, after line-by-line review with the American Legion (other veterans' groups refused to participate in such a review), the script had been revised to a fifth version. Harwit, who oversaw the negotiations and ordered the changes, became trapped between curators who resisted alterations and the veterans' groups, some of them perhaps bent on getting the exhibit canceled. In August 1994, he expressed surprise at how little the exhibit had been altered, a complaint some historians were making and something the veterans' groups feared openly.[36] Yet two months later there had been enough changes to provoke several dozen historians and writers to protest to the Smithsonian secretary that the museum had caved in to censorship and succumbed to "intellectual corruption," and that the fifth draft was "mere propaganda," the result of "historical cleansing." One author attacked the museum for abandoning "history with all its uncomfortable complications" in favor of "feel-good national myths."[37]

Thus, by the fall of 1994, the museum had not succeeded in satisfying the veterans and had alienated many historians; its actions had called into question the credibility of the exhibition's scholarship. Harwit had lost the trust of both groups. Mired in a senseless contest over the number of casualties expected in the planned invasion of Japan—a symbol of whether the bombing was necessary—the museum had become the target of a U.S. Senate resolution demanding history in proper context and exhibits reflecting positively on veterans of the Pacific war; the Smithsonian faced a troubling number of critics and politicians calling for Harwit's resignation or removal and the abandonment of the exhibition as planned. Not until too late did museum leaders realize that they could be forced from the outside to cancel the exhibit.[38]

◆ ◆ ◆

The fourth and fifth strands of the story came together after November 1994 with a speed and power that decided the outcome. First came the largely unexpected victory of the Republicans in the fall congressional elections. For those in the House of Representatives who had made the culture wars central to their critique of American society, canceling this exhibit seemed a necessity essential to rolling back the cultural left in American intellectual life. After the exhibit was canceled, newly installed House Speaker

Newt Gingrich told the nation's state governors that the "Enola Gay fight was a fight, in effect, over the reassertion by most Americans that they're sick and tired of being told by some cultural elite that they ought to be ashamed of their country."[39] As part of the larger battle over American values, the *Enola Gay* exhibit seemed to its critics more emotional, significant, and less ambiguous than the debates over the national history standards, the National Endowment for the Humanities, the National Endowment for the Arts, the Public Broadcasting Corporation, and the suspected left bias of the press and other institutions. If an exhibition that appeared to be openly unpatriotic, planned by a national, publicly funded museum on the fiftieth anniversary of the winning of World War II, could not be shut down or altered, then fashions and institutions more insulated from the levers of power might be truly unreachable. No matter that forcing the cancellation might excite charges of political censorship or the suppression of free speech, open debate, or the search for truth, values the critics professed; stopping the *Enola Gay* exhibition or converting it into a patriotic celebration would have deterrent and collateral effects. The threat of large cuts in the Smithsonian budget and hearings into how the Smithsonian was managed and administered were just the weapons to be wielded for the desired result.

•   •   •

The final part of the story consisted of a new Smithsonian secretary brought in to raise money, who was unable or unwilling even to contest the political pressure to cancel the exhibition. And that pressure was intense. By January 1995, eighty-one members of Congress had called for firing Harwit; twenty thousand subscribers to *Smithsonian* magazine had complained about the exhibit. Some 72 percent of the Smithsonian's operating budget and 77 percent of its construction monies came from federal appropriations; the percentage of federal support had been rising as dollars from the private sector dwindled. In the middle of January 1995, the American Legion, using as an excuse Harwit's intention to change a casualty estimate for the invasion of Japan, suddenly demanded cancellation of the exhibition, called on Congress for help, demanded hearings into the Smithsonian's management, and asked that the *Enola Gay* be transferred to another museum for display in a positive context. The secretary met with legion officials on January 18 and refused; thirteen days later he reversed himself and abandoned the exhibition.[40]

In the weeks before becoming Smithsonian secretary, I. Michael Heyman, a law professor and former chancellor of the University of California at Berkeley, had defended "the independence of the Institution from detailed political direction." Heyman was "especially sympathetic" to the analogy between "the Smithsonian . . . [and] a public university"; the "threat to the Smithsonian budget [was like] . . . an attempt to dictate the books and curriculum to be taught in university courses." Heyman endorsed the idea that the "strength of America is the relative independence of its scholars from political pressures." But by November he had distanced himself from the exhibition. In a carefully reasoned and precisely worded speech to the Commonwealth Club in San Francisco, the new secretary defended the Smithsonian's educational role, the broadening of its museums to include "the full range of communities which share the American experience," the need for "context and interpretation" in exhibits, and the propriety of controversial exhibits, even ones that *"transform* the visitors' perspective." He denied that "the Smithsonian's role" in "presenting American history [was] . . . solely to affirm 'good news' and traditional patriotic values." He argued that "it is possible to respect affirmation without only telling the good news of history." Although NASM's "goal was honorable and important: to provide a context in which to understand the significance" of the airplane's "participation in that epic moment," the exhibit had presented only "half a context." Heyman believed the exhibit needed "to honor the heroism of the American forces in their war against clear Japanese aggression and to recognize that significant numbers of American lives were saved," while respecting "the pain of those affected by the bomb on the ground and the precedent of the use of the bomb in a war." "If we are to capture our audiences' attention and carry out our mission as a national educational institution, we must eschew presenting narrow viewpoints. We must explore and present the complexities of our subjects, including the curator's 'take,' and we must be mindful that most in our audiences are perfectly willing to deal with new ideas and interpretations (not always, of course, agreeing with them) if they do not feel that their own are despised."[41]

Eighty-one days later, when Heyman canceled the exhibit, he had changed his mind about the feasibility of combining commemoration and history. His "one overriding reason" for cancellation was "that we made a basic error in attempting to couple an historical treatment of the use of atomic weapons with the 50th anniversary commemoration of the end of the war." The "veterans and their families were expecting, and rightly so, that the nation would honor and commemorate their valor and sacrifice. They were not looking for analysis, and, frankly, we did not give enough thought to the intense feelings such an analysis would evoke." While the revisions of the script "succeeded in creating plans for a more balanced presentation . . . the problem was more than one of balance," and a "fundamental flaw in the concept of the exhibition" made "our sincere efforts to address everyone's concerns . . . bound to fail. No amount of re-balancing could change the confusing nature of the exhibition." Earlier Heyman had contended that a few "historical objects," such as Charles Lindbergh's aircraft *The Spirit of St. Louis* and "the actual Star-Spangled Banner" that had inspired Francis Scott Key, had a "kind of power" to "speak for themselves"; now "the *Enola Gay* and its crew" had no choice but to do the same.[42]

Before he abandoned the exhibition, Heyman had listened to Harwit argue against cancellation. Harwit warned that the decision would destroy the morale of curators and staff at his museum and throughout the institution and bring on the Smithsonian the opprobrium of scholars across the country for buckling to political pressure; educational opportunities would be lost, along with an excellent exhibit that had undergone four full revisions. Yet Heyman and Undersecretary Constance Newman dismissed these arguments by weighing them against the threat of massive reductions in congressional appropriations and private contributions and the threat to the independence of the institution. The scholars, Newman and Heyman pointed out, were nowhere to be seen defending the Smithsonian, and they would get over it.[43] Less than a month after abandoning the exhibition, Heyman went further, telling an audience at the National Press Club that the Smithsonian had studied its future and would clearly need more money: to use technology "to take the Smithsonian into American homes and schools," to care for the 140 million objects it possessed, to collect, and to mount exhibitions. The institution, however, was "not buffered . . . from the influence of the purse or the suasion of congressional opinion." The "ground rules—not unlike those guiding state legislatures in relating to their public universities"—were that the Smithsonian "is expected to make its own judgment concerning the nature of its programs." But "if new initiatives require Federal funding . . . the Congress rightfully determines whether to make such investments." The primacy of budget came out most clearly in the Senate hearings nearly four months later, when Ted Stevens, a Republican from Alaska and the chairman of the Rules and Administration Committee, told Heyman that "eroding public support threatens the ability of the Smithsonian to continue to be the central depository of our nation's artifacts." "I am worried, because we are going to discuss the budget for the next 5 years, and there is not room in that budget for the projection you have made to manage the institution you have. . . . I believe you should have the money," Stevens said—twice. "But I can tell you, you will not get it from this Congress if we have controversies like this. You cannot expect to have dramatic increases in funding at the time of controversies of this size."[44]

In January 1995 Heyman faced an awful choice. A new Republican Congress, promising major changes—and reductions—in the government, was organizing itself to hammer out a five-year budget agreement. Heyman, sixty-four years old, intended to stay in office only until he reached age seventy. The Commission on the Future of the Smithsonian Institution, only the third such outside body commissioned by the regents in the 150 years since James Smithson's bequest, had concluded that "even with the best imaginable outcomes, improvement in revenues and operating efficiencies will not resolve the financial issues facing the Smithsonian." To deal with these "daunting facts," "choices will have to be made," and the commission recommended many, some requiring more, not less, money.[45]

By canceling the exhibition, the new secretary would repudiate his most popular museum and admit management problems that might require him to impose authority over museums, galleries, research institutes, outreach efforts—institutions and programs that for more than a century had been run loosely, like a major research university. The problem was not "curatorial freedom," for to Heyman, as he put it in his November San Francisco speech, "there are differences between a university and the museum world of the Smithsonian. Most people treat academic work as that of the professor's—either as author or in the context of presentation to a class or scholarly audience. Scholarly work, of comparable quality, translated into an exhibition in a museum, and in particular a national museum, however, is seen as an official statement and a national validation." The pressing problem was imposing from the top guidelines, standards, and policies that might be difficult to apply to diverse activities and that might undermine independence, creativity, and entrepreneurial spirit. In the summer of 1994, the vice president for research at Colonial Williamsburg had ridiculed interference by "nonacademic administrative officers and . . . trustees . . . to abrogate major program initiatives . . . or [to] downplay this or that kind of history" as a "tired old jab [that] lands few solid punches on museums today." Cancellation would constitute exactly such an intervention. As Heyman admitted in his Senate testimony, his willingness to consider top-down initiatives "with regard to exhibition policy and exhibition review is a little shocking to a number of my colleagues, and we are going to have an awful lot of conversation with respect to that." Heyman understood that his action would damage the Smithsonian's reputation, call into question its scholarly integrity, and give the appearance of political censorship.[46]

When the controversy blew up all over again in mid-January just as Congress convened, he had to choose. To cite a conflict between commemoration and history, between celebration and scholarship, offered a cover, although at the hearings the veterans' organizations disputed that and lamented the abandonment of a substantive exhibition. The president of the Carnegie Institution of Washington, a distinguished biochemist who chaired the commission on the Smithsonian's future, reportedly regretted the decision as "a political one . . . cowing to pressure . . . the kind of nightmare that Washington hands out to people who come here to do important jobs."[47] But perhaps the *Enola Gay* exhibit was simply the last straw, following other exhibits denounced for disparaging American culture. As Heyman's predecessor, Robert Adams, had reflected the previous summer, "this may be a good time to be leaving." Michael Heyman was just coming in. By abandoning the exhibition and agreeing to review some earlier controversial exhibitions and to suspend or delay new ones under way, he chose to surrender the Smithsonian's independence in order to save it.[48]

♦   ♦   ♦

History has had many functions in human society, the accurate reconstruction of the past being only one. "What happened, what we recall, what we recover, what we relate, are often sadly different," the scholar of the Middle East Bernard Lewis wrote twenty years ago. "The temptation is often overwhelmingly strong to tell it, not as it really was, but as we would wish it to have been." The conflict over the *Enola Gay* exhibition was in part generational, for to many World War II veterans, a critical presentation of this climactic event on the Washington Mall during the fiftieth anniversary was seen as discrediting everything they had done in a cause that had defined their lives and connected them to U.S.

history. But Americans have frequently fought over how to commemorate anniversaries, design monuments, observe holidays,
and mount displays and exhibitions. The U.S. government, like
other national governments in the last two centuries, has used the
memory of war to construct the identity and to build the cohesion
of the modern nation-state. At the state and local levels, people
have had different agendas. Throughout our history, the memori-
alizations of battles and wars have been important cultural and
political rituals that have had varied and changing meanings for
individuals and groups—something all too easily forgotten as the
fiftieth-anniversary commemorations of World War II come to a
close. Because of its fame and mission, the *Enola Gay*, displayed
alone or in an exhibit fifty years after the event and in a heretofore
celebratory museum in Washington, was sure to arouse passion.[49]

But the causes of the controversy and the cancellation lay in
the diverse circumstances that came together in 1994: an exhibit
designed to provoke its viewers with powerful (perhaps tendentious) interpretations; a difficult relationship between a museum
and an important constituency; long-developing and increasingly
bitter contests over education, social relationships, historical interpretations, public culture, and other issues rending American
society; mistakes of process and response by the National Air and
Space Museum; a new, aggressive, determined Republican majority in the Congress; and a new, peculiarly vulnerable Smithsonian
leader who did not resist pressures generated by an enormous
national outcry. Before we read wider implications for presenting
history in America into this experience, we should remember that
there were specific events and conditions that help to explain the
event, circumstances unlikely to be duplicated in the future.

The historical and museum communities should be sensitive to
the ironies as well as the issues. Some veterans' groups did want a
full historical exhibit; a few, including *Enola Gay* pilot Paul W.
Tibbets, Jr., and the scholar and veteran Paul Fussell, from the
beginning wanted no exhibit other than the airplane; others
worked with the museum to the end, and at least one, the Retired
Officers Association, sincerely deplored the cancellation.[50] An ex-

hibit that provided the context of the entire war; that explained in even tones the decision to drop the bomb from the U.S. government's viewpoint (including the disagreements among historians over American motives); that memorialized the artifacts and the fliers as the original script did; that recounted the effect of the bombs on the ground without attempting to arouse emotion or to use repetition in a way that might appear moralizing; and that explored the implications of the bombs for the future with the ambivalence most Americans have felt about the nuclear age seemed possible to many historians. What was *not* possible was "to honor the veterans" in an exhibition that was, in its first form, essentially antiwar and antinuclear, one that emphasized "the reality of atomic war and its consequences." This was the fundamental predicament, Martin Harwit explained, in a thoughtful essay aptly titled "The *Enola Gay*: A Nation's, and a Museum's, Dilemma."[51]

The controversy could be read to indicate that the American people can tolerate honest history presented in full; that they can detect biased or partisan interpretation; and that they recognize the necessity of independent judgment and interpretation in public historical presentation.[52] Americans know that if the complex, scholarly history of controversial events cannot be presented to the public, the United States will be behaving like its former enemies, the Soviet Union and Japan: one abused history for propaganda; the other is still unwilling to acknowledge fully its behavior during World War II in spite of the harm such silence does to Japanese foreign policy across Asia. As a student of Japanese literature about the bomb wrote recently, "Americans' ambivalence over Hiroshima and . . . Japan's ambivalence over its role in the war, involve a common reluctance to think too carefully or long about anything that threatens the national sense of legitimacy." Perhaps a Briton, the great spy novelist of the Cold War John Le Carré, recognized something deeper at work in American culture in the aftermath of the Cold War. "The fight against communism diminished us," he wrote two years ago, lamenting inaction on the Bosnian situation. "It left in us a state of false and corrosive orthodoxy." "The strength of America is in her frankness, her nobility of mind, her willingness to declare herself, take risks and change. Not in her secrecy."[53]

The tragedy of the cancellation is that a major opportunity to inform the American people and international visitors about warfare, airpower, World War II, and a turning point in world history was lost.[54] Certainly, the *Enola Gay* exhibition, even in its unbalanced versions, would have revealed the power and effectiveness of bombing and of nuclear weapons. Ironically, the results for U.S. foreign policy could have been salutary. Millions of people, including many of the world's leaders, would have seen how destructive nuclear bombs are and how difficult it is to control the passion unleashed in nations during wartime, perceptions that might help prevent nuclear proliferation and deter aggression. Viewers would have seen a reminder of what happens when an aggressor sets out on a war of conquest, attacks American interests, and provokes the American people. Placed just a few blocks from the United States Holocaust Memorial Museum and from the exhibit on the World War II internment of the West Coast Japanese Americans at the Smithsonian's National Museum of American History, the exhibit on the atomic bombing would have attracted many visitors. Those who saw all three might have reflected on the folly of racism and concluded that some wars are worth fighting, World War II being one of them.

6

CULTURE WAR, HISTORY FRONT

· MIKE WALLACE ·

In the summer of 1994, reports flaming through the mass media denounced the Smithsonian's impending *Enola Gay* show as a monstrous attempt to recast the history of World War II. Editorials and opinion pieces, mostly cribbed from a series of articles by John T. Correll, editor of *Air Force Magazine*, the official journal of the Air Force Association (AFA), blasted "anti-American" curators and warned that "revisionists" had hijacked the National Air and Space Museum (NASM) to promulgate "politically correct" history. Over the following months, as inaccurate and malicious accusations tumbled forth in a variety of forums, NASM issued a series of revised drafts of the exhibition script. Each cut out some of the objects and language critics deemed objectionable. Each was greeted by the Air Force Association with renewed demands for additional changes. In the end, the show was canceled, and a minimalist installation substituted in which was embedded the AFA's perspective on the *Enola Gay*'s mission.

Given the Air Force Association's crucial role in the *Enola Gay* affair, it's important to understand the organization's background. The group is routinely described as a veterans' organization. Even NASM's then-director Martin Harwit called it "a non-profit organization for current and former members of the U.S. Air Force." But a perusal of the ads in *Air Force Magazine* makes instantly clear that it's a good deal more than that. In marked contrast to the American Legion's journal, where the wares on sale include hearing aids, power mowers, Florida retirement homes, and talking memo-minders, the pages of *Air Force Magazine* are festooned with glossy advertisements for sleek warplanes produced by various of the AFA's 199 Industrial Associates (whose ranks include Boeing, du Pont, Martin Marietta, Northrop Grumman, Rockwell, and Lockheed, which hawks its F-16 to Correll's readers for only "a $20 million price tag").

The AFA, in fact, is the air wing of what Dwight D. Eisenhower called the military-industrial complex. It was founded in 1946 at the instigation of Henry H. "Hap" Arnold, the commanding general of the U.S. Army Air Forces, with James H. "Jimmy" Doolittle, leader of the famed Tokyo raid, as its first president. Arnold, hyperattentive to public relations, set up the AFA to lobby for creation of an independent air force, to fight postwar budget cutbacks, and to "keep our country vigorously aroused to the urgent importance of airpower." It has been the semiofficial lobbying arm of the United States Air Force ever since.

In succeeding decades the AFA institutionalized relations with the defense industry by regularly sponsoring mammoth expositions of military hardware (known to critics as the Arms Bazaar); opposed John Kennedy's test-ban treaty; denounced Lyndon Johnson's refusal to unleash airpower in Vietnam (a Correll predecessor deplored America's renunciation "of the use of even the smallest of nuclear weapons"); battled the peace movement; railed against the "anti-military, anti-industry" atmosphere of the 1970s; and warned about the dangers associated with a "relaxation of tensions, and an end to the cold war."

But the Cold War did end, as did the glory days of the Reagan buildup, and the AFA turned to fighting the cutbacks in military budgets "demanded by the liberal community." During the period Correll was assaulting the National Air and Space Museum, his magazine featured articles like "Another Year, Another Cut," "Boom and Bust in Fighter Procurement," "This Isn't the Bottom Yet," "More Base Closures Coming Up," and "The Case for Airpower Modernization." When not urging Congress "to shift the burden of the cuts to entitlement spending—and thus spare defense," the magazine's writers were warding off attacks from the army ("They need money," said Correll, "and they are ready to take a bite out of the Air Force to get it") or making preemptive strikes on the navy.

In an era of imperiled budgets and reduced political clout—a function, Correll believed, of the diminishing percentage of veterans in the country and in Congress—the AFA was more concerned with image than ever before. "Attitude surveys show waning desire among young people to join the military," Correll noted, a decline he attributed in part to negative portrayals by the news media and entertainment industry.

Whether one thinks well or ill of the AFA's positions, it should come as no surprise to find it paying meticulous attention to how the premier achievement of American airpower—arguably the one instance in which strategic bombing, not an army invasion or a navy blockade, triumphantly ended a major war—would be treated at the most popular museum in the world.

The AFA, moreover, was dismayed that since 1987, when Cornell astrophysicist Martin Harwit was chosen over an air force general to be the new NASM director, the museum had been moving in unwelcome directions. Harwit had set out to demonstrate the social impact of aviation and space technology—the ways it transformed daily life "both for the good and the bad." This applied to the military sphere, too. "No longer," he said, "is it sufficient to display sleek fighters" while making no mention of the "misery of war."

From the Air Force Association's perspective, the series of new exhibits Harwit had authorized seemed like serpents wriggling their way into the Garden of Eden. People came to the National Air and Space Museum to see old aircraft, Correll claimed. "They are not interested in counterculture morality pageants put on by academic activists." The *Enola Gay* exhibit had gone wrong, he thought, precisely because curatorial "interests and attitudes have shifted." It was imperative that the Smithsonian's "keepers and overseers take a strong hand and stop this slide" and get the museum back on track.

Here one can see the structural fault lines that underlay the surface struggle over texts. How the *Enola Gay* was to be interpreted was important in its own right. But the curators' exhibition plans for the *Enola Gay* were also seen as the latest in a series of museological departures that, taken together, signaled AFA leaders that "their" institution was being taken away from them.

They were determined to get it back. The wrestling match over control of the interpretation was emblematic of the struggle for control of the institution. The AFA, less interested in improving the scripts than in axing its opponents, adopted a policy of taking no prisoners. Convinced that the curators were subverting the museum, it took the short step to accusing them of subverting the Republic.

In the supercharged atmosphere surrounding the fiftieth anniversary of Hiroshima, Correll's charges easily touched off a museological conflagration. But to understand why it developed into a national incident, and why the AFA drive to shut down the show proved successful, the story must be set in a larger context. For the Battle of the Enola Gay was only one of several engagements that broke out that summer, all along the History Front of a wider Culture War.

Historical Correctness

In his 1993 book, *See, I Told You So*, Rush Limbaugh warned his fellow conservatives that "we have lost control of our major cultural institutions. Liberalism long ago captured the arts, the press, the entertainment industry, the universities, the schools, the libraries, the foundations, etc."

"This was no accident," he explained, noting that "in the early 1900s, an obscure Italian Communist by the name of Antonio Gramsci theorized that it would take a 'long march through the institutions' before socialism and relativism would be victorious." If these key institutions could be captured, "cultural values would be changed, traditional morals would be broken down, and the stage would be set for the political and economic power of the West to fall."

In the last twenty-five years, Limbaugh continued, "a relatively small, angry group of anti-American radicals"—the "sixties gang"—finally succeeded in executing Gramsci's master plan. Seizing the commanding heights of the cultural economy, they became "firmly entrenched in all of the key cultural institutions that are so influential in setting the agenda and establishing the rules of debate in a free society." From these redoubts they denigrated American values, policed the nation's thought and speech, promoted victimization theories, exalted women and people of color over white males, and pushed a divisive multiculturalism. At the same time, their allies in the welfare and regulatory bureaucracies were busy squashing entrepreneurial initiative.

Of particular concern were those who "bullied their way into power positions in academia." These professors immediately set about demolishing traditional history, the sort which "was once routinely learned by every schoolchild in America." They promulgated instead "a primitive type of historical revisionism." The essential revisionist message—the core of the "indoctrination taking place today in American academia"—consisted of several propositions: "Our country is inherently evil. The whole idea of America is corrupt. The history of this nation is strewn with examples of oppression and genocide. The story of the United States is cultural imperialism—how a bunch of repressed white men imposed their will and values on peaceful indigenous people, black slaves from Africa, and women."

Up and down this new "politically correct" canon Rush roamed, succoring casualties of the onslaught. Poor Christopher Columbus, accused of wiping out savages (who were in any event "violent and brutal"), was the victim of a hoax perpetrated by the sixties gang, who routinely "ascribe fictitious misdeeds to people not alive to defend themselves." The Pilgrims and Puritans, another trashed group, are "vilified today as witch-burners and portrayed as simpletons" in order to cover up the importance of religion in "shaping our history and our nation's character." The early pioneers had single-handedly "tamed a wilderness"—"nothing was handed to them"—but now their antigovernment vision and self-reliant accomplishments were being "turned upside down" in order to justify the reign of Big Government.

A full response to such falsehoods would take us too far afield, but let me briefly attend to the last two. Pace Limbaugh's portrait of the state of religious studies, scores—hundreds—of scholars have over the past thirty years produced a superb and respectful body of work on religion in American life; one could fill a small library with volumes on religion in the seventeenth century alone. As for Limbaugh's sturdy pioneers, they were among the first to demand—and receive—governmental aid in the form of land grants, roads, canals, railroads, and armies. This quasi socialism passed to their twentieth-century descendants, who vigorously sought agricultural subsidies, military contracts, and the giant irrigation and electrification projects that built up sunbelt/gunbelt states with tax dollars drained from their frostbelt cousins.

But pointing out Rush's errors—a cottage industry these days—is somewhat beside the point. Myths can't be refuted by facts. And Limbaugh was out to launch a crusade, not an academic conference. "As we saw during the 1980s," he told his troops, "we can elect good people to high office and still lose ground in this Culture War. And, as we saw in 1992, the more ground we lose in the Culture War, the harder it is to win electoral victories. What we need to do is fight to reclaim and redeem our cultural institutions with all the intensity and enthusiasm that we use to fight to redeem our political institutions."

Happily a field marshal had appeared with exactly the credentials needed to wage such a war. Newton Leroy Gingrich had long since proven himself a master of the political arts, having battled his way to a leadership role in the House of Representatives. He was also a former professor of history and eager to intervene in the battle against revisionism. In 1993, Gingrich began beaming a twenty-hour college course called "Renewing American Civilization" to more than 130 classrooms across the country and to the ten million subscribers to National Empowerment Television.

Central to the course was an analysis of U.S. history, not a subject in which Gingrich had been rigorously trained. Though he had taken some courses in American history as a graduate student at Tulane, his major was in modern European history, and, at the behest of his adviser, he wrote his 1971 Ph.D. dissertation on "Belgian Education Policy in the Congo, 1945–60." During his professorial years at West Georgia College (1970–78), he spent only four years in the history department—teaching mainly Western civilization and European subjects—before moving over to the geography department and launching an environmental studies program. Most of his time at West Georgia was given over to repeated runs for Congress, leaving little time for scholarly research. Indeed by 1975, having published nothing whatsoever, he realized he had no chance of getting tenure and abandoned the notion of applying for it. Had he not been elected to Congress he would have been out of a job. Yet Gingrich brushed aside questions about his expertise. "I'm not credentialed as a bureaucratic academic," he noted waspishly, "I haven't written 22 books that are meaningless."

In his 1994 lectures, especially one entitled "The Lessons of American History," and in speeches and interviews throughout that year, Gingrich asserted the existence of an "American Exceptionalism," which he believed was rooted in distinctive "American Values." These included individualism, "the religious and social tenets of puritanism," the centrality of private property, freedom from government control, and the availability of opportunity (which left Americans "prepared to countenance very substantial economic inequalities"). He admitted past contradictions between profession and practice—slavery, male-only suffrage—but seemed to believe these had been overcome not by organized struggles but by an ineluctable rippling out of the ideals themselves. Unlike his competent dissertation, or his 1984 book *Window of Opportunity*, which advanced an ersatz-Marxist thesis about a contradiction between America's forces of production (a

computer-driven information revolution) and its social relations
of production (a putatively antitechnological welfare state and
culture), Gingrich's more recent teaching conveyed little sense of
agency, little awareness of how history happens.

Gingrich, in fact, said remarkably little about U.S. history, and
a fair amount of what he did say was wrong. In his work, there was
little sustained encounter with actual historians, although he occasionally waved books at his class (Daniel Boorstin's volumes
were favorite wands), and he was fascinated by Gordon Wood's
suggestion that conservative Republicans should claim descent
from Jefferson, not Hamilton. He did urge students to read biog-
raphies, but as sources of inspiration or for tips on problem solv-
ing. (He himself claimed to have been fortified during his
repeated defeats in Georgia politics by reading lives of Lincoln,
and accounts of Churchill's tribulations had buoyed him in his
single-handed struggle to unseat Speaker Jim Wright.) As had his
hero Ronald Reagan, Gingrich reached back to late 1930s, early
1940s movies for his version of American history, citing *Boys Town*
on orphanages, or *Abe Lincoln in Illinois* on the great rail-
splitter—though he also embraced more contemporary sources,
such as Hollywood's recent version of *The Last of the Mohicans*.

Gingrich invoked classic American myths with little concern for
how true they were as long as they were serviceable as moral
fables. The point of studying the past was not to discover how
things changed but to ransack it for role models. Newt's was a
"McGuffeyite history-of-America-by-edifying-anecdote," as Gary
Wills has noted.[1]

Gingrich's idealized U.S. past was also a static one. For centuries, nothing much happened. Then, in the 1960s, things lurched
into sudden downward motion. From 1607 to 1964, as he put it in
his somewhat discombobulated manner, "there is a core pattern
to American history. Here's how we did it until the Great Society
messed everything up: don't work, don't eat; your salvation is
spiritual; the government by definition can't save you; governments are into maintenance and all good reforms are into transformation." Then, abruptly, "the whole system began decaying."

Why? Because the United States got beguiled by irresponsible, "self-indulgent, aristocratic values." These led, apparently over-night, to the welfare state, drug use, hippies, multipartner sex, and the pregnant poor. "From 1965 to 1994"—an epoch that would seem to embrace the Age of Reagan as well as the Age of John-son—"we did strange and weird things as a country."

The culprits were the same ones Limbaugh had fingered—counterculture elitists who despised traditional values. From the 1770s to the mid-1960s, there had been "an explicit long-term commitment to creating character," crucially by studying history. But secular left-wingers couldn't "afford to teach history because it would destroy the core vision of a hedonistic, existentialist America in which there is no past and there is no future, so you might as well let the bureaucrats decide." For Gingrich, properly taught history was a form of ideological inoculation; without it, we "get drowned in European socialist ideas, and we get drowned in oriental ideas of mandarin hierarchy." Once the booster shots stopped coming, the country swiftly succumbed to a host of moral maladies.

The solution was clear. It was time to return to "teaching the truth about American history, teaching about the Founding Fathers and how this country came to be the most extraordinary civilization in history." We should get back to Victorian basics, burnish up the old fables. "We spent a generation in the counterculture laughing at McGuffey Readers and laughing at Parson Weems's vision of Washington." Cherry tree and little hatchet, redivivus.

Gingrichian history, of course, bore little relation to America's complex and sprawling saga. What he had crafted, rather, was a secularized, sacred narrative that flowed from an Edenic past through a fall from grace in the sinful Sixties into a degenerate present, and on, hopefully, to future redemption through a return to prelapsarian values.

Republican Revanche

Redemption drew nigh in the summer and fall of 1994, as the insurgent "conservative" movement spearheaded by Limbaugh and Gingrich drove toward capturing Congress. It was at this very moment that the *Enola Gay* first appeared on Republican radar screens, courtesy of the Air Force Association. It proved an irresistible target.

Out on the hustings right-wing candidates had been happily beating up on the monstrously powerful thought police and bureaucrats, whose un-American values and policies they blamed for the country's disorder and decay, as well as the declining fortunes of white male voters. Along came an exhibition in which, allegedly, arrogant, "politically correct" curators accused white males (aged veterans, no less) of being racist aggressors. Better still, it supposedly cast the Japanese as victims, rather than as transgressors to be held accountable for their immoral actions. In exactly the same way, the politically correct crowd had claimed victimhood status for blacks, women, and assorted welfare layabouts, who were in fact responsible for their own condition.

The show thus afforded yet another opportunity for shifting (white male) electoral attention away from the Republicans' corporate sponsors, who were assiduously dismantling the nation's industrial economy, downsizing vast numbers of (white male) middle managers and (white male) factory workers into the ranks of the un- and underemployed.

Conservative commentators picked up and amplified Correll's critique. The exhibit script provided clear evidence (according to right-wing columnist John Leo) that "the familiar ideology of campus political correctness" had been "imported whole into our national museum structure." Critics were quick to point out that this wasn't the Smithsonian's first transgression. Back in 1991, the National Museum of American Art's "The West as America" had critiqued the pioneer saga celebrated by Limbaugh-Gingrich-ism, touching off an uproar. Writing in the *Wall Street Journal*, Matthew C. Hoffman of the Competitive Enterprise Institute suggested that, over the previous several years, there had been "a gradual change in the Smithsonian's character." Little by little "a portion of the national heritage it represents has been lost to a campaign of ideological revisionism." It was now in the hands of "academics unable to view American history as anything other than a woeful catalog of crimes and aggressions against the helpless peoples of the earth."

Republican members of Congress—like Sam Johnson (Texas), Tom Lewis (Florida), and Peter Blute (Massachusetts)—feasted on the issue all summer and fall of 1994. In August, for instance, Lewis opined on behalf of five other congressmen and himself that the museum's "job is to tell history, not rewrite it." Republican senators were also active. Slade Gorton (Washington) won passage for a declaration that Congress "expects" the *Enola Gay* exhibit to "properly and respectfully recognize the significant contribution to the early termination of World War II and the saving of both American and Japanese lives." Nancy Kassebaum (Kansas) introduced a "Sense of the Senate" resolution that pronounced even the revised script "revisionist and offensive" and directed NASM to avoid "impugning the memory of those who gave their lives for freedom." With the election less than two months away, this was a formulation that no Democrats, not even liberal ones, were prepared to vote against. More disturbingly, no one, right or left, took issue with the assumption underlying such initiatives— that the federal government had the right to mandate historical interpretations.

Standards Bearer

On October 20, just as the fifth and final *Enola Gay* script was emerging from the latest round of revisions, the history wars escalated once again. Lynne Cheney, former head of the National Endowment for the Humanities, launched a preemptive strike in the *Wall Street Journal* against the *National Standards for United States History,* due to be issued five days later. Several years in the making, and funded in 1992 by the NEH while Cheney was still director, the document was intended as a voluntary guide for teachers. Astonishingly ambitious, it offered broad analytical themes, over 2,600 specific classroom exercises, and suggestions for encouraging historical thinking. More than six thousand teachers, administrators, scholars, parents, and business leaders were involved in the drafting process, which was marked by wide-ranging open debates and the involvement of thirty-five advisory organizations, including the Organization of American Historians, the Organization of History Teachers, the American Historical Association, the National Education Association, and the American Association of School Librarians.

No matter. In her *Wall Street Journal* piece, and in subsequent articles and interviews, Cheney chanted the standard mantra: a core group—gripped by a "great hatred for traditional history," and intent on "pursuing the revisionist agenda"—had, "in the name of political correctness," made sure that a "whole lot of basic history" didn't appear. "Counting how many times different subjects are mentioned in the document yields telling results," she wrote ominously. In her pseudostatistical survey, she found traditional heroes underrepresented and women and minorities mentioned too often; references to (black female) Harriet Tubman cropped up more often than to (white male) Ulysses S. Grant. In addition, the history standards lacked "a tone of affirmation," directed attention to social conflict, and invited debate not celebration. Predictably, she concluded her initial blast with a call for battle against an all-powerful "academic establishment."

Cheney's analysis bordered on the disinformational. The standards weren't a textbook, a dictionary of biography, or a compendium of important facts, much less a pantheon or a catechism. Counting white faces and listing a few famous absentees was therefore disingenuous; the issues and events that the document urged exploring patently required repeated reference to the supposedly spurned generals and presidents. In addition, bean counters more scrupulous than Cheney discovered not only that the vast majority of cited individuals were in fact white males, but that the two members of the genus mentioned most often were Richard Nixon and Ronald Reagan.

Cheney's real objections—assuming they were motivated by more than mere personal ambition and political calculation—seemed to be to the paradigmatic shift the history standards represented. In its pages the American past was not a simple saga of remarkable men doing remarkable deeds. Those deeds were included—despite Cheney's charges, for example, the Constitution was treated extensively—but so, too, were less laudatory dimensions of the historical record. Slavery was examined not to muckrake or denigrate the American past but to understand it. And the standards, like much contemporary scholarship, embraced the experience of ordinary people—as heroes of their own lives and as collective actors on the world historical stage.

Some fellow conservatives—notably Diane Ravitch—were also critical of the history standards but balked at Cheney's demand that they be scrapped altogether. The standards' drafters had, after all, expressed willingness to respond to substantive objections, such as complaints that monetarist economic theories explaining the Great Depression were slighted, or that a few dozen (out of 2,600) classroom exercises could arguably be described as shepherding students to preselected conclusions.

But most of the crew that copied Correll now echoed Cheney. Though few in numbers—far fewer than the multitudes that had fashioned the standards—their command of media megaphones allowed them to manufacture another uproar. Rush Limbaugh weighed in four days after Cheney's initial intervention. With his usual insouciant disregard for facts, he informed his radio audience that the "insidious document" had been "worked on in secret." In truth, the drafts had been hammered into shape in countless sessions of democratic discussion embracing enormous numbers of participants, including twenty-three days of formal (tape-recorded) meetings, and hundreds of copies had been dispatched to all who requested them. Limbaugh pronounced the document "an intellectually dishonest, politically correct version of American history" that ought to be "flushed down the toilet." With tedious predictability, columnist Charles Krauthammer called it "a classic of political correctness." The *Wall Street Journal* bundled letters on the subject under the headline "History Thieves." And John Leo o'er-hastily objected to the elevation of one Ebenezer McIntosh, a "brawling street lout of the 1760s," to the heroic stature of a Sam Adams; unfortunately for Leo, the said McIntosh turned out to be an important leader of the Stamp Act Demonstrations in Boston. Not until three weeks had passed did a major national news story—in the *New York Times*—do much more than parrot Cheney's charges, and by then the election was over.

Victory in November didn't stem the Republican assault on revisionists. Indeed their accession to political power shaped the *Enola Gay* endgame.

Speaker-to-be Gingrich made clear that efforts to enact the Contract With America—a package of proposed legislation meant to dismantle much of the regulatory and welfare state and ladle out breaks to business—would be accompanied by a campaign to "Renew American Civilization." In a postelection interview he said that the new Republican leadership intended to improve the country's moral climate, especially by "teaching the truth about American history." Before the month was out, Gingrich had called for eliminating the National Endowment for the Humanities, in part because it had sponsored the history standards, which he pronounced "destructive for American Civilization."

Almost immediately on taking office, Gingrich, acting (he said) "as Speaker, who is a Ph.D. in history," chose a new historian of the House of Representatives. Christina Jeffrey, not a historian at all, but an associate professor of political science at Kennesaw State University who had helped him launch his course, was given the task of helping "in reestablishing the legitimacy of history." "History" suffered a setback in January 1995 when Gingrich abruptly fired Jeffrey. As it transpired, in a 1986 evaluation of an educational program that included an examination of the Holocaust, Jeffrey had argued that "the program gives no evidence of balance or objectivity. The Nazi point of view, however unpopular, is still a point of view and is not presented, nor is that of the Ku Klux Klan." Moreover, she had characterized the since widely adopted program as embodying a "re-education method" that "Hitler and Goebbels used to propagandize the German people," a method later "perfected by Chairman Mao," and which was "now being foisted on American children under the guise of 'understanding history.'"

With this misstep, initiative passed momentarily to the Senate. On January 18, 1995, Republican senators Robert Dole (Kansas) and Slade Gorton won passage (by 99–1) of a nonbinding Sense of the Senate Resolution. It urged that the present history standards not be certified by the federal government, and that funds for any future ones go only to those that "have a decent respect for the contributions of Western civilization, and United States history, ideas and institutions, to the increase of freedom and prosperity throughout the world." Democrats argued against the resolution but agreed to support it, if made nonbinding.

A week later, House members joined the fray. On January 24, sixty-eight Republicans (including House Majority Leader and Gingrich ally Dick Armey) and thirteen Democrats demanded Martin Harwit's ouster. Representative Blute elaborated: "We think there are some very troubling questions in regard to the Smithsonian, not just with this *Enola Gay* exhibit but over the past 10 years or so, getting into areas of revisionist history and political correctness. There are a lot of questions that need to be answered."

On the twenty-sixth, critics began tying the two issues together. Columnist George Will claimed "the Smithsonian Institution, like the history standards," was "besotted with the cranky anti-Americanism of the campuses." Lynne Cheney, in guileful congressional testimony, seized on one of the 2,600 teaching examples to argue that fifth or sixth graders who learned about the end of World War II from the history standards would know only that the United States had devastated Hiroshima, but nothing of

Japanese aggression. In fact the standards called explicitly for analysis of the "German, Italian and Japanese drives for empire in the 1930s"; moreover, a suggested teaching activity for seventh and eighth graders was to construct a time line that included the "Japanese seizure of Manchuria in 1931."

Also on the twenty-sixth, Speaker Gingrich named Representative Sam Johnson—an ardent critic of the *Enola Gay* show who had alerted him to the issue—to the Smithsonian's Board of Regents. The following day Gingrich announced he had found "a certain political correctness seeping in and distorting and prejudicing the Smithsonian's exhibits," and declared the museum should not be "a plaything for left-wing ideologies."[2]

Four days later I. Michael Heyman, the recently installed Smithsonian secretary, scuttled the *Enola Gay* exhibit.[3] Now in full retreat mode, he also announced "postponement" for at least five years of a planned exhibit on airpower in Vietnam; suggested that critics of "political correctness" in recent interpretive exhibits had a point; and promised the regents he would review and, where necessary, rectify current exhibits that they believed reflected "revisionist history." Heyman refused to fire Harwit, but then a long-time Smithsonian critic, Republican senator Ted Stevens of Alaska, announced he would go ahead in mid-May 1995 with previously threatened hearings on the philosophical underpinnings of the exhibit. On May 2 Harwit resigned. The continuing controversy, he said, had convinced him "that nothing less than my stepping down from the directorship will satisfy the Museum's critics." Regent Sam Johnson immediately made clear that Harwit's departure wasn't enough, that only a full-scale purge of "revisionists" would do.

The actual exhibition opened on June 28, 1995. It proved even more of a retreat than had been anticipated. Heyman claimed it simply reported "the facts," but it was larded with AFA-style interpretation. Apart from a twenty-second video snippet showing the bombs' effects (which may or may not have included the image of a corpse), and label copy saying that the two bombs "caused tens of thousands of deaths" (by most accounts, a serious understatement), there was no confrontation with the destruction of Hiroshima and Nagasaki. "I really decided to leave it more to the imagination," Heyman stated at a news conference on June 27.

The secretary added that "the aircraft speaks for itself in this exhibit"—and indeed NASM scattered additional pieces of the giant plane throughout the exhibition, trying to fill up the embarrassingly bare galleries—but in fact it is the *Enola Gay*'s pilot, Paul W. Tibbets, Jr., who speaks on its behalf, in a sixteen-minute video presentation offering his views of the mission. Not surprisingly, after previewing the exhibition on June 21, Tibbets wrote Heyman he was "pleased and proud" of it. It presented the "basic facts," he argued, without any "attempt to persuade anyone about anything." The final exhibit, he added, "demonstrates the merits and the positive influences of management."

On opening day, twenty-one demonstrators with the *Enola Gay* Action Coalition were hauled away by a U.S. Park Police SWAT team.

Fallout

What are the larger meanings, and likely consequences, of the battle over the *Enola Gay*?

The victors have suggested their own answers to these questions. Newt Gingrich told the National Governors' Association, "The *Enola Gay* fight was a fight, in effect, over the reassertion by most Americans that they're sick and tired of being told by some cultural elite that they ought to be ashamed of their country." The editorial page of the *Wall Street Journal*, that GHQ of reaction, proclaimed it a triumph for the public, which had successfully "stuck its snoot inside the sanctums tended to these many years by the historians."

This is faux-populist hogwash. In truth, this generation of historians and curators has thrown open the historical tent flaps and embraced the experience of a far broader range of Americans than had ever before been represented in museums. Just as opinion polls belie right-wing claims that public broadcasting is an elite-only enterprise, so too the vast number of citizens flocking to public historical presentations (far more than attend professional sports events) contradicts claims that historians are out of touch with the larger culture.

The people packing into history museums, local historical societies, preserved historic places, and National Park Service sites are drawn in part by the novel presence of their forebears' voices and stories. Not only women and people of color are now depicted extensively but vast numbers of white males as well—the farmers and miners and sailors and steelworkers and clerks and professionals who had never before been deemed of sufficient stature to warrant inclusion in the marble mausoleums stuffed with the portraits and possessions of "historically correct" statesmen and entrepreneurs. At long last the American past is as crowded and diverse and contentious and fascinating as is the American present.

Conservative cant about liberating the masses from political correctness is more than just misleading. The only political correctness displayed in the *Enola Gay* affair was the censorship that shut down the real exhibition and barred people from judging it for themselves. It was bad enough watching the show get throttled; it has been insufferable to hear the censors whine about their powerlessness. If this Orwellian recasting of suppression as liberation is not rejected, if the Right is allowed to frame the issue this way, the Smithsonian's humbling may herald further repression.

There is a simple way conservatives might try to expunge the scholarship they detest, or at least keep it bottled up inside the academy—gut governmental funding. Just as Republican congresspeople have invited business lobbyists to the legislative drafting tables, the abolition of NEH and NEA, NPR and CPB will make public history programming, like access to the airwaves, dependent on corporate funders. This will further narrow the range of acceptable historical presentations (few such enterprises will care to be identified with controversial issues) or lead to puff pieces like the histories of transport, energy, and food that Disney "imagineers" crafted for General Motors, Exxon, and Kraft at EPCOT.[4]

But for all the new elite's libertarian professions about reducing the power of big government, they seem drawn to authoritarian solutions. In the case of the National Air and Space Museum, congresspeople laid down an official historical "line" and demanded the firing of curators who did not toe it. Gingrich himself believes our ailing culture can be cured through state intervention, "first of all by the people appointed to the Smithsonian board." Regent Sam Johnson—Newt's first cultural commissar—agrees completely that "this Congress has an opportunity to change the face of America," and makes clear that his goal is "to get patriotism back into the Smithsonian."

Suppression follows all too logically from such premises. If traitors have seized the nation's cultural bastions, it's essential to root them out. The *Wall Street Journal* professes amazement that "the history profession pushed its 'new history' this far without challenge," and seeks to terminate the enterprise forthwith. Historians "fear that one set of assumptions is simply going to be imposed by fiat in place of their own," the *Journal* notes. "That would be unfortunate, we guess. But we don't plan to feel very sorry for these academics."

The new expurgators are busily scrutinizing the "history textbooks, curricula and museum displays" that John Leo believes have become "carriers of the broad assault against American and Western culture." An outfit calling itself the American Textbook Council damned Paul Boyer's update of Merle Curti's classic history survey for, among other things, pointing out the achievements of environmentalists. John Leo blasted the same study using the now time-dishonored technique of counting up biographical references and declaring white male faces insufficiently in evidence. Lynne Cheney censured a textbook by Gary Nash, former president of the Organization of American Historians and codirector of the history standards project, for dwelling on Mc-Carthyism and Watergate and being "gloomier than the story of the United States ought to be."

Even that nemesis of gloom the Walt Disney Company got its corporate wrist slapped by the new censorians. When Disney's America, the proposed history theme park, announced it would "not take a Pollyanna view" of the American past and would even evoke the experience of slavery, conservative apparatchik William Kristol warned, "If you're going to have a schlocky version of American history, it should at least be a schlocky, patriotic and heroic version," rather than something "politically correct," making "suitable bows to all oppressed groups."

Though the new nabobs have so far restricted themselves to a relatively niggling negativism, we should not underestimate how fast and how far things could slide. The United States has never had a State Ministry of Culture to dictate historical "lines," but it's had plenty of private vigilantes patrolling cultural institutions to ensure they promoted "patriotic" perspectives. In 1925, the American Legion declared that history textbooks "must inspire the children with patriotism" and "speak chiefly of success"; during subsequent decades—especially in the 1950s—the organization expended considerable energy demanding that intellectuals it deemed un-American be muzzled or fired.

There are disturbing signs that this rough beast has been waked again. *Air Classics*, a popular magazine for aviation buffs, has been inspired by the November 1994 elections—which proved "Americans are taking control of their government . . . and their institutions"—to set the Smithsonian in its gun sights. It aims to "oust the revisionists who want to forever change history in favor of the enemy," and to establish a permanent committee to "constantly monitor the NASM, and similar institutions to stop a repeat of their nearly successful treachery."[5]

Such assaults, even if restricted to the rhetorical, can lead to museological self-censorship. The NASM has already put off its Vietnam exhibition, and across the Mall, at the National Museum of American History, curators worry openly that fallout from the

Enola Gay affair will contaminate future exhibitions. "Once it's known that Air and Space sat down to a line-by-line review of the script with the American Legion," said one, "who's next? The Christian Coalition."

Yet it won't do to overstate the degree of danger. Serious obstacles confront those who would revive a full-rigged McCarthyism. For one thing, the Cold War is over. The absence of an external communist menace makes it harder to demonize internal opponents. Indeed, the thawing of controls on the practice of history in Russia and Eastern Europe provides an embarrassing counterpoint to newfound U.S. government interest in policing the past. The same issue of the *New York Times* that reported fourscore congresspeople had called for the firing of "defiant" curators also reported that Polish historians "have suddenly begun to savor the newfound freedom to examine and write about their country's history as they see it." Further loosening of ideological bonds abroad will hinder their imposition at home.

In the case of the *Enola Gay*, Japan served as an acceptable substitute for the Evil Empire. Attacks on the exhibition gained strength and plausibility from Japan's egregious approach to its past. Americans (and Asians) had been rightfully indignant at the cabinet ministers, educators, and curators who for decades downplayed or denied Japan's record of aggression, in sharp contrast to Germany's willingness to apologize for the criminal activities of its fascist state. The Hiroshima Peace Memorial Museum presented its city and country solely as martyrs and victims, as if the war had begun the day the bomb was dropped. This allowed critics to charge that the National Air and Space Museum—which was to have borrowed artifacts from the Hiroshima museum—shared (or had been ensnared by) its lender's politics.[6]

But those politics had begun to change. Under pressure from internal critics, particularly Socialist and pacifist groups, Japan had taken significant steps toward accepting responsibility for launching the war and committing atrocities. Historians like Professor Yoshiaki Yoshimi, by irrefutably proving that Korean "comfort women" had been forced to service the imperial army, prodded the government into reversing its denial of responsibility. Leading intellectuals and politicians (including the country's Socialist prime minister, Tomiichi Murayama) called for a parliamentary apology to the Asian countries Japan had invaded. Though this met with vehement opposition from a coalition of conservative parties, bureaucrats, and business leaders, a 1994 poll found that four of every five Japanese believed their country had not adequately compensated the citizens of conquered nations.[7]

In Hiroshima itself, recently elected mayor Takashi Hiraoka argued "that when we think about the bomb, we should think about the war, too." Overcoming opposition from groups like the Great Japan Patriots Party, he won installation of new exhibitry in June 1994, just as the *Enola Gay* affair was heating up, that described in detail the city's role in the war effort.[8]

Thus the Smithsonian's cancellation was particularly ironic: the Americans (under pressure from the Right) were refusing to reflect on the past just as the Japanese (under pressure from the Left) were beginning to confront it. Ironic and unfortunate, in that closing down a public historical enterprise that transcended narrow nationalist interpretations missed an opportunity to bind up old war wounds and reconcile former enemies. Still, if Japan continues along this "revisionist" path, it will be harder for American xenophobes to replicate their triumph at the Smithsonian, which, in any event, was rooted in singular circumstances. And although Japan may be a tough competitor, it's a capitalist competitor, and an ally to boot; it won't be as easy to (as it were) "yellow-bait" intellectuals as it once was to "red-bait" them.

Critics of mainstream academic and public historians face a different kind of problem: you can't fight something with nothing. It's clear what the new censorians don't like—though Gingrich affixes his "counterculture" and "socialist" labels so indiscriminately that his Enemies List lacks the nice precision of Nixon's. What's not so clear is what they would put in place of the historical edifice they seek to tear down.

Most insist history should be heroic. "I think our kids need heroes," says Lynne Cheney. "I think that they need models of greatness to help them aspire." But apart from the fact that the only heroes the Right deems worthy are those already enshrined in the traditional pantheon—the Harriet Tubmans in our past don't seem to cut the mustard—trumpeting great deeds isn't much of a substitute for serious analysis of the nation's historical development; nor is "patriotic" history, not that it's clear exactly what this means.[9]

From Matthew Hoffman's wistful recollection in the *Wall Street Journal* of the days when the Smithsonian stuck to "unapologetic celebration," it would appear that conservatives long for unqualified boosterism. Now, it's completely appropriate to insist that hard-won American accomplishments, like the steady expansion of democratic and constitutional government, be fully recounted in any full-scale historical reckoning. As indeed they are in the works of current practitioners; despite conservative canards, the history standards pay them rich tribute. But does "patriotism" require striking from the public record all instances where practice fails to live up to preachment? Is their slogan "Triumphs sí, tragedies no?" Are we to return to the see-no-evil days when Colonial Williamsburg, Inc., could present its eighteenth-century town purely as a cradle of liberty without mentioning that over 50 percent of its residents were slaves? I suspect most Americans want their historians to pursue the truth, not generate feel-good fantasies. As Secretary Heyman said when he was still resisting closure, it's not the Smithsonian's job "simply to offer a romantic portrait of the nation's past; Hollywood and Disney do that quite well."

What academics have going for them, despite the cartoon characterizations their opponents bruit about, is the immense body of scholarly work they have put together over the past generation. It will be difficult (though not impossible) for opponents to vault over it and sport about in fields of mid-nineteenth-century pieties. Nor will the museums that have so successfully quarried this mine of information and analysis be easily driven back to decontextualized displays of the material culture of a privileged few.

If future *Enola Gay* debacles are to be avoided, however, museums will have to be smarter and tougher than they have ever been before. If the National Air and Space Museum can be faulted for anything, it's for underestimating the tenacity and tactics of its likely opponents, and for not realizing it had *enemies* to deal with. "We've been extremely outclassed," admitted NASM spokesman Mike Fetters back in September 1994. "Had we known how intense the AFA's efforts would be, we'd have moved a bit more promptly and aggressively to get our information distributed to veterans, the media, and Congress."

The way to forestall such disasters is not to retreat into controversy-free blandness; given the current climate, that's probably impossible anyway. Museum planners should instead routinely think through a show's potential political impact. They should identify groups that might be affected by, or have a particular interest in, an exhibition. Once identified, the institution should seek out and, where feasible, engage these groups in authentic dialogue.

Museums, including NASM, have done a lot of this in recent years. But it's been relatively easy so far. Curators have mostly been building bridges to sympathetic constituencies—women, African Americans, Native Americans, and white working-class ethnic communities that shared the goal of making museums more diverse and democratic.

In the future, political impact assessments will have to identify potentially harsher critics as well. If a projected exhibition on the history of urban crime intends to flag handgun availability as a problem, it would be wise to anticipate objections from the National Rifle Association. If designers of a show on the history of public health plan to call attention to preventable lung cancer, they had best be prepared for the wrath of the tobacco industry. Treatments of prostitution, pollution, civil rights, birth control, political corruption, homosexuality, welfare, urban planning, historic preservation, deindustrialization, foreign relations—almost anything, in truth, that tries to set contemporary issues in historical perspective—can be expected to outrage some part of the populace, somewhere along the political spectrum. Should such critics be declared "stakeholders" and given an automatic veto? I think not. There are better alternatives available, options whose feasibility has been tested in practice, options that can enhance rather than foreclose discussion.

One approach is to clearly label a given show as embodying the point of view of the curators. It would be presented as the analogue of an op-ed piece, or a column, rather than a news story. The authors-curators could be clearly introduced up front, with pictures and bios. They could lay out, in videotaped prefaces, what they are seeking to accomplish. This would undercut the notion that exhibitions are the products of omniscient and invisible narrators. It would also allow curatorial convictions to be distinguished from those of the institution, as is done routinely on television in disclaimers that state that the views presented are not necessarily those of the broadcaster. At the end of the exhibit, moreover, both critics and visitors could be given the opportunity of commenting on the presentation, using media formats ranging from simple three-by-five-inch cards tacked on a wall to videotaped snippets playing on monitors.

Another strategy would be to incorporate differing perspectives into the exhibition itself. Museums should not duck debate but welcome it. Fascinating shows could be fashioned by pitting alternative perspectives against each other: creationists versus evolutionists, developers versus preservationists, advocates versus opponents of affirmative action.

In most cases proponents will settle for being participants in a conversation. But what happens if they won't? What happens if the NRA insists that all references to gun control as a desirable response to urban crime be deleted? What happens if fundamentalists object to having their divinely sanctioned beliefs paired with those of secular-humanist Darwinians? What to do when the Air Force Association denounces the very notion of laying out differing perspectives on the Hiroshima bombing as being inherently unpatriotic? How to respond when the very idea of presenting controversies is rejected as controversial?

Here, I think, it's essential that there be standards of professional rights and responsibilities to which individual institutions could refer. Fashioned by the museological community at large, these should be akin to but not identical with standards of academic freedom in that they would apply to institutions, not individuals. A public historical organization might be expected to make use of up-to-date scholarship, follow appropriate rules for gathering evidence in its own research, provide ways for critics and visitors to respond to exhibitions, fairly present a range of opinions on controversial issues, and offer over time a reasonable variety of political perspectives. If museums adhered to such procedures, they would be guaranteed the right to mount whatever exhibitions they chose to, free from political interference.

The standards should state the principles that underlie such a call for relative autonomy, and justify its value to the larger society. Curators are educators of a special kind. They have particular responsibilities to listen to their communities. But they also have valuable skills and information to contribute to that community and a responsibility to pursue the truth. If they carry out their civic and professional obligations in a responsible manner, it is in the best interest of that larger community that they be protected from intimidation.

If and when drafters get around to hammering out principles defending freedom of historical inquiry, they might consider four sentences from a *New York Times* editorial of January 30, 1995, responding to attacks on the Smithsonian. "To reduce the complexities or painful ambiguities of the issue to slogans or historical shorthand is wrong. . . . To let politicians and groups with a particular interest frame the discussion and determine the conclusion is worse. . . . The real betrayal of American tradition would be to insist on a single version of history or to make it the property of the state or any group. . . . Historians and museums of history need to be insulated from any attempt to make history conform to a narrow ideological or political interest."

The existence of such a public historical charter might well bolster the position of beleaguered institutions. But then again, it might not. Paper rights are one thing, power realities another.

What could a museum do if it played by the rules and still came under attack?

In part, it would have to take responsibility for its own self-defense. It should have analyzed in advance who an exhibit's potential allies and enemies were likely to be, and thought through a contingency plan for enlisting the former and fending off the latter. Such a blueprint should include an agenda for action, right on down to identifying the media experts and friendly politicians who could be enlisted at short notice to help explain the institution's position to press and public alike.

But isolated institutions can do only so much. There must be a commitment by the larger museum community to help out. An attack on one museum's freedom of expression should be seen as an attack on all. Most Americans believe museums are dedicated to the pursuit and display of truth. They enjoy a rare reputation among our cultural and political establishments. Any capitulation to political or commercial pressures tarnishes that image. If one institution yields to noisy minorities, or even perceived majorities, the hard-won credibility of all museums will quickly unravel, for who can sustain confidence in institutions whose exhibitions have been purchased or imposed?

In the event of future *Enola Gays*, professional bodies should launch their own investigations. If such inquiries find that an institution has operated in compliance with generally accepted standards, and been subjected to unwarranted harassment, then the entire community should speak out vigorously on its behalf. The museum world should also forge alliances with other cultural institutions—like public libraries, schools, universities, E-mail networks, and publishers of print and electronic media—who now routinely come under fire. Jane Alexander, head of the National Endowment for the Arts, has set a splendid example by traveling to all fifty states and mobilizing grassroots arts groups. If, as I believe, museums have developed and retain a substantial reservoir of popular support, they might consider mobilizing their constituents in defense of freedom of expression.

If all this fails, and we are faced with more shuttered galleries, we may have to consider borrowing methods other dissidents have found useful. The NASM story did not end with the opening of the amputated exhibit. An alliance of scholars, curators, and peace activists engaged in demonstrations, teach-ins, and a counterexhibition, a sort of *musée des refusés*. If the shutdown galvanizes the public historical community into ongoing concerted action, perhaps the Battle of the *Enola Gay*, which now seems a setback, may prove in the end to have been a victory.

7

DANGEROUS HISTORY:
VIETNAM AND THE "GOOD WAR"

• MARILYN B. YOUNG •

Sovietologists have frequently commented on the former Soviet Union's need to revise the past. Moscow subway mosaics, for example, were periodically updated. Each time the tiled images of fallen revolutionaries were carefully removed, their ghostly outlines remained, a vivid assertion of the power of the state over the past. Americans understood this as a peculiarly totalitarian sensitivity to the dangers of history and regularly cited George Orwell's famous dictum to explain it: "Who controls the past controls the future; who controls the present controls the past." The connection between past and present needed constant tending, lest Soviet citizens draw undesirable conclusions. There could be, in such a system, no contending "versions" of the past, only a single, state-sanctioned narrative comprising all one was allowed to know of Truth and all it was safe to know.

Official history in the United States has been less organized, visible, or subject to revision by the state. The publication of a new, critical interpretation of Thomas Jefferson's life, for example, would not require Monticello to be closed down, though it might lead to a few more explanatory placards; new work on the ambiguities of Abraham Lincoln's politics would not have a visible effect on the Lincoln Memorial. Does this mean Americans are always open to rethinking their history? The historian Nathan Huggins suggested that, on the contrary, U.S. history was peculiarly impervious to rethinking. American historians, he wrote, "have conspired with the Founding Fathers to create a national history, teleologically bound to the Founders' ideals rather than their reality." The story thus created, Huggins continued, was "unified" with "no discontinuity between the colonies and the Revolution, nor between the founding and the Civil War, nor between Reconstruction and the present." And the result? "The holy nation thus acquired a holy history. A conspiracy of myth, history, and chauvinism served to create an ideology as the dominating historical motif against which all history would resonate."[1]

The essential American historical metanarrative has been based on a belief in the fulfillment, over time, of the enduring principles of the Founding Fathers. Historical events or institutions that seemed to contradict these principles (slavery or imperialism, for example) have been understood as aberrational, "historical accidents," as Huggins put it, "to be corrected in the progressive upward reach of the nation's destiny."[2] Fundamentally ahistorical, the national story had a fail-safe mechanism: wrongs would always be righted and the originating vision realized in due course. Unaffected by historical events, the promise that lay in the nation's establishment served as armor for the governing national myths rather more effectively than did cleansing the Moscow subways of the Soviet past.

One might, then, have expected the Vietnam War to have been absorbed into the standard historical narrative as but another aberrant event. But for a number of reasons, it came instead to threaten the integrity of the narrative itself. Perhaps the most important reason for this was that the war coincided with the civil rights movement, which had already begun to raise doubts about the nation's morality. The United States was fighting in Vietnam, the public was told, because communism would deny Vietnamese that most signal privilege of a democracy: free elections. Yet on their television screens, night after night, Americans watched as African Americans were set upon by truncheon-wielding police and their attack dogs, swept off their feet by high-powered hoses, beaten, and killed in their effort to exercise the most basic rights of citizenship, including the right to vote. "While I had been off fighting for the freedom of foreigners," General Colin Powell recalls in his memoir, "four little black girls had been killed by a bomb planted in Birmingham's 16th Street Baptist Church."[3] Even more significant than the daily contradiction posed by the denial of civil rights to African Americans was the attention the movement drew to the entire history of race relations in the United States and to the "inescapable paradox," in Huggins's words, of a "free nation, inspired by the Rights of Man, having to rest on slavery."[4]

The issues of the Vietnam War brought into question the founding premise of U.S. history itself. It was an axiom of this history that the United States, from its inception—and as an aspect of that inception—stood for self-determination, freedom, and democracy. The longer the Vietnam War lasted, however, the less tenable that proposition became. The United States was seen as supporting a government that tortured, jailed, and executed those who challenged its rule; its military forces leveled villages, forced their inhabitants into refugee camps, napalmed, carpet bombed, and massacred noncombatants. For an increasing number of Americans, the war seemed to recapitulate the nation's entire past, recalling, in the language and manner in which it was fought, the extermination of Native Americans and the violence of its continental and overseas conquests. Soldiers in the field called Vietnam "Indian country," a phrase whose gloss, historians pointed out, went back to the nation's origins. According to historian Richard Slotkin, America, starting with the annihilation of its earliest inhabitants, developed a culture that found fundamental, regenerative power in violence. Vietnam was an acid bath in which received myths dissolved, and so presented a serious threat to the nation's very sense of self. The traditional narrative, worn thin with use, left history no safer for American governments than it was for the Soviets. Historian Loren Baritz, in his impassioned polemic against the war, *Backfire: A History of How American Culture Led Us into Vietnam and Made Us Fight the Way We Did*, declares that America "must be for freedom, for dignity, for genuine democracy, or it is not America. It was not America in Vietnam."[5] The problem, however, was that many Americans had concluded the reverse: America was never more itself than in Vietnam.

The loss of a common vision of America in the Vietnam era proved a surprising and intolerable constraint on the making of foreign policy. The official response to the popular sense of the war as immoral was to declare it pathological: a Vietnam syndrome existed, whose symptoms included distrust of the government and a reluctance to support sending troops abroad. Treatment took a variety of forms. The Reagan and Bush administrations tried homeopathy, fighting a series of short healing wars whose victorious conclusions, it was hoped, would eliminate the syndrome once and for all. No public official directly confronted the widespread public unease about the war's meaning, nor the diffuse feeling of guilt, often voiced most powerfully by veterans themselves. Jimmy Carter's diagnosis invoked morality, if imprecisely; the war had caused "mutual destruction," as if the United States, like Vietnam, had been a battlefield. Ronald Reagan preferred Christian transcendence: the war had been a "noble crusade."

In a variety of media, those friendly to the government's problems did their best to reconstitute a lost sense of American rectitude. The historian Guenter Lewy, in his book *America in Vietnam* (1978), used his privileged access to Defense Department archives to persuade a younger generation that nothing in the conduct of the war merited censure; the journalist Norman Podhoretz, in his book *Why We Were in Vietnam* (1982), pursued Reagan's noble crusade theme, while Hollywood turned America into the victim, Vietnam into the aggressor, and the war into something that had happened to the United States rather than something it had done to others. In 1985 the movie *Rambo*, though set in the postwar period, took this logic to its conclusion, projecting the Vietnam War not as a high-tech U.S. invasion of another country but as a heroic American guerrilla effort to rescue captive Americans.

Despite such efforts—and there were many as the years passed—Vietnam-induced skepticism about the standard heroic national story retrospectively infected ever earlier periods of American history. Those who wished to preserve that older tale more or less intact found themselves fighting defensively on a number of fronts. When the Smithsonian Institution's National Museum of American Art mounted an exhibit titled "The West as America," which interpreted U.S. expansion as a march of plunder rather than progress, there was an immediate outcry. But although the museum modified some of its more rhetorical explanatory placards, the exhibit as a whole stood, as had an earlier Smithsonian exhibit on the World War II internment of Japanese Americans.[6]

One bastion of America's faith in itself remained safe in these troubled times. Despite the blot of Japanese internment, the most sacred icon of twentieth-century U.S. culture, World War II, remained a symbol of national virtue. Even at the height of the Vietnam War, antiwar protesters never questioned the goodness of their country in the Second World War. Indeed, the war in Vietnam was often portrayed as bad in precise proportion to the goodness of America's fight against German fascism and Japanese militarism. Everyone agreed that the United States had entered World War II because of the vicious attack by an enemy so depraved it had not even given decent warning of its intentions. America had fought enemies of unparalled evil and emerged triumphant. Anne O'Hare McCormick caught the mood precisely. V-J day, she wrote for the *New York Times* on August 11, 1945, anticipating the Japanese surrender, would be "above all an American holiday. . . . America is at the head of the world as literally as Rome was in the Augustan age."[7] Repeatedly, in the years after the Vietnam War, the glory days of 1945 were recalled as both a lost Eden and a permanent measure of Righteousness. "The biggest event in my lifetime was the Second World War," recalled former governor of New York State Mario Cuomo in a recent interview, "and we have never been able to recreate it." The Second World War, he added, "was the last time that this country believed anything profoundly, any great single cause. What was it? That was Tōjō, that was that S.O.B. Hitler, that was Mussolini, that bum. They struck at us in the middle of the night, those sneaks. We are good, they are bad. Let's all get together we said, and we creamed them. We started from way behind. We found strength in this common commitment, this commonality, community, family. The idea of coming together was best served in my lifetime in the Second World War. You never had a war quite like it." Since then, Cuomo complained, there had been nothing "big to believe in. Nothing to wrap your arms around."[8] Even in the grim years after the Vietnam War, it still seemed possible for Americans to warm themselves in the remembered sunshine of 1945.

Then, to commemorate the fiftieth anniversary of the end of World War II, the staff of the National Air and Space Museum decided to exhibit the restored fuselage of the *Enola Gay*, but to do so in accordance with the museum's new approach, one which placed the artifacts of America's military past in historical context.[9] They saw the exhibition of the plane—the solid material embodiment of the end of World War II—as the occasion for public reflection on the act that, in the language of documentary voice-overs, ended one era and opened the next. The museum's historical intent was clear from the title of the initial script: "Crossroads: The End of World War II, the Atomic Bomb, and the Origins of the Cold War." The exhibition's explicit goal was "to encourage visitors to undertake a thoughtful and balanced re-examination of these events in the light of the political and military factors leading to the decision to use the bomb, the human suffering experienced by the people of Hiroshima and Nagasaki and the long-term implications of the events of August 6 and 9, 1945." The curators hoped the exhibit would "provide a crucial public service by reexamining these issues in the light of the most recent scholarship."

The problem with an exhibit that set the *Enola Gay*'s mission in historical context, however, was that it risked revealing that events that once appeared inevitable were actually matters of decision. The bomb *might* not have been dropped, thus perhaps *should* not have been dropped. What had been largely accepted as inexorable now threatened to become contingent. The exhibit turned the destruction of Hiroshima and Nagasaki into acts of choice and so open to moral question. Rather than simply displaying the plane's fuselage along with dates and statistics which implied by their apparent completeness that no questions attended the production of those numbers, the curators sought to explore the possibility that other choices could have produced quite different numbers.

Earlier commemorations of the Hiroshima mission had been more cautious. On the fortieth anniversary, the National Museum of American History limited itself to an exhibit of replicas of the bomb casings of Little Boy and Fat Man displayed behind glass, with simple plaques that allowed them to "speak for themselves." The historian of science Stanley Goldberg, who wrote the script for that 1985 show, explained that he had deliberately made the display as neutral as possible, fearing "the emotional impact the exhibit might have on unprepared visitors."[10] Goldberg did want to make Hiroshima and Nagasaki "real" to visitors, and so he had included some melted roof tiles, borrowed from Japan, and one picture of a badly burned male survivor. The meaning these objects conveyed was simply that nuclear bombs had fallen, done great damage, and ended the war.

On the other hand, the National Air and Space Museum's proposed exhibit—with its melted school lunch boxes and its many photographs of horribly burned women and children—focused the viewer's attention on the actual impact of the bombs at ground level. Moreover, the exhibit raised serious questions about the decision to drop the bomb. To pose such questions was tantamount to desecrating Anne McCormick's American holiday and, worse, implying that the Augustan age had begun with an atrocity. If so, the United States was no longer simply the victim of barbarous Japanese behavior at Pearl Harbor, Bataan, and elsewhere, but capable of barbarism of its own.

The debate over the use of nuclear weapons to end the war in the Pacific had been ongoing among historians since 1965, when Gar Alperovitz argued in *Atomic Diplomacy* that the real target was not Hiroshima but Stalin. While Alperovitz's book created a stir in the profession, it did not penetrate the consciousness of the public at large.[11] It is one of the less visible ironies of the democratic system that the academy's freedom of expression rests securely on its being ignored.

Historians have considered and reconsidered the events of 1945 without disturbing the remaining hairs on a World War II veteran's head. Indeed, the press regularly serves the academy up to the public as a light snack, drawing attention to its esoteric interests, obscurantist articulations, and general foolishness. No one is asked to take professors seriously, and the fulminations of conservatives and reactionaries cause a stir only when people are reminded that tax dollars support some especially foolish-sounding projects. So it was as much the setting of the exhibit as its content that seemed to cause the uproar. As the television journalist Peter Jennings put it in a television special on Hiroshima, the Smithsonian is "our most important national museum,"[12] prominently situated on the Mall, as much a Washington monument as the Washington Monument itself, and its Air and Space division is explicitly dedicated to the celebration of American military technology. It was only when views that challenged the heroic national narrative appeared in such a sanctified public space that there was plenty of response, mostly in the form of outrage. Public, tax-supported, government-monitored space separates official history from the maunderings of scholars in their classrooms, journals, and annual meetings.

While assembling the exhibit, the Smithsonian's curatorial staff did worry about public response, but they seem not to have anticipated the massively negative reaction that occurred. The original script was balanced and did not insist on any particular interpretation of either the decision to bomb or its necessity to end the war. The Smithsonian's sin seems to have been precisely its effort to deal with the bomb as history. For a government institution like the Smithsonian to raise the possibility that there were alternatives to using nuclear weapons was itself an offense. Angry veterans insisted there could be no question about the need to use the bomb. It was a betrayal for the country's official museum even to raise the question. For almost fifty years there had been no official debate on the subject; as Secretary of War Henry L. Stimson asserted in a 1947 *Harper's* magazine essay entitled "The Decision to Use the Atomic Bomb," the bomb ended the war, saving untold numbers of American and, for that matter, Japanese lives; without it an invasion of the Japanese home islands would certainly have been necessary at a cost too terrible to contemplate.[13]

The veterans at the battle of the Smithsonian were old men remembering horrendous island battles from Guadalcanal to Okinawa, remembering themselves as frightened young men in direct danger of being ordered to invade the Japanese home islands. But more than that was involved: to admit the possibility that the war might have ended without either the bomb *or* an invasion could have only one meaning—that the United States was guilty of an atrocity; the cheers soldiers sent up when they heard the news of Hiroshima and Nagasaki became, in retrospect, grotesque. My point is not to argue the merits of the veterans' case, nor that of the curators who worked on the exhibit or of the historians who criticized it, only to illustrate the dangers of history with its potential for exploding myths and stripping the past of a comfortable inevitability. The Smithsonian exhibit seemed to rob many World War II veterans of their feelings of relief and righteousness, leaving their memories of V-J day painfully unanchored.

If, to this day, few Americans believe the Vietnam War was "necessary" (though they may disagree about why it was fought), most are confident that World War II was. The Smithsonian exhibit, from its position of official authority, threatened the certainty that that war, at least, was justly waged. The essential narrative of the "Good War" depended, to a considerable degree, on a clear delineation of evil versus goodness, barbarity versus civilization. By suggesting the possibility that the war ended in an American atrocity, the Smithsonian exhibit called into question the previously unquestionable virtue of the entire war, casting adrift one of the few remaining anchoring points of national mythology.

To put this another way, the fragmentation of national identity that occurred during the Vietnam War has proved retroactively contagious. The Vietnam syndrome has spread to engulf all of American history, most particularly its wars. "The Vietnam syndrome," the literary critic Avital Ronell has written, "is about losing a war and returning home without heroization, mythologization." In terms of history and identity, the Vietnam syndrome has the potential to demythologize all past military endeavors and so pose severe problems for the future. "One reason the Vietnam syndrome cannot be cured," Ronell observes, "is because it is not an illness. Rather, the illness resides in the drive to cure our mature resistance to war."[14] The traditional definition of national identity, in which America always fought fairly and honorably against evil aggression, probably can never be recovered, only replaced. The nature of that replacement is what the struggle over how to remember Vietnam—and the atomic bombings of Japan—has been all about.

The Vietnam War came to signal the end of national innocence. But the *Enola Gay* exhibit, like earlier controversial Smithsonian exhibits, projected this lack of innocence further back in American history. Of course, a consciousness that the nation is not, and has never been, an innocent abroad *could* serve as the foundation for a national identity that is a product of the United States' history rather than of its myths. Remembering Vietnam has been central to creating this possibility, and so too, it is now clear, is examining the way the "Good War" ended. Blocking such reexaminations is an effort, on the contrary, to preserve the sanctity of American wars past and future.

The Smithsonian has now presented the shiny fuselage of the *Enola Gay*, without context, without death, without reference to any meaning outside of itself. There was a Good War: it ended when Good Men flew a Good Plane and dropped a New Bomb on Bad People. What those bombs did had nothing to do with Us, only with Them: their atrocities, their aggressive war, the horror their resistance would have posed to an invading force. To question this is to bring the meaning of the bomb home to us, where it belongs.

8

THE VICTORS
AND THE VANQUISHED

• TOM ENGELHARDT •

Return to Pearl Harbor

On the morning of December 7, 1991, Americans turning on their TV sets could catch a lavish remembrance of the mobilizing morning of "infamy" that, fifty years earlier, had set their country on the path to its greatest military triumph. Nearly three thousand survivors of the surprise attack that, for Americans, began World War II had gathered that week at Pearl Harbor for various memorial events. Among those presiding over the ceremonies were President George Bush, whose torpedo bomber *Barbara* had been shot down over the Pacific in 1944, Colin Powell, chairman of the Joint Chiefs of Staff, and Richard Cheney, secretary of defense. Only months before, these three had presided over a far more massive celebration, a huge "welcome home" parade to honor the troops who had won a brief war against Iraq in the Persian Gulf.

In the week leading up to December 7, much media attention focused on Pearl Harbor. *Time* made it a cover story (though *Newsweek* failed to mention it). *Life* issued a Pearl Harbor "collector's edition" filled with nostalgic—and horrific—images: Bugs Bunny dressed up for war and the USS *Arizona* keeling over, *Esquire*'s "lusty pinup girls" and an American soldier floating face-down in the Hawaiian surf. CBS brought General H. Norman Schwarzkopf of Persian Gulf War fame together with correspondent Charles Kuralt to moderate a two-hour prime-time Pearl Harbor special. ABC had a special of its own, *Pearl Harbor: Two Hours That Changed the World* (coproduced with Japan's NHK TV); while on *Nightline* Ted Koppel conducted a two-part "town meeting" from Tokyo. NBC bought rerun rights to *Pearl*, a thirteen-year-old ABC miniseries, and ran it all week; PBS aired a documentary, *Pearl Harbor: Surprise and Remembrance*.

Government planning for the event culminated in the December 7 ceremonies, carried live on CNN. There, aging veterans, wearing white "Pearl Harbor Survivor" hats, spoke of their experiences or listened to the president, Cheney, and Powell speak for them. There were multigun salutes, military bands, jet flybys, and the navy's latest high-tech ships on display. President Bush delivered not one but two televised "day of infamy" speeches; the first at the memorial to the USS *Arizona*, sunk by Japanese torpedo bombers that long-ago day; the second (to the humiliation of the Japanese government) against the backdrop of the USS *Missouri*, on which surrender documents had been signed on September 2, 1945. In a voice choked with emotion, his eyes brimming with tears, he invoked an American "spirit" that fifty years earlier was "galvanized as never, ever before into a single-minded resolve that could produce only one thing, victory."

For the emotional president, these ceremonies represented the meeting of two streams of triumphalist feeling: that of the "Good War," the global victory which was to usher in an "American Century," and his own post–Cold War victory in Iraq, which was to banish from the land a "syndrome" of defeatism blamed on the Vietnam War and a post–World War II generation. "Once the war for Kuwait began," he said, "we pulled together . . . we were confident, and when it was over we rejoiced in exactly the same way that we did in 1945 . . . and what a feeling! Fifty years had passed but let me tell you—the American spirit is as young and fresh as ever."

Only eight months had passed since Iraq's crushing defeat, yet polls recorded precipitous declines in presidential popularity, indicating that victory in the Gulf was already fading from popular consciousness. Though the six-week war (in fact, a slaughter) had washed over the public in a flood of blood-pumping, all-channel TV coverage, it left almost no cultural residue. The most successful American military venture since the landing at Inchon, Korea, some forty years earlier would not produce a single movie or toy fighting figure, comic book or TV series. Despite instant bumper stickers ("Kick his ass, take his gas") and quickly remaindered General Schwarzkopf dolls, its power to renew an American culture of victory was already in question on that day of Pearl Harbor remembrance.

In subtle yet disturbing ways, a previously unassailable triumphalist tale of World War II in the Pacific also seemed embattled. What, after all, was the role of Japan, that former nation of barbaric jungle fighters and suicidal pilots, in these ceremonies? Was it still to be the enemy? Was it, as some implied, once again setting up a Greater East Asia Co-Prosperity Sphere, even if none of its soldiers had left its shores? Certainly, many veterans who violently opposed any Japanese presence on December 7 felt this way; that the *Missouri* was so visibly positioned in the harbor implied that others, higher up, had similar feelings.

Or was Japan to be our ally? Much administration attention went into removing any hint of anti-Japanese feeling from the ceremonies. Since inviting Japanese dignitaries, for example, seemed inconceivable, no foreign representatives were invited lest the absence be taken as an insult. In addition, the president went to great lengths to call for healing and reconciliation between the former enemies: "[On coming to Pearl Harbor,] I wondered if I would feel that intense hatred of the enemy all of us felt fifty years ago. . . . I have no rancor in my heart towards Germany and Japan. None at all."

Or was Japan even to take on the role of victim, because the United States in its moment of triumph had obliterated two Japanese cities with a terrifying new weapon of mass destruction? In the air was a "Japanese" suggestion that the president apologize for these acts. What could be more disturbing than the thought that an American president should consider apologizing for the weapon that George Bush and so many other veterans felt had shortened the war, saved untold American lives, and brought victory in the Pacific? Nonetheless, appearing on ABC's *This Week* on December 1, the president did address the matter with indignation. "War is hell, and it's a terrible thing. But there should be no apology requested. And that, in my view, is rank revisionism."[1]

No request for such an apology had, of course, come from the Japanese government. As the president's somewhat confused comment indicated, however, the real target of his anger was not the former enemy nation but a vaguer thing called "revisionism," a kind of sneak attack on an American narrative of triumph— though from where and by whom was unclear.

To tune in to any of the TV specials, however, was to sense immediately what the president was lashing out at. If the music in these programs still had the driving style of *Victory at Sea* and warships plowed heroically forward through the waves as in an old *March of Time* newsreel, it was now impossible to tell at a glance whether those ships were ours or theirs. If Pearl Harbor remained a horrifying sneak attack, there was now the American prewar oil squeeze on Japan to take into account. If Ted Koppel caught a Pearl Harbor survivor shedding a few tears while describing buddies trapped in a half-sunken ship, in the next set of images the viewer saw a teary Japanese woman on her tatami halfway around the world watching those American tears. One victim now potentially pointed the way to another, Pearl Harbor to Hiroshima, a mobilizing defeat not so much to sweet victory as to an unmentionable horror.

Perhaps the president could feel not only his personal victory over Saddam Hussein but that victory story of his youth slowly slipping away. In retelling it, he certainly had to incorporate unsettling new elements. He had to say something that should not have needed saying (that no apologies were in order for Hiroshima), while reassuring the Japanese that we, too, did not require anyone to apologize (a new strain in the narrative). Stranger yet, he found that apologies *were* in order, if not to the survivors of Hiroshima, then to the Japanese-American survivors of America's wartime internment camps. ("The whole thing is something that offends our own principles of justice, and it won't happen again.") He had to speak of previously ignored groups—women nurses, "Americans of Japanese ancestry." Although his multicultural tales were couched in the celebratory language of "the tradition of winning," as Colin Powell called it, implicitly they pointed the way to a darker tale about the war.

Fifty years after Pearl, the national story seemed at sea without a defining victory in sight. A president formed in World War II found himself on this December seventh still struggling with an almost two-decade-old defeat in Vietnam and a victory narrative that had to make uncomfortable space for an implicit critique of itself. "Now," the president said, gazing into a sea of empathetic, weathered faces, "we stand triumphant for a third time this century, this time in the wake of the cold war. As in 1919 and in 1945, we face no enemy menacing our security," he added with a kind of puzzlement, though he meant the statement to ring with affirmation. "And yet we stand here today on the site of a tragedy spawned by isolationism. . . . [T]o believe that turning our backs on the world would improve our lot here at home is to ignore the tragic lessons of the twentieth century."

Yet no affirmation that morning could have brought back the Enemy as an organizing principle. What, after all, could such ceremonies mean in a world where any enemy suitable for a global power's victory rites had disappeared? What could they mean when, for women and nonwhites demanding to be let into the narrative, the enemy was the oppressive former narrators?

If there was still a familiar story of American triumph that, for these veterans, Pearl Harbor called powerfully to mind, a continuous arc of victory that began with the first Indian wars and the Revolution, it was increasingly hard to avoid the thought that it seemed to end in 1945, not in 1991. Despite post-Vietnam battle triumphs in Grenada, Panama, and Iraq, despite the collapse of the Berlin Wall, everywhere there were more than hints that a post-1945 victory story was impossible to reconstruct.

The strains of making any such story bridge the Vietnam era showed. Although a new high-tech ship, the improbably named USS *Chosen* (after a military disaster in the Korean War), was given a float-by, there would be no USS *Tet*, nor would there be any but the briefest references to the war that from 1961 to 1975 had consumed the nation. "To those who have defended our country," the president said, "from the shores of Guadalcanal to the hills of Korea, and the jungles of Vietnam to the sands of Kuwait, I say this: We will always remember."

Whatever words were strung together, a disturbing blankness lay between the USS *Missouri* and Desert Storm, between victory and victory, between 1945 and 1991. Americans had once flocked to movie theaters or flicked on TVs to see a story of mobilizing defeats and glorious victories; now, when a new consensus tale tried to stitch in previously missing groups and fill empty narrative space, a consensus audience turned out to be lacking. Not one of the elaborate memorial TV programs was among those most watched that week. Americans were, by and large, not looking; so George Bush's new victory story, which should have taken Americans from Pearl Harbor safely across the years of defeat to the Persian Gulf, sank beneath Honolulu's water, unlike the *Arizona*, unmemorialized.

Four years later, when the moment arrived to celebrate the actual triumphs of 1945, voters had long since sent George Bush into retirement; and all that was left of the Gulf War was Gulf War syndrome, a mysterious complex of disease symptoms. That war's only lasting power lay in the story of a veteran who, in the postwar years, came to see the government as the Enemy and so allegedly bombed the Federal Building in Oklahoma City. With its Agent Orange–like illness and its vet-as-psycho, the Gulf War seemed, if anything, to replicate aspects of the Vietnam experience rather than expunge it from memory.

In 1995, presiding over the increasingly minimalist ceremonies of victory culture was a president who had avoided military service during the Vietnam era, a "draft dodger" who won office with only 43 percent of the vote. His main political opponent, Speaker of the House Newt Gingrich, had also avoided military service during that war, still talked of "radical revolution" in America, and blamed the "counterculture" of his own era for the nation's ills.

In that fiftieth year of triumph, not only was there no one to embody a consensus culture of victory, but no consensus story remained to be embodied. In fact, the only significant public commemoration of 1945 would collapse without ever coming into existence—an exhibit on the *Enola Gay*, the plane that dropped the atomic bomb on Hiroshima, planned for the Smithsonian National Air and Space Museum in Washington, D.C. After months of bitter charges and countercharges by veterans' groups, the Air Force Association, museum curators, congressional representatives, media commentators, antinuclear groups, and historians who had helped put the exhibition together, it proved impossible to mount a show in one of the nation's preeminent museums that combined the triumphant tale of the "Good War" and the horrifying one of nuclear extinction.

Just after noon on May 8, 1995, the fiftieth anniversary of V-E day, thousands of nostalgic English gathered in front of Buckingham Palace to greet the ninety-four-year-old queen mother (just as they had greeted her at that moment of victory half a century earlier), while others jitterbugged in London's Hyde Park as vintage World World II planes buzzed overhead. Meanwhile, leading political figures from France, Britain, Russia, Germany, and the United States (represented by Vice President Al Gore) followed rolling ceremonies from London to Paris to Berlin, pledging "to prevent a repetition of the European cataclysm." In Paris, French president François Mitterrand and guests reviewed 2,500 soldiers parading the flags of the wartime Allies and of postwar Germany down the Champs-Elysées; while in Berlin, a sparkling international assemblage of 1,400 guests marked the moment by listening to speeches and Beethoven's music in Berlin's elegant nineteenth-century theater, the Schauspielhaus.

In the United States, on the other hand, President Clinton visited Fort Myer, a military base close by Arlington National Cemetery, to review troops and give a commemorative speech before "an ethnic rainbow sampling of veterans who were on active duty on May 8, 1945." He spoke "admiringly, and a bit wist-fully," according to the *New York Times*, "of the common purpose that animated the nation half a century ago." Only then did the president depart for the public celebrations—that afternoon he boarded a plane for Moscow. In the United States, neither on V-E nor V-J day would there be significant public ceremonies to mark that best of all triumphant wars, whose story the young Bill Clinton, like the rest of his postwar generation, had undoubtedly seen, heard, and acted out "admiringly" endless times.[2]

But if no Americans were jitterbugging in the parks, if no president, historian, or veteran could offer a convincing consensus tale of what had happened to the United States since that bomb left the *Enola Gay*'s bomb bay, there was a new, minimalist kind of memorializing with which Americans seemed more at home.

Culture of Defeat (America)

Imagine now an American veteran who does not expect his story to be told, who has no reason to believe that anyone will memorialize his war, no less limn its glories. It is an August day in 1979, and Jan Scruggs, Jr., formerly with the 199th Light Infantry Brigade in Vietnam, spends part of it at the movies, where in his youth, heroic images of war, American style, were commonplace. He has gone to see *The Deer Hunter*, one of the first major films (the other two being *Apocalypse Now* and *Coming Home*) that attempt to capture aspects of his war—though as nightmare rather than glorious daydream. Of the three, only *The Deer Hunter* was considered prowar. It was, nonetheless, the most disturbingly un-American of the three, for it stripped war down to endless scenes of American victimization: of panicky retreats, defeats, and captivities, of losses that mobilized no one and from which no ceremonies of victory would ever come. In its final moments, it even managed to turn the song "God Bless America" into an anthem of despair.

According to Scruggs, that night, "alone in the kitchen with a bottle of whiskey," he experienced a "flashback" that might have been out of *The Deer Hunter*. In it, enemy mortars hit an ammunition truck, and he came running to help. "By instinct, he pulled the first-aid bandage from his trousers. Organs and pieces of bodies were scattered along the ground. They belonged to his friends. He had only one bandage. He stood and screamed for help." Feeling shaky, he remembered the faces of the dead and then their names. None of them, he realized, were held in any but memory of the most private sort. For them, there were to be no memorials; about them, no heroic stories the young might admire; of them, no public images that might rally a nation or comfort those who lived on. *This* was what it meant to live in a culture of defeat.

In the morning, Scruggs had a second vision, one that was, in some ways, more hallucinatory than the first. Its crazed quality tells us much about how far Americans had come from the dreams of '45. Scruggs told his worried wife, "I'm going to build a memorial to all the guys who served in Vietnam. It'll have the name of everyone killed."[3]

That the memorial Jan Scruggs envisioned one lonely night would be a multimillion-dollar reality three years later; that it would be built on the Washington Mall at the foot of the Lincoln Memorial without a cent of government money; that its design would come from the mind of Maya Ying Lin, a twenty-year-old Chinese-American art student at Yale University who knew next to nothing about Jan Scruggs's war; that its dedication would involve 150,000 Vietnam veterans gathering in the nation's capital for a "welcome home" parade; that politicians and military figures would turn out en masse; and that the Vietnam Wall, dedicated on Memorial Day 1982, would become Washington's second most popular memorial, a modern shrine, was remarkable.

More remarkable yet is what the wall reveals about the kind of memorializing available to Americans little more than a quarter of a century after bombardier Thomas Ferebee caught Hiroshima in the *Enola Gay*'s bombsight. From the moment the idea of a memorial appeared in Scruggs's mind, it was already, in story terms, so stripped down that only the most abstract of designs could have caught its spirit.

There was, in fact, almost no story of the Vietnam War that Americans could then agree upon. It's no small thing what a culture makes of a war, particularly a divisive one. In our Civil War, for instance, there was obviously no triumphalist story around which Northerners and Southerners could unite. There was, however, a minimalist path of interpretation—an enemyless one—available. This was to treat the war as a white family "tragedy" in need of rites of "reconciliation" rather than ceremonies of victory. For this, narratives of the conflict had to emphasize the bravery of opposing armies, the skills of their generals, and a sense that losers and winners alike had sacrificed heroically for high, if vague, principles. Much of this narrative would be worked out on the former battlefields of the war in rites that grew more elaborate with each passing decade as a "golden mist of American valor" descended on the war's memory.[4]

For the Vietnam War, too, national rites of reconciliation— from Oliver Stone's movie *Platoon* to Tim O'Brien's books to Jan Scruggs's memorial—would largely be led by the war's veterans. But what's more remarkable here is just how bare, how stripped down the postwar vision of Vietnam has been. Not only were the battlefields on which any reconciliation might have taken place ceded to a victorious and embargoed enemy, but Americans were in hopeless disarray about who exactly had been the true enemy in the war—the media, the antiwar movement, corrupt and venal South Vietnamese allies, a will-less public, or the U.S. government—and with whom any reconciliation might take place. Had the Vietnamese (seen mainly as stand-ins for the Chinese or the Russians) lost, they might have proved adequate for the role; but it was impossible for Americans to accept their resistance as an explanation for defeat.

What immediately followed the war was a kind of shocked silence hard to imagine now. When "Vietnam" returned in the Reagan years in movies, TV shows, comic books, novels, and memoirs, what was largely left of a war that, depending on your point of view, had gone on for from one to three decades was the 1965–68 period of American ground escalation, and its central character was the white foot soldier, the grunt, a beleaguered underdog on whom fell the war's tragedy. The catastrophic impact of airpower on South as well as North Vietnam was largely ignored, as were the secret wars in Laos and Cambodia, as was any discussion of the war's origins. Civilian war planners and military strategists were missing in action (and that previously common war-movie genre, the command film, was abandoned). The youthful antiwar movement could be found in cultural memory only in the image of unkempt hippies "spitting" on returning troops. The Vietnamese appeared, if at all, as passing plot devices in an American tragedy.

In *To Heal a Nation*, his book on the making of the Vietnam memorial, Jan Scruggs illustrates one approach to the loss of enemy. He discusses the Vietnam War without once mentioning the Vietnamese. Never had Americans brought such a reduced consensus to memorializing battle. Previously, commemoration of the dead took place within a tale of American progress that gave a larger meaning to each "sacrifice," subsuming private grief in the ever-developing glory of the nation. Take, for instance, Indianapolis's towering, three-hundred-foot-high Soldiers and Sailors Monument, dedicated in 1902. Constructed in part with funds from the state legislature, dedicated to Indiana's "ordinary soldiers," flanked by statues representing war and peace, and topped by the Goddess of Liberty, it was surrounded by smaller memorials to famous Indiana generals and governors associated with military successes from the Indian wars on. A similar monument in Cleveland had nine thousand names of local citizens who had served in the Civil War carved into its walls. Topped with the Goddess of Liberty and embellished with statues of its governors and generals, it, too, placed every American death, every bit of private grief and sorrow, within a stirring tale of advancing freedoms.[5]

Even where only the ordinary soldier was pictured, a larger story was assumed. Take the Marine Corps War Memorial in Washington, D.C., dedicated in 1954 to marine dead since 1775. A one-hundred-ton bronze monument, it replicated the famed Joe

Rosenthal photograph of six marines raising the flag on Iwo Jima's Mount Suribachi. That image—of the first highly publicized flag planted on Japanese territory—was, by then, iconic. As the Treasury Department put it, when launching a 1945 war bond drive based on the photograph, one of the flag raisers (who died on Iwo Jima) had given "everything he possessed, that, among other American ideals, Old Glory might be planted squarely between the eyes of a fanatical and cruel Japanese enemy." The image had been on the front pages of newspapers and the covers of magazines, on a stamp, and at the heart of the first successful combat film of the postwar period, John Wayne's *The Sands of Iwo Jima* (1949). That rising flag—in a memorial built on Iwo Jima, it sprouts directly from the V of victory—was "the victory flag," "the historic colors." In its unfurling lay a three-hundred-year tale of national triumph.[6]

After 1975, however, you could no longer approach a memorial to the war dead as if entering a glorious story in which individual sacrifice led to national enhancement. For a consensus shrine to the Vietnam War to exist, the war experience had to be stripped down to the names of the American dead, so that multiple audiences could bring their multiple, conflicting, often unarticulated feelings and stories to it in the privacy of their minds.

If a visit to the Vietnam Wall can be a deeply moving experience, it is of a new sort in our history. The memorial was created in a belief that, as Scruggs put it, "Vietnam veterans could be honored without commenting on America's Vietnam policy; the warrior could be separated from the war." It is, as everyone knows, a deeply abstract memorial, a giant black V in the earth that entombs both the V of victory of World War II and the peace-sign V of the Vietnam era. Fifty-eight thousand names of Americans who died in Vietnam, chronologically organized without a text, rise in a second upside-down V to a peak of American mortality and fall back to earth. In its shape, then, it is a double V, though unconnected to the Double V—of victory at home as well as abroad—that African Americans fought for in World War II. This is a double V without any specific public meaning.[7]

The granite from which the wall is made has been polished to reflectivity, and so, behind the incised names, you can see your-self. In this is a powerful image of the war as it now exists in public memory. You stand in front of it, seeing yourself in it, bringing your emotions, your stories, your loved ones, your history to it. It is bring-your-own history, as close as we can get to consensus today. The minute any more of anyone's version of a story is incorporated, disaggregation threatens to set in. This is what it means to live in an American culture of defeat.

But the wall tells us more about the state of public memory today, for the V of the reduced consensus does not stand alone on the Mall. Even as it was being constructed, its embrace of defeat, of storylessness, unnerved conservative veterans, congresspeople, members of the Reagan administration, and Ross Perot, who had funded the memorial's design competition. Desiring a heroic memorial closer to the Iwo Jima image—all white and displaying a prominent flag—they attacked Maya Lin's design as a "mass grave," a "black gash of shame." They also effectively blocked a construction permit from the Interior Department until agreement was reached that a "heroic statue" and an American flag would be placed near Maya Lin's wall.[8]

As a result, at a discrete distance, opposite one point of the V, now stands a green-hued statue of three GIs. They face the wall, each appearing to take it in with a dazed stare as if their mini-patrol had just stumbled into a clearing and spotted this remark-able, alien object. The central figure is obviously a blond-haired white man; close behind him stand an African American and a figure of indeterminate ethnicity (perhaps Puerto Rican or Italian). Every crease in their uniforms, every detail of grenade, rifle, canteen, every bulging vein is in place. Near them flies an enor-mous American flag on a sixty-foot pole, one that these blitzed-out infantrymen could never have raised. It's as if some ravaged version of the famed Mount Suribachi statue were indeed here—the raisers, the flag, victory itself—just beyond the aura of the wall, demobilized.

In the post-Vietnam era, even traditionalists found themselves unable to imagine much beyond Vietnam's reduced narrative consensus. No longer could a general in triumph or a Custer in defeat urge the nation toward greater glory. From the former ranks of the soldier-citizen, from the democratic patrol of any old World War II film with its mix of ethnic, racial, and religious types, only a confused fragment remains; just three lost soldiers, exhausted participants in the American ground war. (What the statue most resembles, in truth, is a piece from a 1950s plastic battle playset for children.)

Opposite the other point of the V is a second statue. Here, three nurses await a medivac unit to helicopter out a wounded soldier. A white nurse succors him in her arms, pietà-like, and looks out toward the wall. A black nurse, facing away, looks up awaiting the chopper. Another nurse, white like the first, kneels, head bowed, holding the wounded man's helmet. Unlike the grunts, the women are bonded more to others than to each other. This statue represents in however weakened a form the new multicultural story in which the patrol in defense of democracy doesn't fuse or unite, but each category of variety—in this case, gender—demands its own unique, celebratory place.

So, here we have two statues and a flag, pods of leftoutness, old and new; each a demand and a complaint, each representing a mix of unarticulated emotions. Each has landed in the neighborhood of bring-your-own history. Similar pods of celebration, upset, and confusion could be endlessly multiplied, turning the environs of what had once been *the* American story into a marketplace of fragmentary stories, each deeply meaningful to some but meaningless or repugnant to others. At the center, however, where the V for victory once was, is now entombed victory culture—and on its walls, in grief and pain, are the names of the defeated, a mantra of loss, a healing icon dedicated to the incomprehensibility of defeat.[9]

If the Vietnam Wall was the first official memorial to American defeat and, in 1982, Vietnam still seemed its birthplace, in June 1995, a second (this time involuntary) memorial to defeat would be created at the Smithsonian's National Air and Space Museum. There, in halls that celebrated the glories of airpower and of victory culture, that exhibited as technological wonders the V-1 and V-2 rockets of the defeated Germans, Americans could experience in the fuselage of the *Enola Gay* another kind of Vietnam Wall, connected to quite a different war.

Culture of Defeat (Japan)

In December 1991, while George Bush struggled to re-create a narrative that would obliterate defeat in Vietnam from American memory, and more than a year before the Smithsonian's curators began considering a fiftieth-anniversary, end-of-the-war exhibit around the *Enola Gay*, Haruko Taya Cook and Ted Cook, wife and husband, former Japanese TV producer and American military historian, were in the third year of their exploration of the Japanese experience in World War II. For *Japan at War*, a planned oral history of the war from the Japanese perspective, they had, by then, perfected techniques for meeting another culture's Jan Scruggs. They found themselves taking on the previously unfamiliar roles of detective and undercover agent to ferret out hidden memories of a lost war that did not even have a generally accepted name or publicly agreed upon ways of being told. They followed whispered clues of introduction, met furtively with anxious subjects in "the most impersonal or deserted of public settings . . . benches in the corners of busy railroad stations, back booths of underpopulated coffee shops, . . . paths separating flooded rice fields."

"People were often at a total loss for where to begin their stories," they later reported, "since the war in Japan has no generally accepted beginning point." Interviewees commonly emphasized that they were speaking "only for themselves." Once they started talking, however, a lifetime of repressed experience would pour out. "Almost every interview involved incredible outbursts of emotion. Tears were a commonplace. . . . Voices choked. Bodies were convulsed with sobs. There were actual groans of pain and anguish, even the literal grinding of teeth."

The Cooks soon realized that they had entered a surprisingly shapeless narrative terrain. For Americans, the story of the war in the Pacific had a specific, agreed-upon form. It moved from a mobilizing defeat to assured victory; from the enemy's savagery and our humiliation at Pearl Harbor, Guam, and Bataan to their continued savagery at Iwo Jima and Okinawa, and our justified vengeance in the skies over Japan (followed by our beneficence in the postwar era). It even had a direction, taking us from defeat in the south and east island-hopping north and west to ultimate triumph in Tokyo Bay. Its collective form had been repeated untold thousands of times in the press and magazines, in scholarly journals and pulp fiction, in endless movies and TV shows, in arcade games and children's collective war play. Into this narrative form, any American veteran of the Pacific campaigns could slot his own memories of his war years.

For the Japanese, the Cooks discovered, memories of 1941–42, that brief year of victories, were largely subsumed in "the overwhelming defeats that came later. . . . [In] Japanese memories of the Pacific War . . . the individual wanders through endless dreamlike scenes of degradation, horror, and death, a shapeless nightmare of plotless slaughter. This formless narrative of defeat—of soldiers overwhelmed in battle, or girls escaping a Tokyo air raid, of a student nurse's living nightmare in Okinawa, or a desperate mother's flight for her life in Manchuria—is how they tend to see their war."[10]

More than impending victory or defeat affected the attitude each society brought to its war story. In 1941, Americans were already living in a culture of triumph. As they saw it, from the earliest days of their history, they simply had not lost, could not lose (except, as in the Civil War, to other Americans); certainly not to a savage and treacherous nonwhite people. The fate of such a people was unquestioned, whatever the immediate situation. That Americans were primed for victory was evident even in the days after Pearl Harbor when, from the president on down, they reassured each other of Japan's certain defeat.[11]

For the Japanese, having long experienced the threat of Western encroachment and seen the dominating, even crushing power of the West elsewhere in Asia, a certain desperate self-doubt had been a propelling emotion since the first moments of the Meiji Restoration in 1868. Even in January 1941, with the American fleet seemingly crushed, the British, Dutch, and French humiliated on land and sea, and most of South and Southeast Asia under their control, they generally seem to have feared the worst, not assumed the best; to have felt relief rather than elation; to have doubted the long-term viability of a war against the United States, Britain, and possibly Russia.

From 1943 on, as their military suffered a series of catastrophes in battle, the Japanese, at home and in the occupied lands, saw their tenuous, government-inspired cult of glorious triumph imperceptibly transformed into a cult of triumphalist death. True, as late as 1945, young children could march in schoolyards, imagining themselves to be victorious "little soldiers of the emperor." "It was thrilling," Funato Kazuyo would recall, "carrying out crisp moves to the piercing commands of the physical education teacher." But as U.S. bombing raids intensified, so did rituals of defense and implicit defeat. "We also had air-defense drills. We put on our special fire helmets and, holding our school bags, we hid under the desks in our classroom. You covered your ears with your thumbs and with the remaining four fingers covered your eyes. They said our eyes would pop out and our eardrums burst if we didn't. We also practiced putting out fires by bucket relay."

In such drills, a generation of American children, growing up in the postwar years, might have recognized certain commonalities. They, too, found themselves in a culture saturated with images of victory, but often viewed official triumphalism from under their desks, hands pathetically over heads, while adults warned them that, at some not too distant moment, their eyes might pop out and their ears burst. But if both groups "ducked and covered," practicing a stance of defeat in a world where adults, hinting at monstrous futures, proclaimed their societies invincible, for Funato Kazuyo that implied future arrived all too soon.

On the night of March 9, 1945, hundreds of B-29s, armed

with incendiary bombs, carried out the first massive, low-level firebombing attack on a Japanese city. One hundred thousand or more residents of Tokyo are estimated to have died that night as half of Tokyo burned to the ground. Funato Kazuyo, fleeing in confusion through the firestorm, saw her father, mother, brothers, and a sister swept one by one into the flames and smoke. Her baby brother was burned off her mother's back. She watched her younger sister's protective headgear catch fire and her hands burn raw. Flattened in a ditch, her sister beside her screaming, "It's hot, hot!" she knew exactly where she was. "We were in hell. All the houses were burning, debris raining down on us."[12]

She was among millions of Japanese in hell. For them, defeat was the most cataclysmic and personal of experiences. Life as it had been was now, whether in the streets of Tokyo or the jungles of New Guinea, unrecognizable. For many, what was happening proved so overwhelming, so unprecedented, that it could not be assimilated into any previous framework of experience. In a society that had offered only a promise of ultimate victory or a kind of glorious national annihilation, there was no conventional way to organize, incorporate, or even account for simple survival. Amid the rubble, defeat could only be absorbed in shame as a private agony, every personal hell taking on its own unexpressed shape.

For the citizens of Hiroshima and Nagasaki on August 6 and 9, 1945, there would not even be the waves of bombers, ghostly as silvery insects, to explain their fate; only, possibly, the sound of a single B-29 and then the utter collapse of a world. Here was a defeat so utterly, unbelievably crushing that its scope could not be revealed even to the citizens of the victor nation; yet here, for the first time in three years of defeat, was a place of loss from which a new narrative structure for telling of survival under inconceivable circumstances would someday be organized.

Those who had experienced the obliterating horror of the mightiest air raid in history compressed into a single bomb carried by a single plane were, however privately, now victims. The past with its imperial promises and threats had been swept away as if by a natural cataclysm. A new history—of a defeated nation, a nation of victims—began on August 6, 1945, under the mushroom cloud. Hiroshima's ground zero would be the point of origin for a new era, for a tale of a new nation and a new people (even if still presided over by the emperor in whose name the war had been fought), and ultimately, a rise to a new kind of power. Schoolchildren would be taught a new history of their land, one that would, in essence, end before the previous war began. Movies from the war years would be locked away; nowhere in Japan would screen audiences see heroic Japanese soldiers advancing into battle. At best, in the era to come, fighting would take place in distant feudal times or, defensively, against fantastic creatures of the imagination like Godzilla, who embodied the depersonalized cataclysm so many Japanese felt they had recently experienced.

When Haruko Taya and Ted Cook interviewed survivors of the A-bombs, they noticed that the landmarkless terrain of Japan's failed war story gave way to a new kind of structure in which all experience was again measurable in time and space. As John Whittier Treat has commented in *Writing Ground Zero*, no A-bomb survivor's account would be complete without note of precisely where he or she was "on the morning of August 6 or 9, 1945. This 'where' is expressed in a measure of how far from, or close to, ground zero the writer stood or sat or slept."[13]

History ended and began at ground zero, the place/moment of annihilating destruction. The invasion of China, the Rape of Nanking, the pillaging of South Asia, the brutal mistreatment of Allied POWs—all the horrors an aggressor nation could commit—and all the horrors the Japanese came to experience in those years of defeat would be enshrined in no war museum, only in private memory; in walls of pictures, in alcoves where model ships and planes rested, in the memorabilia of the dead shrouded in the secret nooks and crannies of people's houses.

For Japan, August 1945 came to represent a disjuncture in consciousness. The many continuities between pre-1945 and post-1945 Japan that would make the postoccupation economic "miracle" less than miraculous were largely ignored. In a humiliated country, at a moment of total defeat, there was good reason not to remember "the dark valley" of the prewar and war years in favor of "the new Japan." There was good reason to see August 1945 as the ultimate dividing line in history.[14]

For the victorious Americans, on the other hand, the crucial thing was to pass from August 5 to August 7 as if nothing but the expected victory had occurred.

Beginnings and Endings

Imagine a bomber, the latest development in aviation, the most powerful plane ever built. Named the B-29 Superfortress, it is seventy thousand pounds of power. With a wingspan of 141 feet, four engines of 2,200 horsepower, capable of flying an eleven-man crew 350 miles per hour carrying up to twenty thousand pounds of bombs, it is the first intercontinental bomber. It can undertake a previously unheard of four-thousand-mile mission.[15]

On an August day in 1945, this particular B-29 sits on a runway on the island of Tinian, recently captured from an implacable foe, stragglers from whose defeated army still haunt the island's wastes. It has taken the building of a virtual city in an American desert, two billion dollars in government funds, and years of intense work by an army of scientists and technicians to create, produce, and deliver a single bomb to this plane's specially reconfigured bomb bay. The new weapon represents the latest development in the long history of destructive technology. The way for its use has been paved by a different sort of evolution in warfare—the increasing targeting of civilian populations from the air, whose history extends from German airship bombings of London (1915) by way of Guernica (1937), Shanghai (1937), and Coventry (1940) to the firebombings of Dresden and Tokyo. It even has a history in the human imagination, where for decades writers (among others) have dreamed of the unparalleled release of previously unknown forms of energy for military purposes.[16]

The journalists, movie cameramen, and photographers swarming around the bomber at the behest of the Department of War are uncertain of exactly what they are recording, but sense that they may be close to the final moments in a global war already brought to its triumphant conclusion in Europe. Colonel Paul W. Tibbets, Jr., the pilot, who waves from the plane's cockpit as the photographers snap pictures, has spent the last two years commanding the 509th Composite Group, which he has been training to fly this mission. He has been assured in secret briefings that it will help end the grim war in the Pacific expeditiously.

Thirty years old, with an exemplary record in the European theater, with almost two thousand men under his command, he sits in his plane at a culminating moment in a much desired life trajectory. From youth he has dreamed of being an air force pilot. It was over his father's bitter objections but with his mother's deeply appreciated support that he first joined the Army Air Forces. To honor her role in his life, the previous night he had her name—Enola Gay—painted in large letters underneath the pilot's window.[17]

Although we can't know what he is imagining, he is certainly well aware of the honor roll of airpower pioneers from "Billy" Mitchell to James H. "Jimmy" Doolittle, the first American to take bombers over Japan, whom he might soon join. They are his history, as are the heroes of the Argonne, San Juan Hill, Gettysburg, Bunker Hill, and the frontier wars against the Indians, who brought his nation to this possible moment of ultimate triumph. He has every reason to believe that if success is his, his plane, his crew, his exploits will someday be part of a glorious story of the air force, as well as of a larger national tale of triumph that his children and theirs will invoke with pride.

As the *Enola Gay* lifts off from the specially lengthened runway built for it on Tinian, it carries not only a bomb weighing more than four metric tons but the full weight of American optimism, of the sense that life has progressed for untold millions of years from the primordial soup to this moment; that tens of thousands of years of development have taken Man from the discovery of fire to the mastery of flight; that hundreds of years of expanding freedoms have led from the Magna Carta to a prospective UN charter; and that from the first tentative landings on a new continent, more than three hundred years of American history have led to this potential prelude to an American century. So the *Enola Gay* heads toward Japan with a bomb called Little Boy that must be armed in midair lest it accidentally incinerate the island of Tinian. Its delivery, as the names of plane and bomb suggest, will be imagined as a kind of birthing, for in this act are imagined not just happy endings but glorious beginnings.

Over Hiroshima, the weather is good. Bombardier Thomas Ferebee catches the city in the crosshairs of his Norden bombsight and with the flick of a switch turns the job over to the bombsight computer. Below is the mission's target, the Aioli ("Live Together") Bridge in central Hiroshima. At 8:15 A.M., Hiroshima time, the bomb falls clear of the plane "inscribed with autographs and messages, some of them obscene. [One message reads,] 'Greetings to the Emperor from the men of the *Indianapolis.*'" These scribblings are, in effect, the last human acts of the preatomic age.

Little Boy detonates 580 meters above the city center, creating an instant fireball of several hundred thousand degrees centigrade. Tibbets has taken the *Enola Gay* through a long-practiced sheer turn and is over eleven miles away when, as he put it, "a bright light filled the plane [and] . . . the whole airplane cracked and crinkled from the blast. I yelled 'Flak!' thinking a heavy gun battery had found us." Behind them, the city disappears into a roiling mass of smoke and fire. "If you want to describe it as something you are familiar with, a pot of boiling black oil," reported "Dutch" Van Kirk, the plane's navigator. "I thought: Thank God the war is over and I don't have to get shot at any more. I can go home."[18]

Leaving Hiroshima, in Tibbets's phrase, "hidden by that awful cloud," the *Enola Gay* heads for home. At this point in a war film, the phrase "The End" might appear on screen and the *Enola Gay* be left to soar into celebratory history. Yet Mrs. Gay's boys did not fare well flying into that cultural sunset, for the blinding light from Hiroshima illuminated The End in a new way.

When Little Boy exploded, an American culture of victory was suddenly fused to an incipient culture of defeat. While Tibbets imagined national triumph from above "that awful cloud," within days large numbers of Americans began imagining their annihilation, The End, under it. It was there, at that largely unacknowledged disjuncture in history, that the American frontier—the one that remained deep in the national imagination—truly closed.

What Tibbets himself found beyond the mushroom cloud was a kind of horrifying Oz. It was as if, in flying the *Enola Gay* away from that cloud, he had also piloted it out of victory culture, out of war American style, and into some only superficially familiar alternate universe (as in a plot from *The Twilight Zone*, that popular TV series of the next decade). Among the hundreds of films that Hollywood would make about World War II, only two would include the most famous B-29 of all time: *The Beginning or the End* (1947), a semiofficial explanation of the Hiroshima bombing, vetted by President Truman and his advisers; and *Above and Beyond* (1953), about Tibbets himself. (He was hired as a consultant on the film.) Although *Above and Beyond* was also a semiofficial effort, meant to glorify the A-bomb pilots and effusive in its "gratitude" for the Defense Department's "wholehearted cooperation," it was riddled with anxiety. ("I think mostly I'm scared for my sons, for their world," the eternally tense movie Tibbets says in a letter to his mother the night before the mission. "I'm scared of what can happen if this thing we're unleashing tomorrow doesn't stop this war and all others.")

Each of these films failed as part of an old or the beginning of a new film genre, and each failed to draw a significant audience eager to see the war end again in such a triumph. Both lacked emotional payoff, partly because neither could put onscreen the moment that was always the end for the enemy and the beginning for us. Hollywood simply could not show the enemy dropping in their tens of thousands. That scene of battle triumph, so essential to the American war film, would have been in this case an unviewable atrocity. To put it onscreen in whatever minimal form would have meant acknowledging that something new and terrifying had occurred; and yet, not to be able to show the winning weapon at work destroying people even President Truman had called "beasts" was implicitly a defeat. Not to show it was to imply that The End was not the beginning of something triumphantly American and hopeful.[19]

In the coming years, the *Enola Gay* and its weapon would indeed appear onscreen and the payoff would be enormous. First, though, they had to mutate into all sorts of spaceships and horrifying rays or radioactive monsters and migrate from the war film that couldn't be made into the horror and science-fiction genres. Those films moved under the mushroom cloud in various futuristic settings, where all sorts of monstrous beings and alien creatures did to our cities and towns what we had done to Hiroshima and Nagasaki; and crowds of Americans onscreen screamed and fled and were crushed or mangled, burned or consumed. Finally, in the late 1950s and early 1960s, in films like *On the Beach* and *Dr. Strangelove*, updated versions of the *Enola Gay* flew back into the war film, but one in which the enemy was us and the missile or plane armed with the winning weapon was on what could only be a final mission for us as well as for them.

Almost nowhere in all those years when, hounded by curious interviewers, Colonel (later Brigadier General) Paul Tibbets began to avoid publicity and sometimes even traveled pseudonymously could he find an image of his mission of which he might be proud. John Wayne never piloted the *Enola Gay* into battle heaven, and unlike Audie Murphy, Tibbets was never invited to play himself onscreen. The only time he tried, off screen, proved an embarrassment. "In 1976, he reenacted the Hiroshima mission at an air show in Texas, with a smoke bomb set off to simulate a mushroom cloud, and made plans for a repeat performance the following year until pressure from the State Department (there had been a storm of Japanese protest) caused its cancellation." The only museum that told his story was in the hands of the former enemy who portrayed it as a horror almost beyond the bounds of meaning.[20]

And what of the *Enola Gay* itself? Refitted for but not used in the 1946 Bikini atomic tests, it was stored at an Arizona air base until, on July 3, 1949, Tibbets flew it to Park Ridge, Illinois, and turned it over to representatives of the Smithsonian Institution. In 1953, it came to rest at Andrews Air Force Base near Washington, D.C., where in 1960–61 it was disassembled and put into a deeper form of storage.[21]

The View from Under the Desk

Two nations: one vanquished, its military in a state of disintegration, its cities in ashes, its people starving, its land occupied; the other victorious, its military ascendant, its cities bustling, its people dreaming of homes equipped with fantastic new machines—electric ranges, automated washing machines, television sets—its soldiers the beneficent occupiers of their former enemy's land. The people of the first nation feel they have stepped across an invisible line, that the world has been turned inside out: their flag is an object of shame; their school textbooks rewritten; the paintings, movies, plays, books, poems of recent years have vanished. The people of the second nation feel that they have fulfilled their destiny. Their flag flies proudly; their school textbooks speak of ever greater glories; their culture flourishes as never before; their economy, already booming during wartime, is now supplying the products of peace (and war) to a ravaged world. The Japanese and the Americans, the vanquished and the victors, are two peoples who could not be in more dissimilar situations, though the victors plan to remedy that. Through their occupation, they expect to introduce much of the American way of life—democracy, trade unions, freedom of the press, equality for women—remaking the vanquished in the image of the victor.

There is a further dissimilarity between the two nations, but it is a less expectable one. It is not the vanquished but the victors who would like to forget—to suppress, in fact—the evidence of what their victory weapon with its "new and revolutionary increase in destruction" (as President Truman's initial announcement put it) did to the defeated, of what sorts of death, what sorts of obliteration it offered. That suppression begins in the land of the vanquished, where photos and films of the dead, the dying, and those who survived, along with information about the nature of the human destruction at Hiroshima and Nagasaki, disappear into the inaccessible files of the occupation in Japan or into classified files in Washington.[22]

This suppression is not, however, limited to the land of the vanquished. In the land of the victors, too, the weapon's effects disappear under a cloud of secrecy. Not only are the actual cities of Hiroshima and Nagasaki declared off-limits to American reporters, but evidence of atomic dangers in the United States—where the weaponry was, and continues to be, tested—is carefully kept from the public. With the war over, President Truman requests in the name of "the highest national security" that the media consult the War Department before writing about most nuclear matters. Even the nicknames of the two bombs dropped on Japan, Little Boy and Fat Man, remain classified information.

At least until the late 1960s, images of the human suffering at Hiroshima and Nagasaki are almost impossible to find in the United States. What remains visible, other than images of the mushroom cloud, are photographs of the physical destruction of the two cities; moonscapes that look little different from those of a Berlin or Tokyo pulverized by more conventional arms. If the occupiers have anything to do with it, there will be no "revolutionary" scenes, no carbonized lunch boxes, no keloid-disfigured faces or bodies. This despite the fact that most Americans seem unconflicted about the use of the bomb against Japan and a significant minority only wish more such bombs had been used before the war ended. Nor is it a matter of public squeamishness. In 1945, after all, large numbers of Americans saw revolutionary scenes of another kind, unparalleled images of human suffering in the first newsreels released of the liberation of the Nazi death camps.[23]

Why, then, hide the effects of the atomic bomb? Why suppress images of the ultimate American victory? Because to see what happened to tens of thousands of people in that single instant potentially means to imagine the obliteration of differences between two radically dissimilar nations otherwise experiencing radically dissimilar fates. To look at that in one of the few lands on earth hardly touched by the world war is to experience not the glories of immediate victory but the horrors of possible future defeat; to imagine even newer and more revolutionary weapons that might soon be able to destroy in days, or minutes, what it had taken years of global war to do. Not just cities but whole nations might be turned almost instantaneously into rubble. Under that cloud, victory, atrocity, and defeat, the righteous warriors and their savage foes threaten to become one.

But not to look provides only partial protection. Even with just the carefully crafted information on Hiroshima released by the government the day of the bombing, many Americans quickly grasp the implications of the new weapon. The power to annihilate the world, however concealed, turns Americans toward an obsessive concern with endings. What cannot be seen is transmuted into a riot of imaginings about ever more terrifying finalities. Long before the possibility exists for any nation but theirs to launch devastating atomic attacks, they begin to imagine themselves, their cities, their nation, the world obliterated.

From that first announcement until perhaps sometime in 1947, there is a brief historical moment when a sizable number of Americans seem almost willing to stare defeat in the face. As has been shown by Paul Boyer in *By the Bomb's Early Light*, Spencer Weart in *Nuclear Fear*, and most recently Robert Jay Lifton and Greg Mitchell in *Hiroshima in America*, without even a clear sense of what happened at Hiroshima, Americans immediately begin to reconceive themselves as potential victims under the bomb. These first fantasies about a post-Hiroshima world have all the trappings of "reality," even if it is a reality whose time has not yet come. In the scenarios of destruction that populate newspapers, magazines, radio shows, and private imaginations, millions of people in America and tens of millions elsewhere die horribly in a few days of "battle." Though Americans often "win" the imagined war, the accompanying images of destruction in the homeland are no different than those that might have accompanied defeat.[24]

The idea of a Pyrrhic victory is hardly new, but in the past it always meant calamitous losses suffered by the victors in the course of their putative triumph. Here is a Pyrrhic victory in which the victors claim that their weapon has saved them from such calamitous losses; that is, from an invasion of the Japanese home islands. Here is a Pyrrhic victory in which the victors appear stronger, militarily and economically, afterward. Is it any wonder that the citizens of the richest, most successful country in a largely devastated world cannot accept what their imaginations, their anxieties are telling them: that it is a kind of defeat they are experiencing?

As it happened, after 1947, any sense of that defeat went underground. Yet in that underground, half-conscious fears multiplied, taking on ever stranger forms. The "realistic" images of American victimization that arose spontaneously in August 1945 did not, of course, disappear. In 1953, for instance, a top-secret film, *Operation IVY* (the code name for the H-bomb test), was "screened in the White House . . . for the Cabinet, the Joint Chiefs of Staff, and others. . . . the few dozen people on that level were the entire audience for whom the Air Force and Atomic Energy Commission had made the film. Nobody who saw it was likely to forget its picture of an entire atoll vanished into a crater, or the fireball with a dwarfed New York City skyline printed across it in black silhouette."

But as ever more powerful nuclear weapons and delivery systems proliferated in an atmosphere of heightened secrecy, even leading politicians of the wartime generation began imagining ever more lurid "realistic" endings to the human condition. In 1956, for example, Senator Estes Kefauver, then running for the Democratic party's presidential nomination, suggested that hydrogen bombs could "right now blow the earth off its axis by 16 degrees."[25]

In private dreams and popular culture, a lack of information, of "realism," only led to a splurge of apocalyptic fantasies in which ever more bizarre mutant futures were imagined, all of which put a deformed ending to anything resembling an American tale. In the 1950s, in films like *When Worlds Collide* and *This Island Earth,* the destruction of whole planets, sometimes ours, became a visual commonplace. In private, in silence, in a world in which most of the time few people were conscious that the bomb was even on their minds, fears and anxieties grew and a sense of the future narrowed.

If Americans, like their defeated foe, deeply registered the disjuncture of that moment in August 1945; if, briefly, they looked into the future and saw themselves defeated, that moment was soon overridden by a rising tide of prosperity (as well as the rise of a Communist superenemy). The remarkable economic boom that made the United States the world's powerhouse of goods seemed to confirm the ineluctable nature of the tide of victory that had swept Americans from 1645 to 1945. Was it not logical, then, to see in the new houses, cars, and goods the fruits of victory?

The apparent smoothness of the passage from victorious war to triumphant peace, plus sole possession of nuclear power, led Americans to accept a story of unbroken continuity in which August 6 became just another marker on the path to an increasingly American world. Yet the shock of that "birthing" moment opened fissures in the society through which bubbled up a despairing sense that The End, an end previously unimaginable, was in sight.

What might have happened if that moment of victory-as-defeat had been followed by the return of prewar economic bad times remains in the realm of speculation. As polls showed, however, such an economic possibility had been deeply feared by many Americans during the war. Had nuclear fears fused with the economic ones of a people demobilizing into a crumbling economy, Americans might have drawn quite different mental maps in the postwar world.[26]

As it turned out, the two former enemy nations, Japan and the United States, chose diametrically opposite and extreme ways of absorbing August 1945. For the Japanese, the bomb arrived out of historically empty skies and the modern moment began at ground zero. Left behind was any public confrontation with the war itself or with war responsibility. For a generation of Japanese looking forward out of the rubble, August 1945 represented a rupture in history. For a generation of Americans looking back with pride, the disjunctive nature of that moment was buried and history continued to flow ever upward. In this, a generation in both countries left behind the possibility of taking true responsibility for the world they had helped to create, for the actual world in which they now found themselves living.

Each approach represented a kind of blindness, a kind of willed amnesia. Each culture could have used an infusion from the other's story. Certainly, in the United States, jarring images of defeat and a sense of futurelessness, however unacknowledged, were never far from consciousness. If we do not know what Eisenhower's cabinet made of *Operation IVY*, those men had still less of a sense of what their children made of it (for it was, finally, released to the public). For those who fought or lived through the war, what it was like to be born into a secret culture of despair amid vistas of wealth and seeming promise was too unsettling to grasp.

Their children would huddle under their desks with sirens howling and learn to live with triumphalist despair. Amid the stories of their fathers' triumphs, imagining ashes where there were burgeoning suburbs, they would try to adjust to, find thrills and excitement in this strange new world, while at night, in their dreams, the mushroom cloud would rise again and again. Yet most of the wartime generation could never come to grips with either the final acts of the Pacific war or the postwar view from under those desks.

For more than two decades, the United States was a triumphalist society that lacked a defeat to make tangible its deepest despairs and anxieties. When that defeat finally came, in Vietnam, it provided a kind of confusing relief, for it gave Americans a chance to release long-suppressed doubts and fears. The defeat, though, was blamed on the generation that grew up under those desks. The young, in a collapsing army in Vietnam or protesting at home, "blowing their minds" with drugs or fleeing the city for "the land" as though the bomb had already fallen, were seen (and sometimes defiantly saw themselves) as the losers, the betrayers of an American dream.

Happy Fiftieth, Mrs. Gay!

In December 1984, Smithsonian technicians began restoration work on the *Enola Gay*. Eleven years and forty-four thousand staff-hours later the plane had been returned to its state on the day it took off from Tinian, a state that would "allow [its] preservation . . . for decades and even centuries into the future." Finally, forty-nine years after its mission was completed, the *Enola Gay*, burnished to a ceremonial glow, was ready for a celebratory fate.[27]

Retired Brigadier General Paul Tibbets was still waiting for his story to be told. "I suggest," he said, "that few, if any of the articles, books, films or reports have ever attempted to discuss the missions of August 6th and August 9th *in the context of the times*. Simply stated, the *Enola Gay* and the 509th Composite Bomb Group have been denied a historically correct representation to the public. Most writers have looked to the ashes of Hiroshima and Nagasaki to find answers for the use of those atomic weapons. The real answers lay in thousands of graves from Pearl Harbor around the world to Normandy and back again." Nor, in his own eyes, had he, a man who was, "to the best of my ability, doing what I could to bring the war to a victorious conclusion," been portrayed in a reasonable fashion. "Too many have labeled the atomic missions as war crimes in an effort to force their politics and their opinions on the American public and to damn military history."

These words came from a bitter statement Tibbets made in June 1994 amid a growing controversy over the *Enola Gay* show then being planned at the National Air and Space Museum. Since its establishment, this museum on the Washington Mall has been regarded as a "temple" to aviation history and technology as well as a testament to the air force, a service without battlefields on which to build its memorials. It was the obvious place for Tibbets to expect his plane, his mission, himself to receive their "historically correct representation." The gleaming plane seemed well prepared for such a role. After all, a plane appropriate to a show focused on the "ashes" would have been left in its beaten-up state, a survivor of its own horrors.

But when Tibbets considered the planned show—and media and congressional reactions to it—he once again failed to recognize his mission. Despite the script's respectful and lengthy treatment of the 509th and of Tibbets, labeled a "hero," he saw betrayal and defeat. In this, though for reasons he only half grasped, he was not wrong. In a tone commensurate with fifty years of disappointment, he denounced the show-to-be as a "package of insults." As for the partial plane to be displayed there, he commented, "Resting on an arrangement that will be shaped like a cradle, the sixty-some feet of fuselage and forward bomb bay—without wings, engines and propellers, landing gear and tail assembly—makes for an awesome sight. If nothing else, it will engender the aura of evil in which the airplane is being cast."

In his statement, one can hear not just anger but an old man's plea to be allowed—finally—to pilot the *Enola Gay* out of the mushroom cloud of destruction that had dogged him for most of his life; out of a world in which his story had the power to scare a generation of children into nightmarish sleep, not encourage them to dreams of glory; and into the one that he (and many others) believed America deserved. "What about the airmen who flew those strikes and lost their lives?" he asked. "And those who survived. Are they to be denied recognition for their efforts? Something is wrong with this scenario. . . . [L]et me urge reconsideration and let the exhibition of the *Enola Gay* accurately reflect the American spirit and victory of August 1945. . . . The million or so of us remaining will die believing that we made the world a better place as a result of our efforts to secure peace that has held for almost 50 years."[28]

On the surface, his anger was directed at a group of historians and Smithsonian curators, the organizers of the *Enola Gay* show, most of whom had grown up on the postwar side of August 1945. For them, the world before the Bomb (capitalized by a generation for whom it was a malign deity) was an unattainable screen fantasy. From the start, they had sensed some of the difficulties of a show that bridged the Hiroshima divide. As Tom Crouch, the show's project manager, wrote privately to National Air and Space Museum director Martin Harwit in July 1993, "We can delude visitors into thinking that [the show] is not really about the atomic bomb. . . . Do you want to do an exhibition intended to make veterans feel good, or do you want an exhibition that will lead our visitors to think about the consequences of the atomic bombing of Japan? Frankly, I don't think we can do both."[29]

The organizers of the show had an encompassing and generous vision: to take the stories of a global victory beyond imagining and a global terror beyond comprehension, and create from them a single narrative that all could visit and partake of. However, the first draft document, critiqued for the museum both by "revisionist" historians like Martin Sherwin and Barton Bernstein and by air force historians, was from the beginning more mythical hybrid—half fish, half fowl—than compromise document.

It was entitled "The Crossroads: The End of World War II, the Atomic Bomb, and the Origins of the Cold War." The "roads" crossed at Hiroshima, an ominous X on the Smithsonian map, for this show assumed that the triumphalist story of the war in the Pacific could be yoked in the "ashes" to a nightmarish postwar tale of a burgeoning nuclear arms race and a MAD (the acronym for Mutual Assured Destruction) world; that the burnished plane and the human suffering it caused and continues to cause, smiling shots of boisterous young airmen and unbearable images of seared victims, the consciousness of those who fought World War II and those who grew up in the penumbra of World War III, the celebratory and the crematory, the just and unjust, victory and defeat could exist in a single space. This was a show that would begin at the end and end at the beginning, celebrate that end and deplore that beginning. As an icon, the gleaming fuselage would be both world redeemer and world destroyer.

The idea of presenting such a show in the National Air and Space Museum seems, in retrospect, a kind of atomic madness. Yet in its judicious approach to controversies that in academia have swirled around the *Enola Gay* ever since historian Gar Alperovitz published *Atomic Diplomacy* in 1965, the draft script was clearly an effort in consensus exhibition-making. In its pages, all controversies were invariably open-ended. No matter the strident accusations leveled at the script by military lobbying groups like the Air Force Association and the American Legion, not to speak of the *Washington Post* and Newt Gingrich, it was a remarkably careful, not to say bland, summary of thirty years of historical research and argument. It was also dutiful in its attention to and praise for Tibbets, the 509th Composite Group, all American veterans who fought in the Pacific, and the various political, scientific, and military figures involved in the decision to make and use the first atomic bombs.

The script's shock lay not so much in what it said as in what was missing. Despite years of laborious work restoring the *Enola Gay* to a pristine state, there was no hint of the celebratory feeling that had once been so inextricably linked to victory culture and triumph in the Pacific. The writing remained emotionally almost monotonal until the moment it ducked under the mushroom cloud; the moment a visitor to the exhibit would have left the *Enola Gay*, turned a corner, and entered a gallery marked "Ground Zero: Hiroshima, 8:15 A.M., August 6, 1945/Nagasaki, 11:02 A.M., August 9, 1945."

The first objects to catch that visitor's attention would have been two smashed wristwatches and a wall clock from Hiroshima, stopped at "the precise moment of the explosion of the atomic bomb," followed by Japanese photos of the mushroom cloud as seen from the ground and the first testimony of survivors. ("My strongest impression when the bomb fell was of the clouds . . .

chasing me . . . like a black hand stretched out . . . covering
everyone so that I too would eventually be crushed by it.")[30]

Here, in Washington's most popular national museum, was to
be a full-scale exhibition of the once suppressed images and icons
of Hiroshima; the most forbidden, most forbidding images of the
nuclear age. In this "underground" show would be a dead school-
boy's tattered jacket; a fused rosary; a lunch box belonging to
Reiko Watanabe, a first-year student at Hiroshima's Municipal
Girls' High School, with "the carbonized remains of sweet green
peas and polished rice, a rare, wartime luxury," inside ("No trace
of Reiko Watanabe was ever found"); and a water bottle that once
belonged to schoolgirl Yoshiko Kitamura ("Her body was never
found"). It was also to include photographs of hideously burned
victims in the ashes of Hiroshima as well as of those who lived on,
having experienced "temperatures so high that the dark, heat-
absorbing pattern of their clothing was burned into their flesh."

Keloid-scarred and disfigured *hibakusha* ("explosion-affected
persons") were to be seen not only in frozen images from 1945 but
in a present-day video. ("Only they can tell you what it is like to
survive an atomic explosion.") Like the crew of the *Enola Gay*,
they would testify to their experiences. ("On the following morning I bandaged my head . . . and went to the work site. Many of
the students' . . . eyeballs had popped out, all the way out . . .
the girls' school uniforms were burned off completely; they were
completely stripped . . . naked. It was just like, well, a scene in
hell.")

Here, in full sight, would be images dreamed about and imagined by a generation, transformed for decades into mutated futures or fantasy attacks on America but seldom before seen. These
images of atrocity and slaughter would now be placed near the
center of an American tale. Here was a moment of great significance for both the pre- and post-1945 generations to be displayed
for all to see; and this was to take place not in the former enemy's
land but in the former victor's capital. In a coda, "Crossroads"
played this out by following the survivors of that disastrous moment—that is, whoever was then living on the globe—into a

"World Gone 'M.A.D.,' " a world of "nuclear waste and human experiments," of "nuclear proliferation and nuclear terrorism."

Though the objects and images would have been on loan from the Hiroshima Peace Memorial Museum and Nagasaki's International Culture Hall, the script's sudden surge of emotionality, the underside of victory culture's celebratory impulse, was distinctly from an American consciousness. In it, one could catch the voice of those who grew up amid the dreamy onscreen images of the marines advancing, Americans winning, and the enemy falling comfortingly before our guns; but who, at night, when they drifted off to sleep, found themselves terrified in the blinding light, felt the searing heat rush up an arm flung high to shield the eyes.

Despite its fate, the exhibition was undoubtedly a salutary event, if not a healing one, for which we can thank the curators and historians involved. For it addressed a moment that Americans could still hardly bear to consider, and exposed a slow-motion collapse of the traditional narrative that had been going on for fifty years. An American culture of defeat had long grown unacknowledged, because responsibility for the moment when it arose could not be borne. The anger and blame directed at the curators and historians for their "betrayal," their "anti-Americanism," as at the Vietnam generation or the "counterculture," involved a desperate displacement. For the betrayal had not been the children's. They had simply plunged into worlds their parents had left open to them so many years earlier.

For half a century, suppression of full consciousness of a new kind of defeat had been, in part, possible. Now, the results of that suppression grew more evident as two generations faced each other across a divide made unbearably wider by the experience they shared so differently. Each group had the desire to trace its side of the divide of August 6, 1945, but unless that divide itself was looked at, unless that disjuncture in history was seen, until there was an acceptance of the ways in which the earth *was* knocked off its axis, confusion and anger were bound to displace healing or understanding from the national agenda.

Wailing Walls

If, as in a science-fiction fantasy, we could create a personalized, virtual reality museum on the capital's Mall, two stories might be able to inhabit the same moment in 1945 without contradiction, and Paul Tibbets, too, could have his show: his plane, burnished to a fine shine; his crew, honored for their task; his war, successfully concluded due to his mission. The bomb would once more fall toward a distant Aioli Bridge; Tibbets would once again swerve his plane; that victory cloud would rise; and the *Enola Gay* would fly away into celebratory history, into glory.

But that cloud concealing events below sooner or later enveloped us all, soldiers and civilians, parents and children. Those still dreaming of victory culture in the mid-1990s found themselves in confused and angry mourning over the fact that their children and grandchildren were incapable of telling that victory story for them—or about them—and that they could no longer tell it with conviction themselves.

Among Tibbets's generation, there has been an increasingly strong urge to scream about the desecration of that story. Many feel that historians now tell no tales about them in which they recognize themselves or their country. Even those in power, who want to return the country and its history to an imagined state of grace, find themselves in a strangely oppositional stance. They challenge, often with hysterical vitriol, any tale told, any exhibit mounted, any standards suggested that do not strike them as familiar, but they themselves are unable to tell the tale, any tale; mount the exhibit, any exhibit; write the textbook, any textbook. Deep down, they know that they are incapable of creating a story that might take Americans successfully from the victory cloud to the present moment. Their *Enola Gay* show must always stop at 8:15 A.M. on August 6, 1945, because they cannot pilot that plane into the postwar world.

This is what it is like for the generation of victors (and their putative successors) to find themselves living in a culture of defeat. Even the postwar body of thought meant to suppress literal defeat—the endless varieties of deterrence theory that came with a two-superpower world—has been relegated to the junk heap. Yet the weapons, in all their theoretical uselessness, remain no less horrifying and dangerous. Little wonder that some from the aging generation of victors have the urge to lash out rather than reflect. For them, each familiar tale now seems to exist only as an isolated pool of embattled memory, hardly extending beyond personal experience. Each tale can be challenged, amended, dismantled, but not placed back in a narrative stream.

It is not surprising, then, that defeat in the *Enola Gay* controversy was first implicitly acknowledged not by museum officials but by the plane's pilot. In a June 1994 press conference, Tibbets proposed what would become the second (if this time involuntary) memorial to defeat in the nation's capital. Instead of the "package of insults" the Smithsonian was planning, he urged the museum to display the *Enola Gay* the way it "displays any other airplane. Look at Lindbergh's airplane. There it sits, or hangs, all by itself in all its glory. 'Here is the first airplane to fly the Atlantic.' Okay. 'This airplane was the first one to drop an atomic bomb.' You don't need any other explanation. And I think it should be displayed alone."[31]

On January 30, 1995, I. Michael Heyman, secretary of the Smithsonian, concurred, announcing the exhibit's cancellation. (The museum also quietly postponed a Vietnam War exhibit planned for 1997.) "We made," said Heyman, "a basic error in attempting to couple a historical treatment of the use of atomic weapons with the fiftieth anniversary commemoration of the end of the war."[32]

Opening instead in June 1995 was a minimalist show somewhat like the one Tibbets had suggested. Along with the *Enola Gay*'s impressive fuselage, other bits and pieces of the disassembled plane—engines, a vertical stabilizer, an aileron, propellers, radar antennae—were scattered generously throughout the empty space once to have been occupied by "Crossroads." It was a technician's exhibit. Two of its four rooms were filled with upbeat accounts of the plane's restoration and restorers ("They're saving it . . . for your grandchildren and . . . that's why they have the smile on their face when they come to work"); a video of surviving crew members giving testimony was repeated twice ("a great group of patriotic men . . . we succeeded in bringing that carnage to an end and everybody got to go home"); and various apologetic or defensive statements by the museum along with copious statistics about B-29s adorned the walls. There was even an almost life-size cardboard cutout of the plane's crew.

Missing, of course, were the inhabitants of Hiroshima and Nagasaki, seen only in the crew video in a couple of fleeting shots of wounded bomb survivors and alluded to in just a single wall poster reference to "many tens of thousands of deaths" from the two bombings. But if the horror story of what had happened in those cities had disappeared, the old tale of triumph in the Pacific was almost as hard to find in those dull and unrevealing rooms.[33]

In the end, there was no story Americans could agree upon across that crucial divide of August 6, 1945. We could only strip away all stories, leaving little more than the burnished object, open to whatever story anyone might bring to it. As such, it bore an unsurprising resemblance to the Vietnam Wall, a second historically mute grieving wall for Americans, dedicated to a defeat deeper than we can yet bear to imagine. In front of it, a visitor could, if desired, weep for almost any kind of loss.

You could move close to that highly polished metal, look into it, and, if you were a veteran of the war, perhaps see those young airmen smiling, and you might weep for them and their now inexpressible story. Or perhaps your father was an airman in that war and you would see him grown old, and weep; or perhaps you would see the scarred face of one of the children of Hiroshima and weep for a very different kind of loss; or see a child crouched hands over head under a desk and weep for the ludicrousness of it all. Or perhaps what you would see would not coalesce into an image at all, and you would know that, in the end, there is no way, not in Washington, not in Hiroshima, to adequately memorialize the nuclear age, or to capture in any exhibit anywhere that moment in August 1945 when it all began. Perhaps, finally, you would weep for all the lost selves of the nuclear age, and even for a nation that made the very weapon with which it was defeated in a moment of triumph, more perhaps than any nation could bear.

NOTES

1. Anatomy of a Controversy: Edward T. Linenthal

1. Uday Mohan and Sanho Tree, "Hiroshima, the American Media, and the Construction of Conventional Wisdom," *Journal of American–East Asian Relations* 4, no. 2 (1995): 157–59. In a letter to the *Washington Post*, August 12, 1995, Jefferson Morley observed that his grandfather, Felix Morley, "was a founder of the conservative journal *Human Events* and the editor of the *Washington Post* from 1933 to 1940." He remarked that his grandfather "was most proud" of an article, "The Return to Nothingness," published in *Human Events* in August 1945. There, Felix Morley wrote, "It was pure accident if a single person slain at Hiroshima had any personal responsibility for the Pearl Harbor outrage. . . . Pearl Harbor was an indefensible and infamous act of aggression. But Hiroshima was an equally infamous act of atrocious revenge. . . . Undoubtedly Hiroshima shortened the war. The atomic bomb may well have saved more lives than it has destroyed to date. But to say that is to excuse rather than to explain. . . . The price we have paid for victory is terribly high. And perhaps the cost of this last installment, at Hiroshima, is even heavier for us than for the Japanese. For its measurement is the loss of ideals which, far more than our moral strength, have made America great and distinctive in the long human story."

2. National Air and Space Museum files, hereafter NASM. I used materials from files in the Aeronautics Department and the Director's Office. I also had access to the materials collected by NASM for an outside review of this exhibit.

3. Quoted material from James P. Delgado, "Memories and Memorials to the Dawn of the Atomic Age," unpublished ms., 1995. My thanks to the author for permission to use material from his essay.

4. Michael J. Neufeld, "The 'Enola Gay,' the Bomb, and the National Air and Space Museum," presented at the Yale-Smithsonian Symposium on Material Culture, May 2, 1992, unpublished ms., 4.

5. Carlin Romano, "Enola Gay," *Washington Post*, August 2, 1979; Neufeld, "The 'Enola Gay,' the Bomb, and the National Air and Space Museum," 5.

6. Michael McMahon, "The Romance of Technological Progress: A Critical Review of the National Air and Space Museum," *Technology and Culture* 22 (April 1981): 294.

7. "Give Enola Gay a Place of Honor," *The Blade* (Toledo, Ohio), n.d., NASM.

8. Samuel A. Batzli, "From Heroes to Hiroshima: The National Air and Space Museum Adjusts Its Point of View," *Technology and Culture* 31 (October 1990): 835. Restoration quote from NASM.

9. "NASM Interviews with Martin Harwit: National Air and Space Museum Oral History Program," April 19, 1983. I thank David DeVorkin for calling my attention to these interviews.

10. Ibid., 64.

11. Elizabeth Kaston, "At Air and Space, Ideas on the Wing," *Washington Post*, October 11, 1988.

12. Memo to Martin Harwit from E. T. Woolridge, assistant director, Museum Operations, May 6, 1988; memo to various staff from Lin Ezell and Steven Soter, May 16, 1988. Robert McC. Adams, "Smithsonian Horizons," *Smithsonian*, July 1988, 12; Martin Harwit, "The Enola Gay," *Air and Space*, August/September 1988, 4.

13. NASM Research Advisory Committee meeting, October 24–26, 1988, NASM.

14. Ibid.

15. Steven Soter to Dom Pisano, Martin Harwit, Von Hardesty, April 18, 1988, NASM.

16. Tom Crouch to Martin Harwit, November 8, 1990, NASM.

17. Tom Crouch, "Hey Marge, Are We Still in Air and Space?" *Over the Front: Journal of the League of World War I Aviation Historians* 7, no. 2 (1992): 184; Martin Harwit to Robert McC. Adams, October 22, 1991, NASM; Michael Neufeld to Martin Harwit and Tom Crouch, February 4, 1991, NASM.

18. Martin Harwit to Mike Mansfield, August 19, 1991, NASM.

19. NASM Advisory Board minutes, December 31, 1991, NASM.

20. W. Burr Bennett, Jr., to William Rehnquist, January 13, 1994. See Public Law 87-186 87th Congress, H.R. 4659, August 30, 1961. I thank Michael Neufeld for providing me a copy of the law.

21. For a detailed discussion of similar interpretive issues at the USS *Arizona* Memorial, see Edward T. Linenthal, *Sacred Ground: Americans and Their Battlefields*, 2nd ed. (Champaign: University of Illinois Press, 1993), 173–212.

22. For information on the early years of NASM, see Neufeld, "The 'Enola Gay,' the Bomb, and the National Air and Space Museum," 2; Jennings

Randolph quoted in Dave Dooling, "History of the National Air and Space Museum," *Spaceflight*, July/August 1976, 254; my figures on attendance from Donald Lopez, "Creating the National Air and Space Museum," unpublished ms., NASM.

23. Joseph J. Corn, "Tools, Technologies, and Contexts: Interpreting the History of American Technics," in *History Museums in the United States: A Critical Assessment*, ed. Warren Leon and Roy Rosenzweig (Champaign: University of Illinois Press, 1989), 242.

24. Steven D. Lavine and Ivan Karp, "Museums and Multiculturalism," in *Exhibiting Cultures: The Poetics and Politics of Museum Displays*, ed. Karp and Lavine (Washington: Smithsonian Institution Press, 1991), 8.

25. David DeVorkin interview, May 18, 1995.

26. Daniel S. Greenberg, "New Candor on a Nazi Aerospace Legacy," *Washington Post*, December 8, 1990; Martin Harwit interview, January 12, 1995.

27. Crouch, "Hey Marge, Are We Still in Air and Space?" passim.

28. Ibid.

29. John T. Correll, "War Stories at Air and Space," *Air Force Magazine*, April 1994, 26; "Snoopy at the Smithsonian," *Wall Street Journal*, October 25, 1994. Accompanying Crouch's "Hey Marge, Are We Still in Air and Space?" in *Over the Front* in 1992 was Steven D. Miller's "Gloom and Doom At NASM," which characterizes the exhibit as an "anti-war diatribe" (188).

30. Wilcomb E. Washburn, "The Smithsonian and the *Enola Gay*," *The National Interest* (summer 1995): 9.

31. "Destination Museum: A Conversation on National Radio with Kim Hill and Barbara Kirshenblatt-Gimblett" (New Zealand), August 16, 1994. I thank Barbara Kirshenblatt-Gimblett for sending me a transcript of this interview.

32. Dominick A. Pisano, Thomas J. Dietz, Joanne M. Gernstein, and Karl S. Schneide, *Legend, Memory, and the Great War in the Air* (Seattle: University of Washington Press, 1992), 135; Richard H. Kohn's letter appears in *Air Force Magazine*, June 1994, 6.

33. Peter Novick appeared on National Public Radio's *All Things Considered*, January 27, 1995 (transcript no. 1740-7). Final quote from personal conversation with author. I thank Peter Novick for sending me a copy of this transcript.

34. Exhibition Planning Document: "The Crossroads: The End of World War II, the Atomic Bomb, and the Onset of the Cold War," 15.

35. Martin Harwit to Robert McC. Adams, April 16, 1993, NASM; and "Trip to Japan: Martin Harwit and Tom Crouch," April 1 to 10, 1993, NASM.

36. Robert McC. Adams to Martin Harwit, July 17, 1993, NASM.

37. Tom Crouch to Martin Harwit, July 21, 1993, NASM.

38. Monroe W. Hatch, Jr., to Martin Harwit, September 12, 1993, NASM.

39. Martin Harwit to Robert McC. Adams and Constance Newman, De-

cember 23, 1993; Merrill McPeak to Martin Harwit, December 29, 1993, NASM.

40. Martin Harwit interview with author, March 29, 1995; Edwin Bearss to Tom Crouch, February 24, 1995, NASM.

41. "Comments on Script, 'The Crossroads: The End of World War II, the Atomic Bomb, and the Origins of the Cold War,'" February 7, 1994, NASM.

42. Akira Iriye to Michael Neufeld, February 7, 1994, and April 21, 1994, NASM.

43. Correll, "War Stories at Air and Space," 28.

44. Martin Harwit, "The Enola Gay: A Nation's, and a Museum's, Dilemma," *Washington Post*, August 7, 1994; Martin Harwit, "Enola Gay and a Nation's Memories," *Air and Space*, August/September 1994, 21. This video is quite different from—and far more moving than—the one shown in the eventual exhibition.

45. These terms were used by Tom Crouch in our discussions of the exhibit.

46. "Report to Sec. I. Michael Heyman concerning the Enola Gay Exhibition." Hubert R. Dagley II, telephone interview with the author, July 12, 1995.

47. Correll, "War Stories at Air and Space," passim.

48. Correll memo, November 23, 1993, "The *Enola Gay* Debate," unpublished collection, the Air Force Association. I thank Jack Giese, chief of media relations at AFA, Stephen P. Aubin, director of communication, and John T. Correll for sending me this and other documents. The AFA also complained that while figures like General Leslie Groves were subject to scrutiny, Japanese emperor Hirohito was not, that the Japanese were, in effect, given a free ride.

49. Richard Hallion's comment about the morality of the bomb in R. Emmett Tyrrell, Jr., "Hiroshima and the Hectoring Herd," *Washington Times*, September 2, 1994; Richard Hallion to Tom Crouch, August 9, 1994; Tom Crouch to Richard Hallion, August 12, 1994; Richard Hallion to Tom Crouch, August 15, 1994, all NASM.

50. Luanne J. Smith, "Smithsonian Air and Space Museum's Enola Gay Exhibit," memorandum through director, Support and Outreach, for executive director, April 25, 1994.

51. William Constantine to Martin Harwit, "NASM 'Crossroads' Exhibit Review and Recommendations," May 25, 1994, NASM.

52. "Draft Statement for the Media," September 6, 1994, NASM.

53. Mark Rodgers, director of Office of Government Relations, Smithsonian Institution, "Report of the NASM 'Tiger Team' on the 'Last Act,'" September 7, 1994, NASM. David Armstrong to Alfred Goldberg, July 14, 1993; Edward Drea to World War II Commemoration Committee, July 12, 1994; Alfred Goldberg to Michael Neufeld, September 19, 1994, all NASM.

Luanne J. Smith, "Comments on the Enola Gay Script," memorandum for the record, September 22, 1994.

54. Eugene L. Meyer, "Dropping the Bomb," *Washington Post*, July 21, 1994; "Context and the Enola Gay," ibid., August 14, 1994; congressional letter to Robert McC. Adams, August 10, 1994.

55. Luanne J. Smith, "Enola Gay Exhibit," memorandum for the executive director, August 26, 1994; Luanne J. Smith, interview with the author, August 7, 1995. Air force historian Herman Wolk recounts a telephone conversation with Martin Harwit in August 1994 in which Harwit said he was "taken aback at how little had been done" with regard to the recommendations of military historians. (This story appeared shortly thereafter in the *Washington Times*.) Martin Harwit remembers the conversation quite differently, saying that he was speaking only of some of the criticisms by Richard Hallion and Wolk.

56. Michael Neufeld to Tom Crouch and Michael Fetters, June 6, 1994, NASM.

57. The legion's characterization of the exhibit appeared in a letter from its national commander, William M. Detweiler, to President Bill Clinton, August 12, 1994; American Legion Resolution 391, September 6–8, 1994, NASM.

58. Jack Giese, interview with the author, June 5, 1995.

59. R. Emmett Tyrell, Jr., "Hiroshima and the Hectoring Herd," *Washington Times*, September 2, 1994; Jeff Jacoby, "Smithsonian Drops a Bomb in World War II Exhibit," *Boston Globe*, August 16, 1994; Lance Morrow, "Hiroshima and the Time Machine," *Time*, September 19, 1994; "War and the Smithsonian," *Wall Street Journal*, August 29, 1994; Charles Krauthammer, "History Hijacked," *Time*, February 13, 1995; Rowan Scarborough, " 'Last Act' Curators Pushed Critical Text," *Washington Times*, September 1, 1994; Johnny Morrow, "From Where I Sit," *Mooresville* (NC) *Tribune*, May 18, 1994.

60. "War and the Smithsonian," *Wall Street Journal*, August 29, 1994; Ken Ringle, "A-Bomb Exhibit Plan Revamped," *Washington Post*, August 30, 1994; "Draft Statement for the Media," September 6, 1994, NASM.

61. Tony Capaccio and Uday Mohan, "Missing the Target: How the Media Mishandled the Smithsonian Enola Gay Controversy," *American Journalism Review*, July/August 1995, 21, 26.

62. Martin Harwit to Akira Iriye, December 3, 1994. Iriye had interpreted the graphic imagery of unit no. 400 in striking contrast to exhibition critics. He was increasingly displeased with each revision of the script and wrote Harwit on September 24, 1994: "I never would have thought that the script made the United States look like the aggressor and Japan as the victim. . . . Clearly, the message was that Japan would not have suffered atomic devastations if it had not started its war of conquest. . . . Because the bombings clearly brought the war to an end, it made sense to show why they made such

an impact on the Japanese decision-makers, and this could only be done by showing what happened in Hiroshima and Nagasaki." Martin Harwit to Takashi Hiraoka, November 28, 1994.

Alfred Goldberg believed that the unit on the legacy of the bomb and the Cold War was another important context for visitors to consider. It was, he said, "desirable and useful." Interview with the author, June 27, 1995.

63. Stanley Goldberg to Martin Harwit, September 7, 1994, NASM.

64. Jo Becker to Martin Harwit, October 27, 1994, NASM.

65. Historians' letter to I. Michael Heyman, November 1994, NASM.

66. James R. Currieo, executive director, Veterans of Foreign Wars, to Martin Harwit, October 26, 1994; William S. Anderson to I. Michael Heyman, November 7, 1994, NASM.

67. Hubert Dagley, correspondence with the author, May 19, 1995; Michael Neufeld, telephone interview, February 14, 1995.

68. Brian D. Smith, "Rewriting Enola Gay's History," *The American Legion*, November 1994, n.p.

69. John Ray Skates, *The Invasion of Japan: Alternative to the Bomb* (Columbia: University of South Carolina Press, 1994), 77. See also Rufus E. Miles, Jr., "Hiroshima: The Strange Myth of Half a Million Lives Saved," *International Security* 10, no. 2 (1985): 121–40; Barton J. Bernstein, "Writing, Righting, or Wronging the Historical Record: President Truman's Letter on His Atomic-Bomb Decision," *Diplomatic History* 16, no. 1 (1992): 163–72; and Barton J. Bernstein, "Seizing the Contested Terrain of Early Nuclear History: Stimson, Conant, and Their Allies Explain the Decision to Use the Atomic Bomb," ibid., 17, no. 1 (1993): 35–72.

70. Michael Neufeld to Wayne Dzwonchyk, May 13, 1994, NASM.

71. Michael Neufeld to Martin Harwit, December 7, 1994, NASM.

72. Michael Neufeld's detailed recollections are found in his memo to Tom Crouch, May 17, 1995, NASM.

73. Martin Harwit to Hubert Dagley, January 9, 1995, NASM.

74. Hubert Dagley, personal correspondence, May 19, 1995.

75. William M. Detweiler to National Commander's Advisory Committee, January 4, 1995, "The *Enola Gay* Debate" (courtesy Air Force Association).

76. Washburn, "The Smithsonian and the *Enola Gay*," 6; Richard Kohn to Martin Harwit, June 18, 1994, NASM.

77. "AFA Blasts the Air and Space Museum on Enola Gay Reversal," January 20, 1995, news release.

78. John Leo, "The National Museums of PC," *U.S. News & World Report*, October 10, 1994, 21; Patrick Buchanan, "A Long March to Revile America's Past," *Washington Times*, November 7, 1994; Sam Johnson quoted in "A Museum in Crisis," *U.S. News & World Report*, February 13, 1995, 74.

79. Alfred F. Young, "S.O.S.: Storm Warning for American Museums," *OAH Newsletter* 22, no. 4 (1994): 6 and 8.

80. Martin J. Sherwin, "The Assault on History," *The Nation*, May 15, 1995, 693; Michael Kammen, "History as a Lightning Rod," *OAH Newsletter* 23, no. 2 (1995): 6.

81. Lynn Darling, "Requiem for the Ruin," *Washington Post*, June 10, 1980.

82. Peter Blute quoted in Andrea Stone, "Wounds of War Still Color Enola Gay's Place in History," *USA Today*, October 5, 1994. Herman G. Harrington, Committee on Rules and Administration, May 11, 1995.

2. Three Narratives of Our Humanity: John W. Dower

1. Prime Minister Tomiichi Murayama's speech, the Diet resolution of June 9, and five other Japanese documents reflecting both right-wing and left-wing arguments on the issue of war responsibility are reproduced in translation, with a short commentary, in John W. Dower, "Japan Addresses Its War Responsibility," *ii: The Journal of the International Institute* (University of Michigan) 3, no. 1 (1995): 8–11. The "unofficial" translation of the June 9 Diet resolution made available by the secretariat of the lower house reads:

> The House of Representatives resolves as follows:
>
> On the occasion of the 50th anniversary of the end of World War II, this House offers its sincere condolences to those who fell in action and victims of wars and similar actions all over the world.
>
> Solemnly reflecting upon many instances of colonial rule and acts of aggression in the modern history of the world, and recognizing that Japan carried out those acts in the past, inflicting pain and suffering upon the peoples of other countries, especially in Asia, the members of this House express a sense of deep remorse.
>
> We must transcend the differences over historical views of the past war and learn humbly the lessons of history so as to build a peaceful international society.
>
> This House expresses its resolve, under the banner of eternal peace enshrined in the Constitution of Japan, to join hands with other nations of the world and to pave the way to a future that allows all human beings to live together.

The reasoning behind opposition to an unqualified expression of apology for Japan's misdeeds was succinctly expressed in a petition circulated by an ad hoc "Citizens' Movement Committee on the 50th Anniversary of the End of the War," which claimed to have collected five million signatures. The key introductory paragraphs to this petition, which was presented to the Diet in February 1995, read:

On the occasion of the fiftieth anniversary of the end of the war, there are plans for a Diet resolution that one-sidedly condemns our country's war and expresses our "remorse" and "apology" to the relevant nations.

Such a resolution means that, as an expression of the nation's will, we declare domestically and internationally that in the history of the world our country alone bears war responsibility and is a criminal nation. This inevitably harms the honor of our nation and race [*minzoku*], desecrates our heroes [*eirei*] who died for the nation at its time of crisis, and will become a grave source of trouble for the future of our country and people. We oppose this Diet resolution.

Paying homage to one's war dead resides at the heart of patriotic sentiments everywhere, and it is essential to keep this in mind when addressing the "peculiarities" of postwar Japan's difficulty in coming to grips with its war responsibility.

2. The flood of valuable primary and secondary materials that appeared after Hirohito's death, as well as the considerable evidence of Emperor Hirohito's personal responsibility for Japan's war, is carefully documented and analyzed in Herbert Bix, "The Shōwa Emperor's 'Monologue' and the Problem of War Responsibility," *Journal of Japanese Studies* 18, no. 2 (1992): 295–363.

3. For a trenchant sample of the Japan Communist Party position, which has been influential in scholarly circles, see the party's criticism of the June 9 Diet resolution on Japanese war responsibility in Dower, "Japan Addresses Its War Responsibility."

4. The "Ienaga textbook case"—which occupied the Japanese courts from 1965 to 1989 and involved a suit brought against the Ministry of Education by Professor Saburō Ienaga for requiring revisions in a school history text that he authored—is often correctly cited to illustrate the government's sanitization of the historical record. Less commonly observed is the fact that Ienaga's protracted and extremely well publicized suit constituted a remarkable, concrete, ongoing exercise in raising public consciousness about the government's attempt to censor the teaching of Japanese history. The recent "exposés" concerning Unit 731 as well as the so-called comfort women are themselves fascinating case studies in not only how we remember and forget the past, but also how the "memory" of Japanese war crimes has been influenced by the United States. Both the murderous "scientific" atrocities committed by Unit 731 and the brutal coercion of Asian women forced to sexually service the emperor's troops were known to U.S. authorities in occupied Japan immediately after the war but were suppressed for reasons having to do with America's own perceived self-interest. (The murderous scientists were exonerated from prosecution in return for frank debriefings about the

results of their "biological" experiments. In all likelihood, the issue of the "comfort women" was not exposed and prosecuted for the simple reason that the large Allied occupation force in postsurrender Japan was itself dependent on an extensive network of "voluntary" Japanese prostitution.)

5. For a convenient bilingual volume containing the three history textbooks that currently are most widely used in Japanese middle schools, with English translations on facing pages, see International Society for Educational Information, *Japanese School Textbooks: Japan in Modern History— Junior High School* (Tokyo, 1994). The ISEI is an affiliate of the Japanese Ministry of Foreign Affairs.

6. At the same time, as Tom Engelhardt's and Paul Boyer's essays in this volume indicate, almost from the moment the bomb was dropped the triumphal image of Hiroshima has been accompanied by a darker, apocalyptic (and frequently suppressed) side in American culture.

7. *New York Times*, March 6, 1995. A representative citizens' petition calling for such compensation is included in Dower, "Japan Addresses Its War Responsibility."

8. Paul Fussell, *Thank God for the Atom Bomb, and Other Essays* (New York: Summit Books, 1988), 13–37. The title essay originally was published (under a different title) in 1981.

9. Richard Hallion was quoted as follows: "The basic questions remain: Dealing with a morally unambiguous subject, why did they have to produce two and maybe three scripts to get it right? Why did it take a tremendous public outcry to force changes that were obvious from the start?"; *Washington Times*, August 30, 1994. Hallion himself emerged as a conspicuously ambiguous figure in the controversy over the *Enola Gay* exhibition. As a member of the original advisory committee for the exhibition, he privately offered strong praise for the first draft script for the planned exhibition presented by the National Air and Space Museum's curators. Once the exhibition became an open political controversy, however, Hallion emerged as one of its most vigorous critics. The letter by Sam Johnson and his colleagues, dated December 13, 1994, and addressed to I. Michael Heyman, secretary of the Smithsonian Institution, is included in an unpaginated press kit made available by the Air Force Association: "Congressional Correspondence and Press Releases," part 8 of "The *Enola Gay* Debate."

A more subtle criticism of the proposed Smithsonian exhibition based on moral considerations was offered by retired general Monroe W. Hatch, Jr., executive director of the Air Force Association, who argued that the museum's draft script treated Japan and the United States "as if their participation in the war were morally equivalent"; quoted in John T. Correll, "War Stories at Air and Space," *Air Force Magazine*, April 1994, 26. Such emphasis on moral (as well as political and ideological) differences between the Allied and Axis sides in World War II is certainly appropriate. In the Smithsonian imbroglio, however, this commonly led to a patterned sort of moral obtuseness. Recitation of Japanese atrocities, that is, was simply offered as a way of cutting off any attempt to seriously engage the moral issues raised by the American policy of targeting enemy civilians and ultimately subjecting them to nuclear destruction. Such polemical tactics usually relativize atrocity (what they did was far worse than what we did). They also reflect acceptance of the appropriateness of eye-for-eye, tooth-for-tooth retribution ("they"—meaning Japanese generically—deserved to suffer horribly, considering what "they" did to others). In the Western tradition, we might think of this in terms of Old Testament attitudes, but it should be noted that in these debates such "retributive" sentiments often are passionately conveyed by Chinese who bitterly recall Japan's wartime atrocities and applaud the bombs for simultaneously ending the war and wreaking vengeance on a hated oppressor.

10. Senate Resolution 257, 103rd Congress, 2nd Session, introduced on September 19, 1994, and passed on September 23. The full text of the resolution reads as follows:

> To express the sense of the Senate regarding the appropriate portrayal of men and women of the Armed Forces in the upcoming National Air and Space Museum's exhibit on the Enola Gay.
> Whereas the role of the Enola Gay during World War II was momentous in helping to bring World War II to a merciful end, which resulted in saving the lives of Americans and Japanese;
> Whereas the current script for the National Air and Space Museum's exhibit on the Enola Gay is revisionist and offensive to many World War II veterans;
> Whereas the Federal law states that "the Smithsonian Institution shall commemorate and display the contributions made by the military forces of the nation toward creating, developing, and maintaining a free, peaceful, and independent society and culture in the United States";
> Whereas the Federal law also states that "the valor and sacrificial service of the men and women of the Armed Forces shall be portrayed as an inspiration to the present and future generations of America"; and
> Whereas, in memorializing the role of the United States in armed conflict, the National Air and Space Museum has an obligation under the Federal law to portray history in the proper context of the times: Now, therefore, be it
> Resolved, That it is the sense of the Senate that any exhibit displayed by the National Air and Space Museum with respect to the Enola Gay should reflect appropriate sensitivity toward the men and women who faithfully and selflessly served the United

States during World War II and should avoid impugning the
memory of those who gave their lives for freedom.

11. This petition is partly reproduced in note 1 above. The key evocative
term in the petition is *eirei*, literally "souls of fallen war heroes." On the
Japanese political scene, the Izokukai (Japan War-Bereaved Families Association), a citizens' lobby composed primarily of representatives of bereaved
families, has emerged as one of the more effective conservative voices in the
debates over how to publicly present the war and address Japan's war responsibility. An interesting comparison could be made between the Izokukai's
emotional role in blocking an unequivocal Diet apology for the war and the
American Legion's comparable role in preventing a critical *Enola Gay* exhibition at the Smithsonian's National Air and Space Museum.

12. See, for example, the essays by Edward T. Linenthal and Paul Boyer in
this volume.

13. See John T. Correll's letter to the *Washington Post*, August 14, 1994.
The Air Force Association's major attacks on the Smithsonian's original
scripts, mostly written by Correll, appear in the April, September, and November 1994 issues of *Air Force Magazine*.

14. These congressmen are quoted in the *Washington Post*, August 30,
1994.

15. See, for example, the congressman quoted by Robert Jay Lifton and
Greg Mitchell in the *New York Times*, October 16, 1994.

16. *New York Times*, January 28, 1995.

17. *Wall Street Journal*, August 29, 1994. Another conservative comment
indicted the museum's curators as individuals who "hate their country and
should be fired"; quoted by Lifton and Mitchell, *New York Times*, October 16,
1994.

18. *Washington Post*, January 20, 1995.

19. Jonathan Yardley, "Dropping a Bomb of an Idea," *Washington Post*,
October 10, 1994.

20. The Air Force Association, for example, was very explicit in placing the
proposed *Enola Gay* exhibition in this broader epidemiology of "cultural
interpretation"; see *Air Force Magazine*, April 1994, 27. In this context, it is
noteworthy that when the new secretary of the Smithsonian announced the
institution's unconditional surrender to critics where the *Enola Gay* exhibition was concerned, he simultaneously announced that the critical tone
of the "Science in American Life" exhibition would be tempered, while
a proposed exhibition on the Vietnam War was being postponed indefinitely.

21. U.S. Strategic Bombing Survey, *Summary Report (Pacific War)* (Washington, D.C.: U.S. Government Printing Office, 1946), 26; the same widely
quoted conclusion is repeated in U.S. Strategic Bombing Survey, *Japan's*

Struggle to End the War (Washington, D.C.: U.S. Government Printing Office, 1946), 13.

22. These basic endgame battle plans are translated in U.S. Department of the Army, *Reports of General MacArthur,* vol. 2, part 2 (Washington, D.C.: U.S. Government Printing Office, 1966), 585–86, 601–9.

23. The "Potsdam diary" was made widely accessible to scholars for the first time in Eduard Mark, " 'Today Has Been a Historical One': Harry S. Truman's Diary of the Potsdam Conference," *Diplomatic History* 4, no. 3 (1980): 317–26; this printed version contains some errors derived from misreading Truman's handwriting. The original diary is in the Truman Library in Independence, Missouri.

24. For a detailed summary of historical scholarship on the decision to drop the atomic bombs, see J. Samuel Walker, "The Decision to Use the Bomb: A Historiographical Update," *Diplomatic History* 14, no. 4 (1990): 94–114; also Walker's contribution "History, Collective Memory, and the Decision to Use the Bomb" in the symposium "Hiroshima in History and Memory" featured in ibid., 19, no. 2 (1995): 319–28. Barton Bernstein draws on intimate knowledge of the U.S. archival record in his lengthy contribution to the same symposium: "Understanding the Atomic Bomb and the Japanese Surrender: Missed Opportunities, Little-Known Near Disasters, and Modern Memory," 227–73. A concise conservative criticism of "revisionist" arguments is presented by Robert James Maddox in "The Biggest Decision: Why We Had to Drop the Atomic Bomb," *American Heritage* 46, no. 3 (1995): 70–77.

25. The plane was named *Bock's Car,* after pilot Fred Bock. On the Nagasaki mission, however, Bock himself piloted one of the accompanying airplanes.

26. Taro Takemi, "Remembrances of the War and the Bomb," *Journal of the American Medical Association* 250, no. 5 (1983): 618–19. Takemi was a young physicist when the bombs were dropped, and participated in identifying the Hiroshima bomb as a nuclear weapon. He later became the head of the Japanese counterpart to the American Medical Association. Through marriage, Takemi also had close connections with high imperial circles, and one purpose of his "reminiscence" was to divorce Emperor Hirohito from the militarists. In this 1983 essay, he expressed his personal belief that the majority of Japanese people had come to agree that the Hiroshima bomb "saved" Japan. This is dubious, but it certainly is true that the Nagasaki bomb is almost unanimously viewed as an atrocity.

27. See, for example, Edward T. Linenthal, *Preserving Memory: The Struggle to Create America's Holocaust Museum* (New York: Viking, 1995), esp. chap. 1.

28. See, for example, the three widely used textbooks reproduced in International Society for Educational Information, *Japanese School Textbooks,*

152–53, 343–44, 514–15. There are in fact no official Japanese figures for atomic bomb–related deaths, although various estimates have been offered by different sources at different times. Much of the difficulty lies in uncertainty concerning the populations of Hiroshima and Nagasaki at the time the bombs were dropped. Many residents were fleeing the cities while, on the other hand, large numbers of military personnel as well as conscripted Korean laborers were moving through. City records, as well as residents, were obliterated.

Immediately after the war, both the U.S. and Japanese governments estimated fatalities in Hiroshima and Nagasaki at approximately 75,000 and 40,000, respectively. These figures are now widely regarded as far too low, although they sometimes are repeated in presentations by Americans. In 1950, city officials released the implausibly precise figures of 73,884 fatalities and 74,909 injuries from the bomb in Nagasaki. In 1953, officials in Hiroshima estimated that roughly 200,000 individuals had been killed by the bomb there. In 1976, a report to the United Nations from the Japanese government put estimated deaths from the Hiroshima bomb considerably lower, at approximately 140,000. Other Japanese sources in the late 1970s tended to endorse the estimates of 140,000 deaths in Hiroshima and 70,000 in Nagasaki, plus or minus 10,000 in each case. The great majority of these deaths occurred immediately or within a short time after the bombs were dropped.

The confusing inflation of numbers in more recent years derives from a complex and highly politicized national policy of formally recognizing as *hibakusha* or atomic bomb "survivors" anyone who was within two kilometers of the epicenters at the time or in the days after the bombs were dropped. When such individuals die, *of whatever causes*, they are identified as deceased *hibakusha*—and their names are inscribed as such at the peace memorials in Hiroshima and Nagasaki. As of August 1994, the number of deceased *hibakusha* thus named in Hiroshima was 186,940. The corresponding figure in Nagasaki was 102,275. (Many of those killed, including thousands of Koreans, naturally remain unidentified and thus nameless and unlisted). At the same time, as of March 1995, a total of 328,629 living Japanese officially possessed papers identifying them as *hibakusha*; when they die, they too will be entered into the memorial lists in Hiroshima and Nagasaki. The potential for misinterpreting and misrepresenting these deaths as ones caused by the bombs is obvious but rarely pointed out in Japan. Much of this confusing data appears in publications issued by the two cities in 1995. See Genbaku Higai Taisaku-bu, Eisei-kyoku, Hiroshima-shi (Atomic Bomb Damage Policy Section, Public Health Bureau, Hiroshima City), *Genbaku Hibakusha Taisaku Jigyō Gaiyō* (Outline of Matters Pertaining to Policy Toward Atomic Bomb Victims), esp. 14, 18, and the counterpart publication under the exact same title issued by the Genbaku Hibaku Taisaku-bu (Atomic Bomb Casualty

Policy Section) of Nagasaki, esp. 7, 45, 105–7. I am grateful to Hideki Tarumi of the Japanese Ministry of Health and Welfare for providing me with materials on this issue.

29. For a recent documented summary of this fact, see Arjun Makhijani, " 'Always' the Target?" *Bulletin of the Atomic Scientists* 51 (May/June 1995): 23–27. This has been well known to researchers for some time, as have most of the imperatives discussed in the paragraphs that follow here; see Walker's historiographic overview in "The Decision to Use the Bomb," and Martin Sherwin's pathbreaking study of the decision to develop and use the atomic bombs, *A World Destroyed: Hiroshima and the Origins of the Arms Race* (New York: Vintage, 1987; this includes a new introduction to the original 1973 work).

30. See Makhijani, " 'Always' the Target?" 26. James Byrnes actually wrote these words before he became Harry Truman's secretary of state—in a memorandum to President Franklin D. Roosevelt dated March 3, 1945. He and others subsequently emphasized the same point to Truman.

31. Oppenheimer is quoted in Sherwin, *A World Destroyed*, 145. Victor Weisskopf's less well known reflections appear in an article titled "Sweetness, Shame of the A-Bomb" in the Massachusetts Institute of Technology newspaper *MIT Tech Talk*, October 2, 1991. Michael Sherry places the development of strategic bombing policy in the context of "technological fanaticism" in *The Rise of American Air Power: The Creation of Armageddon* (New Haven: Yale University Press, 1987). Even afterward, despite misgivings about what they had created, Oppenheimer and others continued to find the challenge of nuclear development—for example, in moving on to a hydrogen bomb—"technically sweet"; see, for example, his 1954 testimony quoted in Charles Weiner, "Anticipating the Consequences of Genetic Engineering: Past, Present, and Future," in *Are Genes Us? The Social Consequences of the New Genetics*, ed. C. Cranor (New Brunswick, N.J.: Rutgers University Press, 1994), 32–33.

There is a larger dimension to the scientific and technological imperative, involving hubris, that really falls in the province of traditional humanistic concerns. Oppenheimer himself was sensitive to this when he observed that in developing the bomb the physicists had "known sin." As he later explained, in saying this he was not thinking of the deaths that came about as a result of their work, but rather "that we had known the sin of pride . . . the pride of thinking we knew what was good for man"; quoted in Bernstein, "Understanding the Atomic Bomb," 169–70.

32. Compton is quoted in Sherwin, *A World Destroyed*, 213; see also ibid., 117–18, 218. See also James G. Hershberg, *James B. Conant: Harvard to Hiroshima and the Making of the Nuclear Age* (New York: Knopf, 1993), 229, 293, 818. The proposal to demonstrate the destructiveness of the new weapon on a noncombat target was presented in the "Franck Report" of June

11, 1945—another example of materials that only belatedly became known to scholars. Top-level scientists such as Robert Oppenheimer, Enrico Fermi, and Ernest Lawrence concurred in rejecting this proposal (drafted by a group of concerned Manhattan Project scientists, led by the émigré physicist James Franck) on the grounds, in part, that actual use of the bomb on Japan might improve the prospects for peace in the future; see also Bernstein, "Understanding the Atomic Bomb," 270–71; Sherwin, A World Destroyed, 210–19.

33. In the public debates of 1994–95 centering on the *Enola Gay* controversy, scholars such as Gar Alperovitz and Martin Sherwin were particularly forceful in arguing that failure to pursue the option of a conditional surrender may even have prolonged the war. This thesis is most extensively laid out in Gar Alperovitz, *The Decision to Use the Atomic Bomb—and the Architecture of an American Myth* (New York: Knopf, 1995). As it happens, this particular aspect of the contemporary debate illuminates an interesting ideological somersault in American political discourse. In the present-day political and polemical milieu, the case for offering Japan a conditional surrender generally is identified as a "leftist" position. In 1945, however, it clearly represented an extremely conservative policy option—and was vigorously attacked as such in public by liberal and left-wing voices such as Owen Lattimore, I. F. Stone, and publications such as *The Nation* and *Amerasia*. Joseph Grew's well-known support for the Japanese imperial system was widely denounced as the most reactionary sort of appeasement. After all, the argument went, Emperor Hirohito was the focal point of imperial Japan's externally aggressive and internally repressive "emperor-system" ideology. Any guarantees of his—or the imperial institution's—preservation could thus be seen as a repudiation of the very ideals of "freedom and democracy" for which the Allies presumedly were fighting. The ideological ambiguity of the Alperovitz-Sherwin position also emerges when one looks at it from a Japanese perspective. In the postwar Japanese milieu, up to the present day, the argument that Emperor Hirohito was seriously seeking peace and should have been offered a compromise surrender would be categorized as a conservative or even a right-wing argument. Among other things, this position tends to exonerate the emperor and his military and civilian leaders from serious responsibility for prolonging the war. It dovetails neatly with the "Hiroshima as victimization" consciousness that concerned and progressive Japanese themselves are struggling to revise.

34. To argue that Truman should have abandoned the "unconditional surrender" policy at the last moment minimizes the political uproar this would have provoked not only in the United States but in the Allied camp generally. Why should a neophyte president, on the verge of total victory, have abandoned a policy enunciated two years earlier by his esteemed and just recently deceased predecessor? Why should he have offered Japan a conditional surrender when Germany had been forced to surrender uncondi-

tionally only a few months before? While elitists such as Joseph Grew (and his conservative counterparts in Britain) may have admired the Japanese monarchy on its own merits, or at least believed it to be essential to maintaining stability in a populace too immature for self-governance, public opinion in the Anglo-American camp and in China and much of the rest of Asia as well ran strongly against any form of appeasement of the emperor and imperial system.

Examined from the Japanese side, the so-called peace overtures to the Soviet Union can most charitably be described as vague. More realistically, they must be seen as the almost incoherent fumblings of a regime hog-tied by its own fight-to-the-bitter-end rhetoric and virtually paralyzed by the prospect of impending doom. These desultory overtures possessed a wishfulness bordering on sheer fantasy, for essentially the Japanese were attempting to stave off their inevitable total defeat by offering to cut some sort of deal with the still-neutral Soviet Union whereby the two countries would stand together and Japan would be able to preserve at least a portion of its crumbling empire in Northeast Asia. The pettifogging chaos within the imperial high command, beginning with the emperor himself, was immense, and no serious overtures regarding conditional surrender ever were officially conveyed to the Allied powers actually engaged in war against Japan. Had the U.S. government broached some sort of conditional surrender in June or July 1945, the imperial government almost surely would have responded either by ignoring these overtures (just as it chose to ignore the Potsdam Proclamation in July) or by coming back with a shopping list of queries on exactly what concessions the Allied powers had in mind. Would *all* the emperor's prerogatives be retained? (Anything less would have constituted lèse-majesté.) Would such a conditional surrender ensure Emperor Hirohito's personal continuation on the throne? Would the Allied powers agree to leave such issues as war crimes trials in the hands of the Japanese? Would the United States, or the Allies generally, guarantee that the "occupation" of defeated Japan would be essentially symbolic and tokenistic, with real administrative authority remaining in the hands of the imperial government? For a recent close analysis of the Japanese side in the closing stages of the war, see Herbert Bix, "Japan's Delayed Surrender: A Reinterpretation," *Diplomatic History* 19, no. 2 (1995): 197–225. The feasibility of a negotiated surrender also is viewed with skepticism in Bernstein, "Understanding the Atomic Bomb," 238–44.

Critics who argue that it might have been possible to avoid using the bombs by abandoning unconditional surrender often buttress their argument with the observation that once the surrender was effected, the United States did, in fact, preserve the throne. Some also argue that the U.S. government did, in effect, offer assurances about the throne when, in the last-minute postbomb exchanges between the two governments, it gave murky assurances that the future form of Japanese governance would be decided "in accordance with the freely expressed will of the Japanese people." This is misleading. From the outset, U.S. occupation officials in defeated Japan based their absolute authority on insistence that Japan had surrendered unconditionally. Moreover, by initially keeping deliberately vague the future status of both the imperial institution and Emperor Hirohito personally, they were able to more effectively pressure the Japanese elites into actively cooperating with basic initial reform edicts. (Hirohito was not even formally exempted from indictment as a war criminal until early 1946.) The new constitution imposed on Japan early in 1946 did substantively alter the emperor's status: he became simply "the symbol of the State and of the unity of the people." The "moderate" civilian elites who staffed the Japanese administration at the time were aghast at this change and agreed to it only when it appeared that the alternative might be elimination of the throne entirely. As Japanese scholars of the occupation commonly emphasize, it was largely by agreeing to "preserve" the emperor in this conspicuously altered "symbolic" form that General Douglas MacArthur and his reformist staff were able to force the Japanese government to accept the other basic features of the new national charter—namely, explicit affirmation of popular sovereignty, extensive human rights provisions, and the highly idealistic "no war" statements in both the constitution's preface and its famous Article 9. None of this would have been possible had the Americans agreed to a conditional surrender.

35. For a sample of the "Keep 'Em Dying" sloganeering, with an illustration of a slant-eyed, bucktoothed Japanese soldier in the crosshairs of a rifle, see the March 1942 issue of the Marine monthly *Leatherneck*. A classic cartoon reference to the Japanese as monkeys appeared in the October 1942 issue of *American Legion Magazine* (p. 56). In this, a Caucasian man is observing monkeys in a zoo who are posting a sign on the wall that reads, "Any similarity between us and the Japs is purely coincidental." Some years ago, when publishing a book on the war (*War Without Mercy: Race and Power in the Pacific War*), I asked the American Legion for permission to reproduce this graphic and received a courteous letter turning my request down on the grounds that the cartoon reflected sentiments the legion was not proud of and believed best left at rest. Truman's characterization of the Japanese as beasts was made on August 11, in response to an August 9 letter from the general secretary of the Federal Council of Church of Christ, and is cited in Bernstein, "Understanding the Atomic Bomb," 267–68. The final air raid is discussed in Dower, *War Without Mercy*, 301.

36. After being declassified in the late 1960s, this confiscated footage was edited in 1970 into a short documentary film produced by Erik Barnouw and titled *Hiroshima, Nagasaki—August 1945*. For Barnouw's account of the suppression of the Japanese footage, see Erik Barnouw, "Iwasaki and the Occupied Screen," *Film History* 2 (1988): 337–57. I have dealt with U.S. censorship of reportage about the effects of the bombs within occupied Japan

itself in "The Bombed: Hiroshimas and Nagasakis in Japanese Memory," *Diplomatic History* 19, no. 2 (1995): 275–95. On the immediate Japanese response to the bombs in general, see also my foreword to the new 1995 edition of Michihiko Hachiya, *Hiroshima Diary: The Journey of a Japanese Physician, August 6–September 30, 1945* (Chapel Hill: University of North Carolina Press, 1995), v–xvii. On the bombs in American consciousness, see Paul Boyer, *By the Bomb's Early Light: American Thought and Culture at the Dawn of the Atomic Age* (New York: Pantheon, 1985); Paul Boyer, "Exotic Resonances: Hiroshima in American Memory," *Diplomatic History* 19, no. 2 (1995): 297–318; and Robert Jay Lifton and Greg Mitchell, *Hiroshima in America: Fifty Years of Denial* (New York: Putnam's, 1995).

37. For a sensitive analysis of the sacralization of American battle sites, and military icons generally, see Edward T. Linenthal, *Sacred Ground: Americans and Their Battlefields*, 2nd ed. (Champaign: University of Illinois Press, 1993).

38. Paul Tibbets, "Our Job Was to Win," *The American Legion*, November 1994, 28ff. "Our sworn duty was to God, country and victory," Tibbets declared. The Japanese counterpart to this perfectly formulaic phrasing would be "Emperor, country and victory."

39. *Washington Post*, May 31, 1994.

40. Yoshida Mitsuru, *Senkan 'Yamato' no Saigo*; translated into English by Richard Minear under the title *Requiem for the Battleship 'Yamato'* (Seattle: University of Washington Press, 1985). This famous work, framed as an extended prose poem by a young survivor of the *Yamato*, was written in 1946 but initially suppressed from publication by U.S. occupation authorities. This censorship is a cause célèbre among Japanese conservatives.

41. For a sample of criticism of the proposed exhibition of the lunch box, see *Air Force Magazine*, April 1994, 24, and September 1994, 61. There are in fact two well-known lunch boxes in the collection of the Hiroshima Peace Memorial Museum—one belonging to a seventh-grade girl and the other to a seventh-grade boy. Original plans called for bringing the first of these to Washington. Ornamented with a design of bamboo, this had belonged to a girl named Reiko Watanabe who disappeared in the destruction of Hiroshima. The lunch box was found on a wall by a temple, and its contents—white rice and peas—were in fact unusual, for by this time in the war few Japanese were eating white rice. Reiko's mother had prepared this meal as a special treat for her daughter, who had been mobilized along with other youngsters to engage in some kind of outdoor public work. The second lunch box belonged to a boy named Shigeru Orimen, who had been mobilized to help remove buildings for a firebreak. An ordinary lunch box with more typical contents—a mixture of soybeans and barley—this was found by Shigeru's mother after the bombing, beneath a child's corpse charred beyond recognition. That is how she identified the body as her son's. While the

National Air and Space Museum originally intended to exhibit the young girl's lunch box, later plans called for replacing this with Shigeru's plainer charred relic. According to a confidential account, Reiko's mother ultimately refused to let this last reminder of her daughter travel to the United States, where it might be treated disrespectfully. The lunch box later exhibited at American University in July 1995—in an "alternative" atomic bomb exhibition mounted as a protest against the Smithsonian's cancellation of its original *Enola Gay* show—was Shigeru's. For samples of the Japanese icons of nuclear destruction, see the special commemorative issue of the weekly magazine *Aera* (August 10, 1995) entitled "Genbaku to Nihonjin: Hiroshima Nagasaki o Wasurenai" (The Atomic Bombs and the Japanese: Do Not Forget Hiroshima and Nagasaki), which reproduces photographs and depicts relics that in a number of instances were among the materials originally scheduled to be displayed in the National Air and Space Museum. See also *Asahi Shimbun*, August 3, 1995. Both of these sources include a photograph of and brief commentary about Shigeru Orimen's lunch box. According to the *Asahi*, Shigeru's mother asked that when this was displayed at American University, it be used to convey the message that "as long as there is one atomic bomb, there is no peace."

42. For a typical example of this argument, see *Air Force Magazine*, September 1994, 61.

43. Richard Minear, following Justice Radhabinod Pal, pursues this argument most relentlessly. See his essay "Atomic Holocaust, Nazi Holocaust" in *Diplomatic History* 19, no. 2 (1995): 347–65, esp. 354–55.

44. This issue is discussed in Dower, *War Without Mercy*, 38–41.

45. Bonner Fellers is quoted in ibid., 41. The moral issue as confronted by American policymakers at the time is succinctly addressed in Barton Bernstein, "The Atomic Bombings Reconsidered," *Foreign Affairs*, January/February 1995, 135–52.

46. Henry Wallace is quoted in Bernstein, "Understanding the Atomic Bomb," 57. Truman gave the order not to drop any more atomic bombs without his authorization on August 10. It was the following day, however, that he rationalized the Hiroshima and Nagasaki bombs in terms of "dealing with a beast."

47. Truman's underlining of Horatio's soliloquy is noted in Merle Miller, *Plain Speaking: An Oral Biography of Harry S. Truman* (New York: Berkley Books, 1973), 248.

3. Patriotic Orthodoxy and American Decline: Michael S. Sherry

The author thanks Laura Hein, Lane Fenrich, Edward T. Linenthal, and Tom Engelhardt for their valuable advice and useful leads. In addition to their input and the sources noted below, I have adapted arguments developed in my book *In the Shadow of War: The United States Since the 1930s* (New Haven: Yale University Press, 1995). An earlier version of this essay appeared in the *Bulletin of Concerned Asian Scholars* 27, no. 2 (1995).

1. John M. Blum, *V Was for Victory: Politics and American Culture During World War II* (New York: Harcourt Brace Jovanovich, 1976), 217–18.

2. Walter Millis, *Arms and Men: A Study of American Military History* (New York: New American Library, 1956), 268–69.

3. Newt Gingrich, *To Renew America* (1995), quoted in Joan Didion, "The Teachings of Speaker Gingrich," *New York Review of Books*, August 10, 1995, 8.

4. Stephen Ambrose, *Nixon: The Triumph of a Politician, 1962–1972* (New York: Simon and Schuster, 1989), 126.

5. John T. Correll, "War Stories at Air and Space," *Air Force Magazine*, April 1994, 26. Jack Giese quoted in "Enola Gay Baiting," *Washington City Paper*, September 27, 1994, 8.

6. Jack Giese quoted in "Enola Gay Baiting," 8.

7. A mountain of scholarship on these points is available, but for the most recent work, see Robert Jay Lifton and Greg Mitchell, *Hiroshima in America: Fifty Years of Denial* (New York: Putnam's, 1995), and Gar Alperovitz, *The Decision to Use the Atomic Bomb and the Architecture of an American Myth* (New York: Knopf, 1995).

8. "Hiroshima: A Controversy That Refuses to Die," *New York Times*, January 31, 1995.

9. For an account of the NASM fracas, see "Enola Gay Baiting," 8. On dominant frameworks in 1945, see Michael S. Sherry, *The Rise of American Air Power: The Creation of Armageddon* (New Haven: Yale University Press, 1987), chaps. 9–10 (Henry L. Stimson quoted on 324). *Herald Tribune* quote in Paul Boyer, *By the Bomb's Early Light: American Thought and Culture at the Dawn of the Atomic Age* (New York: Pantheon, 1985), 6.

10. Paul Tibbets quoted in "Enola Gay Baiting," 8.

11. Among much scholarship on these matters, see Edward T. Linenthal, "War and Sacrifice in the Nuclear Age: The Committee on the Present Danger and the Renewal of Martial Enthusiasm," in *A Shuddering Dawn: Religious Studies and the Nuclear Age*, ed. Ira Chernus and Edward T. Linenthal (Albany: State University of New York Press, 1989); Karal Ann Marling and John Wetenhall, *Iwo Jima: Monuments, Memories, and the American Hero* (Cambridge: Harvard University Press, 1991).

12. Thomas Leonard, *Above the Battle: War-Making in America from Appomattox to Versailles* (New York: Oxford University Press, 1978), 148.

13. Eric Schmitt, "Somalia's First Lesson for Military is Caution," *New York Times*, March 5, 1995.

14. Lifton and Mitchell, *Hiroshima in America*, 240.

15. Ibid., 286, describing *USA Today* commentary. Crewman's claim offered in *Rain of Ruin: Bombing Nagasaki* (PBS, August 8, 1995). On the early history of imaginative linkages between Nazi and atomic holocausts, see Lane Fenrich, "Imagining Holocaust: Mass Death and American Consciousness at the End of the Second World War" (Ph.D. diss., Northwestern University, 1992).

16. Irving Kristol quoted in David Remnick, "Lost in Space," *New Yorker*, December 5, 1994, 86.

17. Original cartoon in *Orange County Register*, as reprinted in the *New York Times*, February 11, 1995.

18. "Enola Gay Baiting," 8.

19. On this point, see Lifton and Mitchell, *Hiroshima in America* (Sheen quoted on 81), and Alperovitz, *The Decision*.

20. Barry Goldwater quoted in Chris Bull, "Right Turn," *The Advocate*, September 7, 1993, 35.

21. See "Enola Gay Baiting," cited above; "Enola Heterosexual" for the *Arkansas Democrat-Gazette*, reprinted in the *New York Times*, January 29, 1995; "Enola Sexually Undifferentiated" by Bok for the *Akron Beacon Journal*, also appearing in the *Washington Post*, September 3, 1994; Barney Frank–Richard Armey cartoons for the *Orlando Sentinel* (circa January–February 1995) and for the *San Francisco Chronicle*, January 31, 1995.

22. Norman Podhoretz quoted in Edward T. Linenthal, "Restoring America: Political Revivalism in the Nuclear Age," in *Religion and the Life of the Nation*, ed. Rowland A. Sherrill (Urbana: University of Illinois Press, 1990), 29.

23. "Anti-Flag Burning Drive Begins: Veterans Rally in Support of Constitutional Amendment," *Chicago Tribune*, March 1, 1995.

24. See Edward T. Linenthal, *Sacred Ground: Americans and Their Battlefields* (Urbana: University of Illinois Press, 1991).

25. Here I draw on comments made by indignant historians at a session on "The Practice of American History," Organization of American Historians convention, March 31, 1995, and on a letter to me recalling that session from Edward T. Linenthal, July 31, 1995.

26. Advice from Mike Wallace was helpful to me on this point.

4. Whose History Is It Anyway? Paul Boyer

The author extends warm thanks to Tom Engelhardt and Edward T. Linenthal for their thoughtful criticisms and editorial suggestions.

1. Shinto priest quoted in Geoffrey M. White, "Memory Wars: The Politics of Remembering the Asia-Pacific War," *Asia Pacific Issues*, no. 21 (July 1995): 6.

2. Ted Stevens quoted in Page Putnam Miller, "NCC Washington Update" (E-mail newsletter) 1, no. 26 (1995).

3. "Japan Protests U.S. Plans for Stamp on A-Bomb," *New York Times*, December 4, 1994; "At White House Behest, Postal Service Scraps A-Bomb Stamp," ibid., December 9, 1994; "The Images of War," *The Economist*, December 10, 1994, 32.

4. Paul Boyer, " 'Some Sort of Peace': President Truman, the American People, and the Atomic Bomb," in *The Truman Presidency*, ed. Michael J. Lacey (Washington and New York: Woodrow Wilson International Center for Scholars and Cambridge University Press, 1989), 176–80; Gar Alperovitz, *The Decision to Use the Atomic Bomb and the Architecture of an American Myth* (New York: Knopf, 1995), 501–70, esp. 515–30.

5. Paul Boyer, *By the Bomb's Early Light: American Thought and Culture at the Dawn of the Atomic Age* (New York: Pantheon, 1985; reissued with a new introduction by the author, Chapel Hill: University of North Carolina Press, 1994), 183–84.

6. Alperovitz, *The Decision*, 448–97, quoted passages on 449; James G. Hershberg, *James B. Conant: Harvard to Hiroshima and the Making of the Nuclear Age* (New York: Knopf, 1993), 294–300.

7. Jack G. Shaheen and Richard Taylor, "*The Beginning or the End,*" in *Nuclear War Films*, ed. Jack G. Shaheen (Carbondale, Ill.: Southern Illinois University Press, 1978), 3–10; Michael J. Yavenditti, "Atomic Scientists and Hollywood: *The Beginning or the End,*" *Film and History*, 8 (1978): 73–88; Mick Broderick, *Nuclear Movies: A Filmography* (Northcote, Victoria, Australia: Post-Modem Publishing, 1988). Neither of these otherwise forgettable movies was notably successful, but as part of a larger stream of mass-culture material reinforcing the official version of the A-bomb decision, and as evidence of Hollywood's readiness to help promulgate that official version, they merit attention.

8. My thanks to Anthony A. Harkins for calling this story to my attention.

9. For a fuller discussion of this ethical discourse, see Boyer, *By the Bomb's Early Light*, part 6, "The Crisis of Morals and Values," 179–240.

10. Rodney Barker, *The Hiroshima Maidens: A Story of Courage, Compassion, and Survival* (New York: Viking, 1985), esp. 3–12, 95, 135–41.

11. For a somewhat fuller treatment of the polemical uses of Hiroshima and Nagasaki by antinuclear campaigners, see Paul Boyer, "Hiroshima in American Memory," *Diplomatic History* 19, no. 2 (1995): 297–318.

12. Stanley Goldberg, "Racing to the Finish: Why the Atomic Bomb Ended World War II," American Historical Association annual meeting, Washington, D.C., January 6, 1995; Hershberg, *Conant*, 229.

13. Boyer, "Hiroshima in American Memory," 305–6, 308–9, 315.

14. Gar Alperovitz, telephone interview with the author, August 23, 1995;

Alperovitz, *The Decision*, 5–7; *Who's Who in America, 1994* (New Providence, N.J.: Marquis *Who's Who*, 1993), 1:58–59 (Gar Alperovitz entry).

15. I am not arguing here that the "revisionist" interpretation of the A-bomb decision was merely a by-product of the radicalism and turmoil of the 1960s—a charge leveled by some conservative critics. One can note the ways in which the larger political/cultural climate helps shape the direction and thrust of historical scholarship while also recognizing the importance of the profession's long-standing tests of scholarly merit: the ability to marshal relevant and persuasive evidence, draw logical inferences from that evidence, remain faithful to the known facts of past events, and so on. A "revisionist" view of Truman's decision motivated solely by "radical" ideology, unsupported by research or convincing argument, would have quickly collapsed as it came under critical scrutiny. In fact, just the reverse occurred: the "revisionist" view not only has survived the political era in which it first arose, but has gained substantial (though not unanimous) support within the history profession.

16. Michael Kammen, "History as a Lightning Rod," *OAH Newsletter* 23, no. 2 (1995), 6.

17. Barton J. Bernstein, "The Struggle over History: Defining the Hiroshima Narrative," in *Judgment at the Smithsonian: The Bombing of Hiroshima and Nagasaki*, ed. Philip Nobile (New York: Marlowe, 1995), 160–68.

18. "Dole Sounds an Alarm on Education," *New York Times*, September 5, 1995.

19. Boyer, *By the Bomb's Early Light*, 198–99. The poet Langston Hughes, in the persona of his fictional character "Jess B. Simple," wrote in his *Chicago Defender* column on August 18, 1945: "Them atomic bombs make me sick at the stomach. Why wasn't the bomb used against Germany? They just did not want to use them on white folks. Germans is white. So they wait until the war is over in Europe to try them out on colored folks. Japs is colored" (ibid., 199).

20. As a broad generalization, one can say that the "revisionist" view of Truman's decision has made less headway among U.S. military historians than it has among American historians at large, and certainly among U.S. diplomatic historians. For example, Gerhard Weinberg, *A World at Arms: A Global History of World War II* (New York: Cambridge University Press, 1994) largely ignores the work of Alperovitz, Sherwin, and others, and uncritically repeats the justifications for the bomb initially advanced by President Truman, as does the historical popularizer David McCullough, the author of a best-selling biography of Truman. Robert P. Newman, *Truman and the Hiroshima Cult* (East Lansing: Michigan State University Press, 1995) is sharply critical of historians who have challenged the official version of the A-bomb decision, as is Stephen Harper, *Miracle of Deliverance: The Case for the Bombing of Hiroshima and Nagasaki* (London: Sidgwick and Jackson, 1985).

And, of course, Paul Fussell, whose scornful ridicule of the "revisionist" A-bomb scholars is discussed later in this essay, is a professor at the University of Pennsylvania with a considerable reputation in the field of English literature. For an overview of how these issues have played themselves out within the history profession, see Karen J. Winkler, "50 Years Later: The Debate Rages over Hiroshima," *Chronicle of Higher Education*, April 21, 1995, A10, 18–19.

21. Air Force Association quoted in Tony Capaccio and Uday Mohan, "Missing the Target: How the Media Mishandled the Smithsonian *Enola Gay* Controversy," *American Journalism Review*, July–August 1995, 20.

22. Edward T. Linenthal, "Can Museums Achieve a Balance Between History and Memory?" *Chronicle of Higher Education*, February 10, 1995, B1.

23. Paul Fussell, *Thank God for the Atomic Bomb and Other Essays* (New York: Summit Books, 1988), 19, 23, 27.

24. Paul Boyer, "The Bomb and the 'Good War,'" *Chronicle of Higher Education*, August 4, 1995, A36. Some of the ideas developed in the present essay appear in much abbreviated form in this *Chronicle* piece.

25. I. Michael Heyman quoted in White, "Memory Wars," 6.

5. History at Risk: Richard H. Kohn

An earlier version of this essay appeared in the *Journal of American History* 82 (1995): 1036–63, under the title "History and the Culture Wars: The Case of the Smithsonian Institution's *Enola Gay* Exhibition." Portions of this essay were presented to the Strategic Studies Program at the Paul H. Nitze School of Advanced International Studies, Johns Hopkins University, and to the 1995 annual meetings of the Organization of American Historians, the Society for Historians of American Foreign Relations, and (jointly) the North Carolina Literary and Historical Association and the Federation of North Carolina Historical Societies. The author thanks Henry X. Arenberg, Tami Davis Biddle, Kenneth R. Bowling, Mark Clodfelter, Eliot A. Cohen, George M. Curtis III, Tom Engelhardt, W. Miles Fletcher, Alfred Goldberg, Martin Harwit, Edward T. Linenthal, Anna K. Nelson, Alex Roland, Wilcomb E. Washburn, Gerhard L. Weinberg, and Herman S. Wolk for help with sources and criticism of the text.

1. Stephen Budiansky et al., "A Museum in Crisis: The Smithsonian Heads into Rough Times after the Enola Gay Debacle," *U.S. News & World Report*, February 13, 1995, 73–75; *Washington Post*, February 24, 1995, C2; Martin Harwit to Richard H. Kohn, February 6, 1995 (in my possession).

2. See, for example, *New York Times*, January 30, 1995, A14; *The Miami Herald*, February 23, 1995, 13A; Barton J. Bernstein, "Guest Opinion: Misconceived Patriotism," *Bulletin of the Atomic Scientists* 51 (May–June 1995):

4; John W. Dower, "How a Genuine Democracy Should Celebrate Its Past," *Chronicle of Higher Education*, June 16, 1995, B1–B2; Robert Jay Lifton and Greg Mitchell, *Hiroshima in America: Fifty Years of Denial* (New York: Putnam's, 1995), chap. 5; American Association of University Professors Resolution, "The Smithsonian Institution and the Enola Gay Exhibition," *Academe* 81 (July/August 1995): 56; and Mike Wallace, "The Battle of the Enola Gay," *Radical Historians Newsletter*, no. 72 (May 1995): 1–12, 22–32. Although Wallace's article contains characterizations and interpretations with which I disagree, it is the most complete and analytical narrative of the controversy yet published. George Orwell, *Nineteen Eighty-Four* (1949; New York: Signet Classics, 1950), 32.

3. Alex Roland, "Celebration or Education? The Goals of the U.S. National Air and Space Museum," *History and Technology* 10, nos. 1–2 (1993): 86; Joseph J. Corn, "Tools, Technologies, and Contexts: Interpreting the History of American Technics," in *History Museums in the United States: A Critical Assessment*, ed. Warren Leon and Roy Rosenzweig (Urbana: University of Illinois Press, 1989), 241–44.

4. Howard Means, "The Quiet Revolutionary," *Washingtonian*, August 1987, 96–101, 146–51, esp. 149, 150, 151, 146.

5. This assessment of Martin Harwit's tenure is based on my observation of the National Air and Space Museum (NASM) beginning in 1982, frequent discussions with NASM staff and other history and museum professionals beginning in the early 1980s, and service on three NASM advisory committees: special advisory committee on research, 1986; Collections Management Advisory Committee, 1988–91 as chair; and Advisory Committee on Research and Collections Management, 1991–present as chair. My views are supported in part by "Statement by I. Michael Heyman, Secretary Smithsonian Institution," May 2, 1995 (in my possession). In my judgment, Harwit's direction of NASM was designed to conform its activities to the understanding of the role of the Smithsonian originally articulated in the Smithsonian's first circular: not merely to entertain and amuse the public, or to inspire them and celebrate national achievements, but to educate and to advance the frontiers of knowledge. See G. Browne Goode, *Plan of Organization and Regulations* (1881) in G. Carroll Lindsay, "George Broom Goode," in *Keepers of the Past*, ed. Clifford L. Lord (Chapel Hill: University of North Carolina Press, 1965), 132–33, 137. Compare Goode's ideas with those that inspired NASM, according to Roland, "Celebration or Education?" 77–89.

6. As chief of air force history at the time and at my own request, I advised the planning committee and attended many of the events. I recognized the air force's interest in, and sensitivity to, public interpretations of military aviation history and strategic bombing, especially involving atomic and nuclear weapons. My purpose was to encourage the museum to present a broad

range of the best scholarly interpretations and the voices of the most knowledgeable and thoughtful participants, to avoid moralizing or politically inspired perspectives that were not based on solid research or high-quality
analysis, and to position the museum "above the battle" of conflicting interpretations about strategic bombing and the use of the atomic bombs in 1945.
The original slate of speakers was in my (and others') opinion heavily tilted
toward criticism of strategic bombing, the development and use of atomic
weapons, and the meaning and impact of the nuclear age, and it did not
include the most knowledgeable veterans or those scholars most current in
researching the field. The museum rectified this bias in the program and
participants. Harwit made clear that the program should introduce museum
staff to the best scholarship and most knowledgeable veterans in preparation
for the *Enola Gay* exhibit.

7. "Exhibition Planning Document July 1993. Tentative Exhibit Title:
The Crossroads: The End of World War II, the Atomic Bomb, and the Onset
of the Cold War. Projected Dates: May 1995 to January 1996," NASM, 2, 16
(in my possession). "A Proposal. Hiroshima and Nagasaki: A Fiftieth Anniversary Exhibit at the National Air and Space Museum," 1993, NASM, 4; Tom
Crouch to Martin Harwit, memo: "SUBJECT: A Response to the Secretary,"
July 21, 1993, NASM, 2. See Robert Adams to Martin Harwit, July 17, 1993,
NASM. Adams said he found much of the planning document "compelling.
There could be an exhibit here that would do the Smithsonian credit. On the
other hand, there are some, fairly fundamental aspects of it with which I am
no more in agreement now than when we have discussed them on previous
occasions." Adams listed seven points, asked for changes, and clearly expressed his unease about aspects of the interpretation, at one point using the
phrase "increasing the risk to SI." Crouch warned Harwit about tampering
with the exhibit piecemeal to meet Adams's objections: "What we will accomplish is to transform a good, powerful, and honest exhibition into a mass
of confused messages on the basis of ten million nickel-and-dime changes."

8. Martin Harwit, conversation with the author, July 18, 1995. On combining scholarship with commemoration in the exhibit, see "Presenting History: Museums in a Democratic Society," conference sponsored by the
Smithsonian Institution and the University of Michigan, Ann Arbor, Michigan, April 19, 1995. An audiotape of the conference can be purchased from
the Smithsonian's Center for Folklife Program and Cultural Studies, Washington, D.C. See also *Washington Post*, April 20, 1995, A7; *Philadelphia In-
quirer*, April 20, 1995, A7, and April 24, 1995, D1.

9. "The Crossroads: The End of World War II, the Atomic Bomb, and the
Origins of the Cold War," first draft script, January 12–14, 1994, NASM (in
my possession). For a diagram of the sections, with major artifact place-
ments, see *New York Times*, February 5, 1995, E5.

10. "Crossroads," 100:5. (Each part of this draft script bears a number in
the hundreds and is separately paginated, so 100:5 is page 5 of part 1.) Ibid.,

200:1, 56; 100:6. See also ibid., 16, 23, and 54. Ibid., 200:25, 26; Stanley Goldberg, "Smithsonian Suffers Legionnaire's Disease," *Bulletin of the Atomic Scientists* 51 (May/June 1995): 30. See Wallace, "Battle of the Enola Gay," 2–5.

11. Mike Wallace points out that most "of the pundits . . . relied on a series of articles by John T. Correll, editor of *Air Force Magazine*," a judgment that confirms my own reading of columns and press reports. See Wallace, "Battle of the Enola Gay," 2. For a glaring example, see "The Shame of Enola Gay," *Popular Mechanics*, August 1995, 45–49. The story title on the cover of the magazine reads "Enola Gay: From Glory to Dishonor. Our Shameful Treatment of the World's Most Famous Airplane."

12. I detected this bias in my first reading of the script and communicated my concerns in a letter, accompanied by specific criticisms: Richard H. Kohn to Martin Harwit, June 18, 1994 (in my possession). Other historians read this or later scripts similarly according to Gerhard L. Weinberg, conversation with the author, July 17, 1995, and Alfred Goldberg, conversation with the author, July 18, 1995. This bias in the script coincided with that apparent to me in 1989–90, in the museum's planned program of films, lectures, and symposia. I and others warned the museum that it could and should air different interpretations, but that if the exhibit did not stand above the battles over interpretation and tilted toward an attack on airpower, the air force, or American behavior in the war against Japan, the museum might forfeit support in the aviation and space community and incite an assault from the military.

13. "Crossroads," 100:2.

14. Ibid., 100:5, 6, 17–28. The three parts of "A Fight to the Finish" were: "Combat in the Pacific," "A Torch to the Enemy: The Strategic Bombing of Japan," and "Two Nations at War."

15. Ibid., 200:28, 31, 56, 66.

16. "Exhibition Planning Document, July 1993," NASM, 12.

17. See John T. Correll, "War Stories at Air and Space," *Air Force Magazine*, September 1994, 24–29; John T. Correll, " 'The Last Act' at Air and Space," ibid., 58–64; John T. Correll, "The Three Doctors and the *Enola Gay*," ibid., November 1994, 8–12; and John T. Correll to editor, *Washington Post*, August 14, 1994, C9. On the reactions of veterans of the 509th Composite Group, see *Chicago Tribune*, September 2, 1994, 1, 7, and *Miami Herald*, February 23, 1995, 13A. The author of the last article, Kate Cannon, the daughter of a 509th veteran, teaches at the University of Miami and Florida Atlantic University and is finishing an American history Ph.D., doing a "good bit of research . . . on World War II veterans." She wrote that "the American Legion's accusations that the exhibit made Americans look like 'butchers' and 'aggressors' . . . worked," inducing "some veterans" at the last 509th reunion to make "hysterical charges about the exhibit."

18. "Crossroads," 500:1, 15, 18.

19. On recent trends in museum exhibits, see Eric Gable and Richard Handler, "The Authority of Documents at Some American History Museums," *Journal of American History* 81 (June 1994): 119–20, 121, 134; Cary Carson, "Lost in the Fun House: A Commentary on Anthropologists' First Contact with History Museums," ibid., 143–50; Barbara Franco, "The Communication Conundrum: What Is the Message? Who Is Listening?" ibid., 153–63; and Cary Carson, remarks, "Enola Gay Exhibit: A Case Study in Controversy," panel at "Presenting History."

20. For Tom Crouch's explanation of the exhibit's purpose and the curators' goals, see Tom Crouch, remarks, in "The Enola Gay Exhibit" panel, "Presenting History." See also his testimony, statement, and answers to questions in U.S. Congress, Senate, Committee on Rules and Administration, *Hearings on the Smithsonian Institution: Management Guidelines for the Future*, 104 Cong., 1st sess., May 18, 1995, 72–78, 89–90, 92–93, 95–98. As late as August 1994, Martin Harwit expressed his goals for the exhibition as both a commemoration of the veterans' contributions *and* "an accurate portrayal that conveys the reality of atomic war and its consequences." *Washington Post*, August 7, 1994, C9.

21. For the meeting and its immediate aftermath, I have relied on Goldberg, "Smithsonian Suffers Legionnaire's Disease," 29–30; and on conversations over the last year with Martin Harwit, Tom Crouch, Edward T. Linenthal, and Herman Wolk. I have seen in its entirety only one written critique from the February meeting that was filed before the Air Force Association attacked the exhibit publicly: [Herman Wolk], "Comments on Script, 'The Crossroads . . . ,' " [February 1994] (in my possession). Excerpts from other comments are printed in Tom Crouch's statement in Committee on Rules and Administration, *Smithsonian Institution: Management Guidelines for the Future*, 77. My own views of the first and fourth scripts were communicated in Richard H. Kohn to Martin Harwit, June 18, September 19, 26, 1994, January 31, 1995 (in my possession). For the reactions of other historians critical of the exhibit scripts, I have relied on Weinberg, conversation; Goldberg, conversation; Edward J. Drea, "Memorandum for DOD WWII Commemoration Committee," April 13, 1994, and "Memorandum for DOD WWII Commemoration Committee," July 7, 1994 (both in my possession); Harold W. Nelson, "Memorandum for Executive Director 50th Anniversary of World War II Commemoration Committee," April 19, 1994, ibid.; Richard Hallion to Tom Crouch, April 13, 1994, ibid.; and [Herman Wolk], "Comments on 'The Last Act: The Atomic Bomb and the End of World War II,' " second script, July 1994, ibid.

22. Correll, " 'The Last Act' at Air and Space," 59–60.

23. The first public attack was issued as a documented "Air Force Association Special Report" titled "The Smithsonian and the Enola Gay" and published as Correll, "War Stories at Air and Space." Six months earlier, the

association's executive director had written Harwit that "the new concept does not relieve my earlier concerns and, in some respects, it seems even less balanced . . . than the earlier concepts were. . . . [Y]ou assure me that the exhibition will 'honor the bravery of the veterans,' but that theme is virtually nonexistent in the proposal as drafted." The plan "dwells, to the effective exclusion of all else, on the horrors of war"; the "concept paper treats Japan and United States in the war as if their participation in the war were morally equivalent. If anything, incredibly, it gives the benefit of opinion to Japan, which was the aggressor." "Balance is owed to all Americans, particularly those who come to the exhibition to learn. What they will get from the program as described is not history or fact but a partisan interpretation." Monroe W. Hatch, Jr., to Martin Harwit, September 10, 1993 (in my possession). In 1993, at the request of the museum, I discussed the proposed exhibit with General Hatch, with whom and for whom I had worked in the 1980s when he was inspector general of the air force, vice commander in chief of Strategic Air Command, and vice chief of staff of the air force. (In 1988, when he was my supervisor's boss, I had shared some concern about the exhibit with him.) While both General Hatch and I recognized the broader purposes and activities of the association, the general was emphatic in saying that he "represented a veterans organization," which I interpreted as a statement by him of the association's primary reason for taking such intense interest in the *Enola Gay* exhibit. On the Air Force Association, see James H. Straubel, *Crusade for Airpower: The Story of the Air Force Association* (Washington, D.C.: Air Force Association, 1982); and Wallace, "The Battle of the Enola Gay," 10–11.

24. For my initial reading of Correll, "War Stories at Air and Space," see Richard H. Kohn to editor, *Air Force Magazine*, June 1994, 6.

25. Correll, "War Stories at Air and Space," 24. For air force involvement in the museum's founding, see Roland, "Celebration or Education?" 80–88.

26. "Clearing the Way for the Air Force Memorial," *Air Force Magazine*, August 1995, 80–82.

27. My thinking derives from Edward T. Linenthal, *Sacred Ground: Americans and Their Battlefields*, 2nd ed. (Urbana: University of Illinois Press, 1993).

28. Correll, " 'The Last Act' at Air and Space," 64; Vago Muradian, " 'This Is What We Wanted:' How a Veteran's Letter Launched a Campaign to Honor the Enola Gay," *Air Force Times*, February 13, 1995, 17; Goldberg, "Smithsonian Suffers Legionnaire's Disease," 33. In his statement to the Senate, on May 11, 1995, R. E. Smith, national president of the Air Force Association, stated: "The question does not end with the *Enola Gay* exhibit. What about the next exhibit and the one after that? We would like to see the museum putting its main effort on its primary mission which is to collect, preserve, and display historic aircraft, spacecraft, and aeronautical artifacts.

There are most certainly indications of change; the main one being the resignation of the director. . . . It was unfortunate that matters came to that, but it was probably inevitable." Committee on Rules and Administration, *Smithsonian Institution: Management Guidelines for the Future*, 29.

29. For a sampling of reaction and analysis of the public campaign, see *St. Louis Post-Dispatch*, June 9, 1995, 1; "Atom Bomb Exhibit Hit," Council on America's Military Past, *Headquarters Heliogram*, July–August 1994, 1, 8; *Washington Post*, August 14, 1994, C8; *Boston Globe*, August 16, 1994, 5; *Wall Street Journal*, August 29, 1994, A10; Charles Krauthammer, "An Exhibit Infused with Revisionism on Hiroshima Bomb," *Chicago Tribune*, August 19, 1994, 13; ibid., September 2, 1994, 1, 6; Lance Morrow, "Essay: Hiroshima and the Time Machine," *Time*, September 19, 1994, 94; *Washington Times*, December 21, 1994, 6; A. J. Bacevich, "Rewriting 'The Last Act,'" *World and I*, December 1994, 78–83; *Chicago Sun-Times*, January 26, 1995, 21; and *Raleigh News and Observer*, February 2, 1995, 9A; Muradian, " 'This Is What We Wanted,' " 17. For an analysis of the press coverage of the controversy, see Tony Capaccio and Uday Mohan, "Missing the Target," *American Journalism Review* 17 (July/August 1995): 18–26.

30. A particularly incendiary example was George F. Will, "Score Big Points: Kill the Monster at Smithsonian," *Chicago Sun-Times*, January 26, 1995, 21. Otis Graham connected the controversy over a proposed Disney history park with the *Enola Gay* exhibit battle, arguments in the Santa Barbara high schools over ethnic studies, and debate over the national history standards. See Otis Graham, "Editor's Corner: Who Owns American History?" *Public Historian* 17 (spring 1995): 8–11. See also Karen J. Winkler, "Who Owns History?" *Chronicle of Higher Education*, January 20, 1995, A10–11, A18; Wallace, "Battle of the Enola Gay," 6–8.

31. *Wall Street Journal*, August 29, 1994, A10; *Washington Post*, February 11, 1995, 21. An editorial in the leading newspaper in the city where the American Legion has its headquarters said, "Americans who love their country are increasingly disgusted with the carping of elitists dedicated to tearing down national morale, insulting national pride and debasing national achievements." The editorial called for firing Martin Harwit and canceling the exhibit. "This isn't the first instance of arrogant revisionism on the part of Smithsonian curators. And it isn't likely to be the last unless Congress intervenes forcefully." *Indianapolis Star*, January 25, 1995, A12.

32. See Martin Harwit to editor, *Air Force Magazine*, May 1994, 4; *Raleigh News and Observer*, August 12, 1994, 21A; and "*Enola Gay* and a Nation's Memories," *Air & Space*, August–September 1994, 18–21.

33. Martin Harwit, "Comments on *Crossroads*," April 16, 1994 (in my possession). This memorandum became public almost immediately. See Correll, "Three Doctors," 8, 9–10.

34. For the role of the veterans' organizations, see Committee on Rules

and Administration, *Smithsonian Institution: Management Guidelines for the Future*, 13–40, 116–17, 157–60. This process apparently began in July. See ibid., 14. On "negotiation" with outside groups, see Edward T. Linenthal, *Preserving Memory: The Struggle to Create America's Holocaust Museum* (New York: Viking, 1995); Daniel Martinez, remarks, "Enola Gay Exhibit" panel, "Presenting History"; and Barbara Franco, "Doing History in Public: Balancing Historical Fact with Public Meaning," *Perspectives: American Historical Association Newsletter* 33 (May–June): 5–8.

35. Martin Harwit has told me that overwhelmingly the changes desired were insignificant from a scholarly standpoint. For the dangers in negotiations, see Alfred F. Young, "S.O.S.: Storm Warning for American Museums," *OAH Newsletter* 22 (November 1994): 6, 8; Martinez, remarks, "*Enola Gay* Exhibit" panel; Barbara Clark Smith, remarks, "Museums in a Democratic Society" panel; and Richard Kurin, remarks, "Wrap-Up Session" panel, all in "Presenting History."

36. Herman S. Wolk, "Subject: Conversation with Dr. Martin Harwit," memorandum, August 23, 1994 (in my possession). On June 21, lead curator Michael J. Neufeld had sent the revised (second version) script to the exhibit advisory committee members, but his cover letter ruled out any further substantive changes. "If you find any factual errors or if you object strongly to certain formulations in the revised script, I would be happy to hear them. But, if the exhibit is to be opened in late May 1995, as planned, we must now move on to the production and construction phase. This script therefore must be considered a finished product, minor wording changes aside." Michael J. Neufeld to Edwin Bearss et al., June 21, 1994, ibid.

37. William Allison et al. to I. Michael Heyman, November 11, 1994, ibid. See also "Enola Gay Controversy Continues," *OAH Newsletter*, February 1995: 3; "Teach-Ins to Foster Discussion of Atomic Bomb Exhibit," ibid., May 1995, 15. The fifth and last version of the script, "The Last Act: The Atomic Bomb and the End of World War II," October 26, 1994, is copyrighted by the Smithsonian and can be purchased from its Office of the General Counsel. This script, considerably shorter than the original, in my judgment is not as imbalanced as the first version but errs on the other side by simplifying the history and arguing one-sidedly for the necessity of the bomb and its agency in ending the war in the Pacific. *New York Times*, October 8, 1994, E15. See also ibid., January 31, 1995, A11; and Bernstein, "Guest Opinion: Misconceived Patriotism," 4.

38. Thomas J. Kilcline, remarks, "Museums in a Democratic Society," panel, "Presenting History"; *Washington Post*, January 19, 1995, C1; *New York Times*, January 26, 1995, A6; Budiansky et al., "Museum in Crisis," 73–75.

39. Budiansky et al., "Museum in Crisis," 73–74.

40. *Washington Post*, January 19, 1995, C1; *New York Times*, January 26, 1995, A6; Budiansky et al., "Museum in Crisis," 73–75. Senator Ted Stevens

stated that 85 percent of the Smithsonian's funding came from the public treasury. See Committee on Rules and Administration, *Smithsonian Institution Management Guidelines for the Future*, 42–43. For the 1994 figures cited in the text, see *Smithsonian, Year 1994: Annual Report of the Smithsonian Institution for the Year Ended September 30, 1994* (Washington, D.C.: Smithsonian Institution, 1994), 83–100. The American Legion gave the impression that it withdrew its support for the exhibition because Martin Harwit changed the estimate of potential American casualties in an invasion of Japan. In reality, that change was inconsequential from an interpretive standpoint, and American Legion leaders had already decided to oppose the exhibition before receiving Harwit's letter informing them of the change. See John T. Correll, "Political Exhibit Crashes at the Smithsonian," *Air Force Magazine*, March 1995, 12; "Last Act" exhibition label "Invasion of Japan— At What Cost?" January 18, 1995 (in my possession); and Thomas B. Allen and Norman Polmar, "Blown Away," *Washingtonian*, August 1995, 110.

41. I. Michael Heyman, "Smithsonian Perspectives," *Smithsonian*, October 1994, 9; I. Michael Heyman, "The Smithsonian: From the Spirit of St. Louis to Enola Gay," November 10, 1994 (in my possession). In his "installation address," September 19, 1994, Heyman "commented . . . that our first script was deficient." See Committee on Rules and Administration, *Smithsonian Institution: Management Guidelines for the Future*, 67. In a February 1995 speech to the National Press Club (in my possession), Heyman said: "We need to distinguish between opinion and fact. We need to contribute to light rather than heat. And we need to avoid 'instructing' people or telling them how to think." Yet "there should always be room at the Smithsonian to explore important contemporary issues lest our great potentialities as an educational institution be wasted."

42. I. Michael Heyman to "All Smithsonian Employees," memo, January 30, 1995 (in my possession); Heyman, "Smithsonian," ibid. In his testimony of May 18, 1995, Heyman stated that in January he had believed the exhibition possible, but that he changed his mind because of "renewed efforts to have the exhibition canceled." Committee on Rules and Administration, *Smithsonian Institution: Management Guidelines for the Future*, 68.

43. Martin Harwit, conversation with the author, February 2, 1995.

44. I. Michael Heyman, speech at the National Press Club, February 23, 1995 (in my possession); Committee on Rules and Administration, *Smithsonian Institution: Management Guidelines for the Future*, 43, 99. See also ibid., 42, 55, 108.

45. Joshua Steinberg, "The Bomb in the Nation's Attic," *Dartmouth Alumni Magazine*, May 1995, 27; Smithsonian Institution, *E Pluribus Unum: This Divine Paradox. Report of the Commission on the Future of the Smithsonian Institution* (Washington, D.C.: Smithsonian Institution, 1995), 23.

46. Heyman, "Smithsonian." This distinction between university and mu-

seum was endorsed by Robert R. Archibald, "From the President," American Association for State and Local History, *Dispatch* 10 (May 1995): 3. See also James L. Abrahamson to editor, *OAH Newsletter* 23 (February 1995): 36. Both reply to Young, "S.O.S.," 1, 6–8. Carson, "Lost in the Fun House," 149–50; Committee on Rules and Administration, *Smithsonian Institution: Management Guidelines for the Future*, 99.

47. See Committee on Rules and Administration, *Smithsonian Institution: Management Guidelines for the Future*, 4–8, 16, 30, 34; Steinberg, "Bomb in the Nation's Attic," 27.

48. Martin Harwit, conversation with the author, February 2, 1995. Both Senator Ted Stevens and Senator Wendell Ford, the ranking Democrat on the committee, cited other controversial exhibits. See Committee on Rules and Administration, *Smithsonian Institution: Management Guidelines for the Future*, 42–43. I. Michael Heyman may have been affected by an article in a conservative weekly published in Washington: Stephen Goode, "Political Correctness Comes Out of the Attic at the Smithsonian," *Insight on the News*, January 2, 1995, 30–32. For his reply, see I. Michael Heyman, "Mission of the Smithsonian Is to Teach *and* Celebrate," ibid., February 13, 1995, cited in Wilcomb E. Washburn, "The Smithsonian and the *Enola Gay*," *National Interest*, no. 40 (summer 1995): 46. For an analysis of Heyman's actions, see ibid., 46–48. Heyman denied that he "negotiated any arrangement concerning the *Enola Gay* exhibit" with Newt Gingrich. "I came to the decision to scale it back independently. I then consulted the Smithsonian Regents." I. Michael Heyman to the editor, *New Republic*, April 10, 1995, 1.

49. Bernard Lewis, *History: Remembered, Recovered, Invented* (Princeton: Princeton University Press, 1975), 71. My thinking on commemorations is derived from John Bodnar, *Remaking America: Public Memory, Commemoration, and Patriotism in the Twentieth Century* (Princeton: Princeton University Press, 1992); John R. Gillis, ed., *Commemorations: The Politics of National Identity* (Princeton: Princeton University Press, 1994); G. Kurt Piehler, *Remembering War the American Way* (Washington, D.C.: Smithsonian Institution Press, 1995); Edward T. Linenthal, "Committing History in Public," *Journal of American History* 81 (December 1994): 988–91; Edward T. Linenthal, "Can Museums Achieve a Balance between Memory and History?" *Chronicle of Higher Education*, February 10, 1995, B1–2; Linenthal, *Sacred Ground*; and Linenthal, *Preserving Memory*.

50. See Committee on Rules and Administration. *Smithsonian Institution: Management Guidelines for the Future*, 4–8, 16, 30, 34; and Charles D. Cooper, "Editorial Comment: The *Enola Gay*—Mission Aborted," *Retired Officer Magazine*, March 1995, 4.

51. Martin Harwit, "The *Enola Gay*: A Nation's, and a Museum's, Dilemma," *Washington Post*, August 7, 1994, C9. Many Department of Defense historians and I believe a full exhibition that avoided this conflict was possi-

ble, according to Goldberg, conversation with the author, July 18, 1995; Herman Wolk, remarks, *"Enola Gay* Exhibit" panel, "Presenting History"; Tony Capaccio, "DOD Historians Lauded Revisions in A-Bomb Script," *Defense Week,* July 3, 1995, 1.

52. For strong, balanced historical reporting, see Evan Thomas, "Why We Did It," *Newsweek,* July 24, 1995, 22–28, 30; and Gerald Parshall, "Shock Wave," *U.S. News & World Report,* July 31, 1995, 44–59. A recent Gallup Poll indicates that while "senior citizens still narrowly approve of the bombing, . . . younger Americans, particularly those under the age of 30, believe that dropping the bomb on Japan was wrong." Thus accounts that question the American action would be accepted by some viewers to an exhibit. See Thomas, "Why We Did It," 22. Media coverage of the anniversary of Hiroshima indicates a general awareness and willingness to consider alternative interpretations of the event. See William Lanouette, "Why We Dropped the Bomb," *Civilization* 2 (January/February 1995): 28–39; Murray Sayle, "Letter from Hiroshima: Did the Bomb End the War?" *New Yorker,* July 31, 1995, 40–64; *New York Times,* August 6, 1995, 1, 9; ABC News, Peter Jennings Reporting, "Hiroshima: Why the Bomb Was Dropped," August 2, 1995.

53. On historical interpretation in the Soviet Union, see *Washington Post,* June 21, 1991, A21; ibid., November 20, 1991, D1. On Japanese division over a war apology, see *USA Today,* August 26, 1994, 7A; *New York Times,* June 7, 1995, 1; ibid., June 12, 1995, A1, 4; Kenzaburo Oe, "Denying History Disables Japan," *New York Times Magazine,* July 2, 1995, 28–29; David E. Sanger, "Coloring History ~~Their~~ [sic] Our Way," ibid., 30–31. The contrast with Germany's confronting of its Nazi period is often remarked; see *New York Times,* June 9, 1995, A7; and Ronnie and Rolf Lynton to Lynne and Richard Kohn (from Berlin, describing the program of sponsored visits for refugees from political persecution in the Third Reich), May 9, 1995 (in my possession). *New York Times,* June 25, 1995, E15; John Le Carré, "The Trap Has Opened, So Let's Be Free," *International Herald Tribune,* May 6, 1993, p. 7.

54. A poll last year showed "60 percent of Americans are unable to name the President who ordered the nuclear attack on Japan, and 35 percent do not know that the first atomic bomb was dropped on Hiroshima. One of every four people surveyed for the America's Talking/Gallup Poll did not even know that Japan was the target of the first atomic bomb." See *New York Times,* March 1, 1995, A19.

6. Culture War, History Front: Mike Wallace

1. Newt Gingrich's immobilized past stands in stark contrast to his vision of a flexible future. He seems oblivious to the contradiction, perhaps because he thinks he needs a fixed base from which to launch his Third Wave revolution. But this is to deprive himself of the historical tools that might be used

to understand (and help shape) the way a society moves from one era to another.

2. It's hard to imagine that if Gingrich had ever actually stepped foot in the National Air and Space Museum, he wouldn't have been pleased with at least one exhibition his allies detested—the revised World War I galleries. He claims as a transformational defining moment his visit, at age fifteen, to the Verdun battlefield. There he peered through the windows of an ossuary containing the bones of 100,000 unidentified bodies. "I can still feel the sense of horror and reality which overcame me then," he wrote in his 1984 book *Window of Opportunity*. "It is the driving force which pushed me into history and politics and molded my life." The World War I exhibition features a giant photograph of the Verdun ossuary. Pity he's intent on denying others even an echo of the experience he found so moving and instructive.

3. President Bill Clinton, whose past and present relations with the military left him in no position to challenge the decision, observed with his usual caution that while "academic freedom" was an issue here, he "nonetheless felt that some of the concerns expressed by veterans groups and others had merit."

4. Newt Gingrich is a trailblazer here too. Of the wealthy donors who picked up the six-hundred-thousand-dollar tab for the first year of his "Renewing American Civilization" lectures, those contributing over twenty-five thousand dollars were "invited to participate in the course development process"—giving a new twist to the notion of a "free market in ideas."

5. In June 1995 the Bradbury Science Museum in Los Alamos mounted an exhibition on the atomic bomb prepared by a Santa Fe peace group. In featuring photos of ground devastation, it infuriated veterans and former Manhattan Project workers. Not having seen the exhibit, I can't comment on its interpretive perspective. But it's a chilling sign of NASM fallout that Harold Agnew, former director of the Los Alamos National Laboratory (which owns the museum), wrote a veterans' group that if the show was not changed, staff members' jobs might be at risk. "We got rid of the Smithsonian curator over the *Enola Gay* fiasco," he said. "Hopefully the Bradbury staff will understand."

6. "They are bending over backwards it looks like to accommodate the Japanese," said Sam Johnson. Ironically, curator Tom Crouch was on record as being "really bothered, angered, by the way that the Japanese find it so difficult to put wartime issues in real context. Their view is to portray themselves as victims." Crouch, however, saw parallels in this country. "As I listen to the folks who criticize this [exhibit], I hear something similar to that. There's real discomfort about looking at destruction on the ground. . . . I hear critics saying, 'Don't tell part of the story.' " "They want to stop the story when the bomb leaves the bomb bay."

7. A "Japan Committee to Appeal for World Peace '95," composed of

scholars and cultural workers, called for an "apology and compensation for damages to the Asian peoples whom we victimized," and urged the Japanese government and Diet to "clearly articulate the government's self-reflection on Japan's responsibility for past colonial rule as well as the Asia-Pacific War."

The political establishment teeters back and forth on this issue. Prime Minister Tomiichi Murayama went to Beijing in the spring of 1995 and said, "I recognize anew that Japan's actions, including aggression and colonial rule, at one time in our history caused unbearable suffering and sorrow for many people in your country and other Asian neighbors." He also wrote a scroll, "I face up to history."

The Japanese nationalist right did not. Shigeto Nagano, justice minister and former chief of staff of the army, insisted in May 1995 that the massacre of hundreds of thousands of Chinese at Nanking in 1937 was a "fabrication" and reaffirmed that Japan, in invading Asian countries, had been "liberating" them from Western colonial powers.

On May 12, 1995, however, a Tokyo High Court ruling of the previous October was affirmed, which had supported Japanese historian Saburo Ienaga's thirty-one-year struggle against the Education Ministry for white-washing schoolbook accounts of the massacre. It also revoked the ministry's power to determine historical "truth."

On June 6, 1995, the right-wing Liberal Democratic Party forced a compromise on the parliamentary apology front. A resolution carried the lower house expressing remorse for causing "unbearable pain to people abroad, particularly in Asian countries." But the wording was ambiguous enough to allow for varying interpretations (thus *hansei* could mean "remorse," or merely "reflection"). The upper house refused even to consider such a resolution. A week later, on June 14, the government responded by establishing a fund to provide medical and social welfare assistance to former comfort women. Although it fell short of what some of the women had demanded, it was accompanied by a statement of remorse and apology. This will clearly be an ongoing struggle.

8. Similarly, Tokyo's Metropolitan Edo-Tokyo Museum mounted a major exhibition for the March 1995 fiftieth anniversary of the city's being firebombed. Though retaining a focus on domestic suffering, it included information on 1930s and 1940s militarism. (Video clips showed Japanese bombers attacking Chongqing.)

9. More irony: A small industry has sprung up in Japan that caters to youth "searching for heroes in an uncertain world," by producing books, comics, and computer games (like Commander's Decision) in which World War II history is rewritten in Japan's favor, granting it retroactive victory, while omitting all mention of wartime atrocities.

7. Dangerous History: Marilyn B. Young

1. Nathan Huggins, "The Deforming Mirror of Truth," new introduction to *Black Odyssey: The African American Ordeal in Slavery* (New York: Vintage Books, 1990), xii, xiii.

2. Ibid., p. xii.

3. Colin Powell quoted by Henry Louis Gates, Jr., "Powell and the Black Elite," *The New Yorker*, September 25, 1995, 66.

4. Huggins, *Black Odyssey*, xi.

5. Loren Baritz, *Backfire: A History of How American Culture Led Us into Vietnam and Made Us Fight the Way We Did* (New York: William Morrow, 1985), 341.

6. See Mike Wallace, "The Battle of the Enola Gay," in *Radical Historians Newsletter*, no. 72 (May 1995), for an account of a new, contextualized display of the V-2 rocket and its 1991 transformation of the World War I galleries. Michael Harwit, appointed director of the National Air and Space Museum in 1987, "set out to demonstrate the social impact of aviation and space technology—the ways it transformed daily life, 'both for the good and the bad.' This applied to the military sphere too. 'No longer is it sufficient to display sleek fighters,' he said, while making no mention of the 'misery of war' " (12).

7. She warned, however, that this might be only a "fleeting moment in history, for the scepter passes," and worried that Americans were not ready to assume the responsibilities of their immense new power.

8. *New York Times*, March 19, 1995, 41.

9. Wallace, "The Battle of the Enola Gay," 22. The positive response to Harwit's departures from standard NASM exhibits "cleared the way for the Enola Gay."

10. Stanley Goldberg, "Smithsonian Suffers Legionnaire's Disease," *Bulletin of the Atomic Scientists*, May/June 1995.

11. The controversy over the Smithsonian exhibit has remedied this situation. Alperovitz's new book, *The Decision to Use the Atomic Bomb and the Architecture of an American Myth* (New York: Knopf, 1995), was in its second printing before it even reached the bookstores. Peter Jennings interviewed Alperovitz and listed his books as sources for his ABC special on Hiroshima that aired on July 27, 1995. Alperovitz's publisher, Alfred A. Knopf, then used the special to advertise the book: "A must for all who saw (and all who missed) last night's ABC Television Special." In the preface to his new book, Alperovitz writes that the focus of *Atomic Diplomacy* was not on the decision to bomb as such, but rather the impact of that decision on subsequent U.S.-Soviet relations. Critics of his work have nevertheless understood it as a monocausal explanation of the use of the atomic weapons.

12. Peter Jennings, quoted in Walter Goodman, "Fifty Years Later, Still the Day After," *New York Times*, July 30, 1995.

13. That same year, Hollywood provided the visuals for Henry L. Stimson's essay. In a script heavily censored by Manhattan Project director General Leslie Groves, *The Beginning or the End* worked to block any sense that the United States had acted with ruthless brutality against a helpless victim: the citizens of Hiroshima are showered with warning leaflets (a courtesy the Japanese had failed to extend at Pearl Harbor), and the *Enola Gay* must fly through heavy anti-aircraft fire before it can fulfill its mission. The reality of the raid, the complete absence of any warning against an undefended civilian target, disappeared, along with any reference to the bombing of Nagasaki. See Robert Jay Lifton and Greg Mitchell, *Hiroshima in America* (New York: Putnam's, 1995).

14. Avital Ronell, "Activist Supplement: Papers on the Gulf War," in *Finitude's Score: Essays for the End of the Millennium* (Lincoln: University of Nebraska Press, 1994), 296.

8. The Victors and the Vanquished: Tom Engelhardt

My special thanks to my patient editors, critics, and friends: Sara Bershtel, Jonathan Cobb, Peter Dimock, John Dower, Yasuko Dower, Nancy Garrity, Beverley Gologorsky, Vicki Haire, Ed Linenthal, Paul Tough.

1. Michael Wines, "President Rejects Apology to Japan," *New York Times*, December 2, 1991. All Pearl Harbor quotes are taken from tapes of the televised ceremonies. Excerpts from one of George Bush's Pearl Harbor speeches can be found in the *New York Times*, December 8, 1991, 24.

2. John Darnton, "At Buckingham Palace, Solemn and Joyful Echoes of 1945"; Stephen Kinzer, "Allies and Former Enemies Gather to Pledge Peace"; Todd S. Purdum, "Clinton Pays Homage to an 'Extraordinary Generation,'" *New York Times*, May 9, 1995, A10. When, on September 2, 1995, V-J day plus fifty, Bill Clinton marked the anniversary of the end of the war with a speech, carried on CNN, at the National Memorial Cemetery of the Pacific, he, like George Bush four years earlier, meant to mobilize memories of an ascendant America. But unsurprisingly, his speech, even more than Bush's, had an abiding post-Vietnam ring to it. It emphasized the war's destructiveness ("It ravaged countrysides . . . cost a total in lives of 58 million people . . . civilians and prisoners felled by disease and starvation . . . millions wiped out in the gas chambers"); made covert reference to the atomic bombings of Hiroshima and Nagasaki ("It destroyed whole cities . . . [left] children buried in the rubble of bombed buildings"); replaced the fused democratic patrol of wartime propaganda with multicultural

lists of race and ethnicity ("the whites, the blacks, the hispanics, the Asian-Americans who served including Japanese-Americans, the Native-Americans including the famous Navaho code talkers"); and where the enemy had once been, left a blankness. If he invoked a half-century-old moment when "we found . . . unity in a shared mission, strength in a common purpose," it now seemed only a sad plaint for the disunity, the lack of common purpose, of 1995.

3. Jan C. Scruggs and Joel L. Swerdlow, *To Heal a Nation: The Vietnam Veterans Memorial* (New York: Harper and Row, 1985), 7–8.

4. For more on rites of reconciliation after the Civil War, see Edward T. Linenthal, *Sacred Ground: Americans and Their Battlefields* (Urbana: University of Illinois Press, 1991), esp. 90–96, 105–8, 119.

5. John Bodnar, *Remaking America: Public Memory, Commemoration, and Patriotism in the Twentieth Century* (Princeton: Princeton University Press, 1992), 81, 94–5.

6. Parker Bishop Albee, Jr., and Keller Cushing Freeman, *Shadow of Suribachi: Raising the Flags on Iwo Jima* (Westport, Conn.: Praeger, 1995), 109, 120, 139.

7. Perhaps the only American war memorials similar to the Vietnam Wall were, as John Bodnar has suggested, the "beautiful cemeteries, 'cities of the dead' " that Southerners built after the Civil War "where people could honor those they had lost and express their grief." And those, too, arose from a culture of defeat. Bodnar, *Remaking America*, 5, 28.

8. Ibid., 5; Scruggs and Swerdlow, *To Heal a Nation*, 80ff.

9. Already the Mall is filling with new-style memorials. Across from the Vietnam Wall is the Korean War Veterans Memorial, dedicated in July 1995. With its own black reflective wall (etched with ghostly faces rather than names), its centerpiece is a patrol of nineteen stainless-steel, seven-foot-high soldiers. As James Reston, Jr., has written, "These G.I. Joes are moving forward, up a slight incline toward their goal: the American flag. . . . This is a tribute to military action itself. . . . Only sentiments of duty and country draw them forward." Although the memorial is indeed more traditional in intent than the Vietnam Wall—with sentiments like "Freedom is not free" and "Our nation honors her sons and daughters who answered the call to defend a country they never knew and a people they never met" etched into wall and ground—the patrol is something else again. With flesh pressed in on eroded cheeks, theirs are death's-head faces, while their bulky ponchos look like shrouds. They are walking collections of bones, their stainless steel seeming to fade to a ghostly gray in sunlight. While they are portrayed talking and gesturing to each other, they clearly have no idea we are there. As we "forgot" them and their war, so now they plod on (more likely retreating from the Chosen Reservoir than advancing across the 38th Parallel), like some land-bound Flying Dutchman; another grim, if possibly only half-conscious entry

in America's memorialization of its culture of defeat. South of the Vietnam Wall, a site has already been approved for a Black Revolutionary Patriots Memorial. More such are undoubtedly to come. James Reston, Jr., "The Monument Glut," *The New York Times Magazine*, September 10, 1995, 48–49.

10. Haruko Taya Cook and Theodore F. Cook, *Japan at War: An Oral History* (New York: New Press, 1992), 8–14. As is obvious, I have relied heavily on this remarkable book here.

11. For a full discussion of victory culture in America, see Tom Engelhardt, *The End of Victory Culture: Cold War America and the Disillusioning of a Generation* (New York: Basic Books, 1995).

12. Cook and Cook, *Japan at War*, 343–49; see also Michael S. Sherry, *The Rise of American Air Power: The Creation of Armageddon* (New Haven: Yale University Press, 1987), 273–82, for a particularly striking account of the firebombing of Tokyo.

13. John Whittier Treat, *Writing Ground Zero: Japanese Literature and the Atomic Bomb* (Chicago: University of Chicago Press, 1995), ix.

14. For a powerful essay on those ignored continuities, see John W. Dower, *Japan in War and Peace: Selected Essays* (New York: New Press, 1993), 9–32.

15. Richard Rhodes, *The Making of the Atomic Bomb* (New York: Simon and Schuster, 1986), 584–85.

16. On these early atomic dreams of destruction, see Spencer Weart, *Nuclear Fear: A History of Images* (Cambridge: Harvard University Press, 1988), 17–35.

17. Rhodes, *The Making of the Atomic Bomb*, 703; "The Crossroads: The End of World War II, the Atomic Bomb, and the Origins of the Cold War," draft script, National Air and Space Museum, 231–33.

18. Rhodes, *The Making of the Atomic Bomb*, 709–11; "Crossroads," 278; Cook and Cook, *Japan at War*, 382–83.

19. Robert Jay Lifton and Greg Mitchell, *Hiroshima in America: Fifty Years of Denial* (New York: Putnam's, 1995), 29, 359–68.

20. Ibid., 231.

21. "Crossroads," 258, 261.

22. For one interesting example of this suppression of evidence, see Erik Barnouw, "Iwasaki and the Occupied Screen," *Film History* 2 (1988): 337–57 (kindly sent to me by the author).

23. For the fullest account of this suppression, the exceptions to it (especially John Hersey's *Hiroshima* and the case of the Hiroshima Maidens), as well as the ways these images finally entered the culture in the 1970s and 1980s, see Lifton and Mitchell, *Hiroshima in America*, esp. 40–64, 86–92, 245–63.

24. For the best account of these fantasy scenarios (and much else about the effects of the bomb on American culture), see Paul Boyer, *By the Bomb's Early Light: American Thought and Culture at the Dawn of the Atomic Age* (New York: Pantheon, 1985).

25. Weart, *Nuclear Fear*, 157, 187.

26. John Morton Blum, *V Was for Victory: Politics and American Culture during World War II* (New York: Harvest/HBJ, 1976).

27. "Crossroads," 258, 261. The figures come from a wall poster from the actual Smithsonian exhibition.

28. "Statement Offered by Brigadier General Paul W. Tibbets (USAF Retired) at the Airmen Memorial Museum on June 8, 1994 Upon the Acceptance of the Air Force Sergeants Association's Freedom Award," press release.

29. Tom Crouch memo from National Air and Space Museum Files (supplied by Edward T. Linenthal).

30. All quotes here and to follow from "Crossroads," 300ff.

31. Paul W. Tibbets, Jr., news conference, June 9, 1994, quoted in John T. Correll, " 'The Last Act' at Air and Space," *Air Force Magazine*, September 1994, 64.

32. I. Michael Heyman, Smithsonian news release.

33. Quotes taken from the final truncated Smithsonian exhibit; see also *Enola Gay, the First Atomic Mission*, the Greenwich Workshop, 1995, the video of testimony from the *Enola Gay* crew produced for the exhibit.

THE CONTRIBUTORS

PAUL BOYER is Merle Curti Professor of history and director of the Institute for Research in the Humanities at the University of Wisconsin, Madison. Among his many books are *When Time Shall Be No More: Prophecy Belief in Modern American Culture* (1992), *By the Bomb's Early Light: American Thought and Culture at the Dawn of the Atomic Age* (1985), and *Salem Possessed* (coauthor, 1974), winner of the John H. Dunning Prize of the American Historical Association and nominee for a National Book Award. He serves on the national advisory board of the public television series *The American Experience*, and is editor in chief of the *Oxford Companion to American History* (forthcoming, 1998).

JOHN W. DOWER is Elting Morison Professor of History at the Massachusetts Institute of Technology. His books include *Japan in War and Peace* (1994), *War Without Mercy: Race and Power in the Pacific War* (1986), winner of the National Book Critics Circle Award and, in Japan, the Ohira Prize, as well as *Empire and Aftermath: Yoshida Shigeru and the Japanese Experience, 1868–1954* (1979). He was executive producer of the documentary film *Hellfire: A Journey from Hiroshima*, an Academy Award nominee. He is at work on a history of the occupation of Japan to be jointly published by W. W. Norton and the New Press.

TOM ENGELHARDT, former editor of Pacific News Service and former senior editor at Pantheon Books, is the author of *The End of Victory Culture: Cold War America and the Disillusioning of a Generation* (1995) and *Beyond Our Control: America in the Mid-Seventies* (1976). His media criticism and cultural commentary have appeared in magazines and newspapers ranging from *Harper's* and the *New York Times* to *The Nation* and in numerous European publications. He has received a John Simon

Guggenheim Memorial Fellowship. He is now Consulting Editor for Metropolitan Books.

RICHARD H. KOHN, former president of the Society for Military History, is professor of history and chair of the Curriculum in Peace, War, and Defense at the University of North Carolina, Chapel Hill, as well as executive secretary of the Triangle Institute for Security Studies. He is the editor of *The United States Military under the Constitution of the United States, 1789–1989* (1991) and author of *Eagle and Sword: The Federalists and the Creation of the Military Establishment in America, 1783–1802* (1975). From 1981 to 1991, he was the chief of air force history for the United States Air Force, and since 1986 he has served on three advisory committees for the National Air and Space Museum, most recently as chair of the Research and Collections Management Advisory Committee.

EDWARD T. LINENTHAL, professor of religion and American culture at the University of Wisconsin, Oshkosh, is the author of *Preserving Memory: The Struggle to Create America's Holocaust Museum* (1995) and *Sacred Ground: Americans and Their Battlefields* (1991). While a research fellow in the Arms Control and Defense Policy Program at the Massachusetts Institute of Technology, he wrote *Symbolic Defense: The Cultural Significance of the Strategic Defense Initiative* (1989). He served on the advisory committee of the Smithsonian Institution's National Air and Space Museum during the *Enola Gay* controversy and worked for the National Park Service at the fiftieth-anniversary events at the USS *Arizona* Memorial at Pearl Harbor in 1991. He is the coeditor of *American Sacred Space* (1995).

MICHAEL S. SHERRY, professor of history at Northwestern University, is the author of *The Rise of American Air Power: The Creation of Armageddon* (1987), winner of the Bancroft Prize for Distinguished Books in American History and Diplomacy, and *Preparing for the Next War: American Plans for Postwar Defense, 1941–1945* (1977). His most recent book is *In the Shadow of War: The United States since the 1930s* (1995).

MIKE WALLACE, professor of history at John Jay College (CUNY), is most recently the author of *Mickey Mouse History and Other Essays on American Memory* (1996). With Edwin Burrows, he is writing a history of New York City to be published by Simon and Schuster. He is an editor of the *Radical History Review*.

MARILYN B. YOUNG is currently chair of the Department of History at New York University. She is the author of *The Vietnam Wars, 1945–1990* (1991), which won the Berkshire Conference of Women Historians Book Prize. She is also the coauthor of *Transforming Russia and China: Revolutionary Struggles in the 20th Century* (1980) and author of *Rhetoric of Empire: American China Policy, 1895–1901* (1968). She coedited *Vietnam: A Documented History* (1995) and was the editor of *Women in China: Studies in Feminism and Social Change* (1973).